The
RED MARK
on GOD'S FOREHEAD

Explaining The Way Of God More Accurately To His People

RABBI DARRYL WEINBERG

 FriesenPress

One Printers Way
Altona, MB R0G 0B0
Canada

www.friesenpress.com

ISBN
978-1-03-914555-9 (Hardcover)
978-1-03-914554-2 (Paperback)
978-1-03-914556-6 (eBook)

1. RELIGION, BIBLICAL CRITICISM & INTERPRETATION

Distributed to the trade by The Ingram Book Company

Table of Contents

Chapter 1—Antinomianism............................1
Purpose of the Law   6
No Longer Under the Law   11
Salvation vs. Obedience   19

Chapter 2—Manmade Traditions 25

Chapter 3—Christmas...............................34
Should believers celebrate the birth of Messiah?   35
Should we celebrate on December 25 and in the manner we do?   39
Symbols and Traditions of Christmas   47
The Christmas Tree   51
Santa Claus   53
Even if the origins are pagan, what if that's not what it means to me?   56
Won't the Father redeem or sanctify it?   57

Chapter 4—Other Holidays 61
Easter   61
Valentine's Day   66
Halloween   70

Chapter 5—Gentiles Don't Have To 74
Torah   81
Circumcision   84

Chapter 6—The Sabbath 92
The Number Seven   95
The Eighth Day   98
Scripture Verses Regarding the Shabbat   104
Verses "Proving" Sunday Worship   109
The Lord's Day   111
The Didache   118
Any Day   120
An Appointed Time   123

Chapter 7—God's Appointed Times **128**
Passover 135
Unleavened Bread 140
First Fruits 145
The Counting of the Omer 147
Shavuot (The Feast of Weeks) 148
The Feast of Trumpets 154
The Days of Awe 160
The Feast of Tabernacles 170
Hoshana Rabbah (The Great Salvation) 172

Chapter 8—Food **179**
Scripture 185

Chapter 9—Anti-Semitism **196**
A Blessing to Others 201
The Early Assembly 206
The Church Fathers 207
Marcion 210
Justin Martyr 213
Constantine 218
John Chrysostom 222
Augustine 224
The Crusades 227
Blood Libel 229
The Spanish Inquisition 231
The Reformation 233
The Holocaust 237

Chapter 10—The Messianic Way **242**
The Messianic Lifestyle 245
Terminology 247
The Commonwealth of Israel 249

Acknowledgements **254**

Endnotes **257**

Introduction

A number of years ago, I began to get an image. God often works with me in that way. A picture starts to form in my head. Sometimes it's about what a person is like spiritually, like the time my wife and I were discussing the temperament of someone and suddenly I pictured a scorpion. She said that not only was this person born under the Scorpio sign, but they had a tattoo of one and a pet scorpion at one time. Now I don't put any credence into astrology per se, but people can open up spiritual doors and take on characteristics of things that demons are only too happy to oblige to fulfill for you, and this certainly was the case concerning this person's personality.

This image I began to receive came as I was thinking about how God looks at us sometimes. God is perfect and truly amazing, and He chose to work out His plan of redemption through us. Terry Woychowski says, "It remains a mystery to me as to why God, who is all-powerful and self-sufficient, still chooses to accomplish His work through people. He must not be overly concerned about maximizing productivity or efficiency, because **_working_** through mortals is hardly a way to achieve either goal." (Wochowski 2007) [1] God in His infinite wisdom chose His fallen imagers, humanity, to bring about His completed work. That is truly astounding, and it demonstrates His long-suffering. The term "long- suffering" comes from the Hebrew (*erekh appayim*) and literally means "long of nose." In Hebrew, adjectives describe actions. Long of nose indicates slow, steady breathing. On the other hand, anger is described by short, rapid breathing and the flaring of the nostrils. Therefore, long of nose means patience and being slow to anger (Ex 34:6). But how we must test God's patience!

This image I got was of God sitting on the throne of heaven looking down on creation, with His hand slapped against His forehead in total bewilderment at how ridiculously humanity behaves, especially the Body of Messiah. To a certain extent, we understand that those who don't believe in God, or in Yeshua (Jesus—I use His Hebrew name, as we will discuss in a later chapter) can continue to live their lives in opposition and outright rebellion to His will. But how He must be grieved and exasperated at times with those who have come to faith and accepted the atoning work on the cross for their sins yet continue to miss the mark so badly. I can just see him smacking His head in frustration and turning to Gabriel and asking, "Who told them to do that? Did I tell them to do that?" Poor Gabriel is just shrugging his shoulders, not knowing what to say. Think about it. It's almost comical if it weren't so tragic in its results. Thus, the name of this book is *The Red Mark on God's Forehead*.

God's Word is simple, if we look at it in the proper context. For the most part, it's easy to understand if we apply proper interpretive techniques, which are basic foundations in Bible colleges and seminaries. However, over the centuries, many different influences have crept into the Assembly (the Church—again, we'll address terminology later) that have caused us to veer off course and out of the will of God. We now resemble Paul's words in Romans 7:15: "*For what I am doing, I do not understand; for I am not practicing what I would like to do, but I am doing the very thing I hate.*" We have come to the point in Christianity where we're doing the things we aren't supposed to do and not doing the things we should be doing, and then we're bewildered when we don't experience the miracles, the power, or even the blessings promised. Why is there so much confusion? How can there be (according to the *World Christian Encyclopedia*) over 33,000 denominations of one faith around the world today?[2] Even if we accept that many of these denominations are variations of the same thing, that is still a staggering figure that cannot be ignored. There is something fundamentally wrong with how we interpret the Bible.

In this book, I hope to show how many of the theological positions accepted as fact today and believed to be true are either misinterpretations of what was originally intended or, more insidiously, a result of the oldest and most pernicious hatred in history. Most believers would be shocked to know that much of mainstream Christianity's doctrine comes from men who had less than favourable attitudes toward the Jewish people, which shaped how they interpreted things such as the days we worship on, circumcision, what foods we can and cannot eat, etc. In fact, it could be argued that anti-Semitism is one of the leading causes for how far off track the Body has gotten in its interpretation and practices of the Christian faith today.

After a detailed analysis of these various issues, my prayer and hope are that more people will begin to awaken from the slumber that has engulfed God's people to the point where His Word says that in the end times, there will be such a great deception that most of those who claim to be believers will fall away from the faith. Christian theology has become so watered down in many churches today that the language and the practices of believers are virtually indistinguishable from the rest of the world. From our original calling to be radically different from the world and its system, we have become so syncretized with the ways of unbelievers that it's hard to differentiate us from those we're trying to reach. Whether it be seeker-sensitive churches assuring us that God loves us just the way we are and we're ok to stay that way, or the prosperity gospel churches emphasizing that if we just have enough faith (and give enough money), we can enjoy a successful and prosperous life without much inconvenience, we're being sold a bill of goods. Even when churches and denominations attempt to preach holiness, we have to ask what exactly that means and what is it based on. If everyone is doing what is right in their own eyes, as the book of Judges condemned Israel for, thousands of denominations show that not much has changed since then. Many of our practices today aren't based on God's Word but rather on human traditions, and we were expressly warned against adopting these things. No wonder we're in such a mess and much of the world ridicules us.

If you're reading this and aren't a committed follower of Yeshua of Nazareth, or aren't even sure if there is a God, that's ok. Perhaps you've been raised in an environment where God wasn't much of a concern but you're wondering if He's real. Maybe you grew up in the church but were hurt and turned away from what was presented as the true faith. Wherever you're at, I welcome you to join in this journey anyway. Just understand that I've made certain presuppositions when writing this—mainly that God exists, Yeshua (Jesus) is the promised Messiah who came in the flesh, and the Bible is to be trusted as the inerrant and complete revelation of God to His creation. When I write these details, I presume them to be true, and the tone of the book will reflect that. You may not believe any or all of these but are still curious. If you find the tenor of my arguments a little strong, I ask that you would suspend disbelief and consider what I'm saying as a possibility. The Bible *assumes* the existence of God; it doesn't try to make a case for it, and neither do I. If certain statements in the book offend you, please keep in mind that many truths have been accepted only after strong initial resistance. I can write a whole book just on my experiences with that alone. Proverbs 27:17 says that *"As iron sharpens iron, so one person sharpens another."* I am grateful for the opportunity to share God's truth with you and hopefully aid in the sharpening process.

Our return to the truth of God's Word, God's way, will eliminate the confusion and weakness from His Body and unleash the power of the Holy Spirit to see a revival of repentance, miracles, healings, and people growing in their faith so that we can provoke the world to jealousy. May your journey of seeking deeper truth lead you to greater faith and understanding of who God is and His will for your life.

Darryl Weinberg
10/25/2020

Chapter 1—Antinomianism

"Not only can man not escape the obligation to keep God's law, but man's decision to keep God's law because it is God's law is a sign of grace, not a sign of being unconverted or having a legalistic spirit, as the antinomians argued."

Unknown

"The antinomians essentially 'confound' justification and sanctification and insist that true sanctification is nothing but believing the gospel more and more."

Mark Jones

"So you think that Gentiles shouldn't eat pork." The question was asked as I sat down to enjoy a pizza lunch with the others on the team. It was 2008, and I and a few others from the ministry I served with at the time were in Dearborn, Michigan during the Dearborn Arabic Festival. Dearborn was at the time home to the largest Arab community in the US. Henry Ford, being extremely anti-Semitic, brought in Arabs, predominantly Lebanese people, to work his car plants. During this festival, you could turn any which way and get great tasting shawarma, falafel, and baklava; hear Middle Eastern music; and feel like you were in the Mediterranean.

We had gone down to join in a street evangelism group composed of people from all over North America who would spend the next few days sharing the gospel with these folks. We spent a couple of days learning about Islam and how to effectively witness to those who might be open to the gospel message. I met some terrific friends, including a former PLO terrorist who got saved in an Israeli jail. Did they ever have fun introducing me on the streets! When we were in front of a mosque on a Friday evening, it was absolutely priceless to watch the Imam's face as I joined the conversation he was having with a couple of our folks and he looked over at me, looked away, and then his eyes slowly came back as he saw my tzit-tzit (tassles) and Star of David on my shirt.

We had just finished going door to door and our team came to the pizza parlour late, as we'd been in a great conversation with one family. The pizzas had already been ordered, and when I asked the team leader what was on them, she replied "pepperoni." I stated that we don't eat pepperoni because it was pork, and she quickly apologized and ordered another one without meat for us. I sat down at the table with about twenty others, and my friend across from me heard the conversation and decided to ask his question. Have you ever been asked something and your first response was "uh oh"? I paused for a moment before answering (I know. You're all shocked.) The individual who asked had already caused quite a few problems while on the trip and was quite antagonistic, even almost causing a riot on the streets with about ten thousand people around us. I seem to recall that he was even sent home early.

I realized this was probably not going to end peacefully; however, I answered and said, "Well, since you asked, no I don't believe they should eat pork." It's amazing how when you stand for righteousness, trouble finds you (2 Tm 3:12). I never commented on what he was eating. I was just making sure I was living by my own convictions and those of the people with our ministry.

He looked at me and replied, "Well, I enjoy my freedom in Christ." He then proceeded to bite into a piece of his pepperoni pizza with emphasis. In the immortal words of Wayne Campbell from *Wayne's World*, it was "game on." After ten minutes of me explaining what the Bible actually says about unclean things and gently persuading him that he was unwittingly mistaken about his interpretation of certain passages, he began to indicate he was no longer interested in our friendly discourse ("I don't want to talk about this anymore." The woman beside him then elbowed him and responded, "Shut up. I want to hear this.") However, I was on a roll and decided he needed a little dose of his own medicine. I was finally convinced by a brother at the other end of the table to stop before I made the poor man cry, since everyone was a spectator to our little tete-a-tete by now.

Now, I confess that the flesh probably did enter into my response a little, and perhaps just maybe I enjoyed his discomfort too much, but when one is minding his own business and then gets slapped with the proverbial gauntlet, one needs to stand his ground. I've always maintained that I don't necessarily set the rules of engagement, but if you're going to set them, don't complain when things don't turn out the way you expected them to. Also, don't bring a nerf gun to a shootout.

I share this story because over and over I've come across people who not only insist on living according to their "freedoms" but demand that you live by them too. They even get upset and hostile when you disagree. I had a gentleman from a denomination with which I once served threaten to have me and my entire ministry "excommunicated" from the organization because I shared with him that I believed the moedim (feast days) were for all believers, not just Jews. His father was Jewish, by the way. Although I emphasized that it's not up to me to convict anyone, I believe what the scriptures say about being eternal, perpetual, and everlasting ordinances for everyone alike, whether Jew or Gentile. Why did he get so upset? Why do so many believers get so perturbed and sometimes downright indignant when you disagree with them? It's a complicated question, which I hope to adequately address.

Theopedia.com says that "Antinomianism comes from the Greek, meaning lawless. In Christian theology it is a pejorative term for the teaching that Christians are under no obligation to obey the laws of ethics or morality. Few, if any, would explicitly call themselves "antinomian," hence, it is usually a charge leveled by one group against an opposing group."[3] Or as Webster's puts it: "one who holds that under the gospel dispensation of grace the moral law is of no use or obligation because faith alone is necessary to salvation."[4] In other words, an antinomian believes that the commandments of the Torah (Genesis-Deuteronomy or the "Pentateuch," meaning five) are not applicable to the life of a believer because we already have salvation. Therefore, since we can't earn that, we don't have to do anything once we do have it. Many would say that if you believe in keeping the commandments, you are practising legalism, or the keeping of the commandments, to be saved.

I once had a conversation with a woman about this issue. She presented the usual arguments about no longer needing to observe the commandments because Jesus died, and she claimed that suggesting that we do need to keep them was being legalistic because she was saved by grace. I responded, "Why is it that every time the issue of the commandments comes up, *you* Christians (I was not identifying with her as one at this point) always bring up the issue of salvation? We're not talking about salvation. We're talking about how we live once we're saved." There appears to be a default response from most believers the moment obedience to the commandments comes up that we're adding to salvation by doing so. In all the conversations I've ever had about the Torah and the keeping of the commandments, not once have I ever said that the keeping of any of them helps me obtain my salvation. Never. Yet it's what I'm constantly accused of. I was having breakfast with a pastor one morning, and when he understood that I believed we need to keep the Sabbath (Saturday) and that none of the commandments were done away with, told me that he felt I was putting a burden on my congregants.

How did we get to the point where we call the commandments of God a "burden?" First of all, 1 John 5:3 tells us *"For this is the love of God, that we keep His commandments; and His commandments <u>are not burdensome</u>"* (emphasis mine). The apostle himself told us almost two thousand years ago that this was going to be an issue. I quoted this passage to the pastor, and he didn't know what to say, yet years ago I was threatened with being kicked out of a mainline denomination because of this stance. I was once asked to help plant a Messianic synagogue in the northern US, and when it was discovered I still believed that the food commands from Leviticus 11 were relevant, the plug was pulled on the entire project. No congregation was planted because I was accused of causing confusion with this belief. This was right after we'd held a Passover Seder with 190 people in attendance—an enormous success.

In the Sermon on the Mount, Yeshua was likely addressing the Qumran community, famous for producing the Dead Sea Scrolls, as much of the language of Matthew 5–7 lines up with what we find in the scrolls, such as the Community Rule (previously known as the Manual of Discipline). Yeshua assured them that as the Messiah, He held the Torah in the highest esteem and would continue to uphold it. In Matthew 5:17, He says:

"Do not think that I came to abolish (destroy) the Law or the Prophets; I did not come to abolish but to fulfill. For truly I say to you, until heaven and earth pass away, not the smallest letter or stroke shall pass from the Law until all is accomplished. Whoever then annuls one of the least of these commandments, and teaches others to do the same, shall be called least in the kingdom of heaven; but whoever keeps and teaches them, he shall be called great in the kingdom of heaven."

Dr. Michael Lake says, "the Greek word here for destroy is kataluo, which means to 'destroy, dissolve, disunite, bring to naught, and overthrow,' By the way, fulfill in the Greek is pleroo, which means 'to make full, cause to abound, to flourish,' and finally, 'to fulfil, i.e. to cause God's will (as made known in the law) to be obeyed as it should be, and God's promises (given through the prophets) to receive fulfilment.' Jesus makes it clear that He did not come to see the Law of God set aside; rather He came so that we might properly understand it and execute it."[5]

Despite the fact that He clearly said that until heaven and earth pass away, every single commandment of the Torah will be in effect, most Christians today don't believe that. Many will say that since Yeshua kept the Law and died for our inability to keep it, we are now freed from doing so. That's like saying that because the answers to the questions in my math textbook are written in the back, I don't have to do the questions. Yet in the very next verse (v. 19), He says that anyone breaking the least of the commandments and teaching others to do so will be called least in heaven. How many pastors are dedicating their entire lives for the sake of the gospel yet when they get to heaven will find out that their works will be burned up because they held God's Law in disdain? In Luke 16:17, Yeshua reiterates, *"But it is easier for heaven and earth to pass away than for one stroke of a letter of the Law to fail."* Not one of the over six hundred commandments of the Torah shall be done away with until God destroys heaven and earth, and the new heaven and new earth are created. This could not be any clearer.

Michael Lake says again, "The only antidote to paganism is the Torah because God gave it to a people that were coming out of 400 years in pagan bondage as slaves."[6] If we're truly going to turn from our ways to His, we must first know His ways. By rejecting the Law of God, we now define what is right and wrong ourselves.

Purpose of the Law

Much of the objection to keeping Torah stems from not fully understanding why it was given in the first place. People tend to narrowly define something by using only one reference while ignoring other ones that would give a different definition or purpose. As a biblical example, Israel is called the Chosen People. Chosen for what, though? Many things, in fact. They were chosen chiefly to glorify God (Is 49:3), but they were also chosen to bring the Word of God to the world (Rom 3:2) and also the Messiah (Rom 9:5) and salvation (Jn 4:22) into the world. Israel has many purposes. The same can be said of the Torah. Many Christians give the sole purpose of the Law from Galatians 3. The Apostle Paul says:

"But before faith came, we were kept in custody under the law, being shut up to the faith which was later to be revealed. Therefore, the Law has become our tutor to lead us to Messiah, so that we may be justified by faith. But now that faith has come, we are no longer under a tutor" (Gal 3:23–25).

It would seem from this passage that the purpose of Torah was to lead people to faith, but once it did, it wasn't necessary anymore. Paul seems to reiterate this in Romans 6:14 where he tells us *"for you are not under law but under grace."* That might be true if Torah didn't have any other purpose. As is usually the case with God, though, everything He makes is multi-purposed.

In addition to helping us understand our sinfulness and the need to come to Yeshua as Saviour and Lord, the Torah was also Israel's constitution. Dr. Daniel J. Elazar said:

"The Jewish political tradition ... emphasizes the ordering of the polity through a written constitution. Here Israel has had to confront a basic conflict, unresolvable under contemporary conditions. That is, whether the Torah as the traditional constitution of the Jewish people must serve as the basis for the state's basic law or whether Israel is to adopt a modern civil (or secular) constitution."[7]

It would also seem that in the Millennial Kingdom, when Yeshua rules and reigns for a thousand years, the Torah will once again be the constitution for not just Israel but the entire world. Speaking of the Levites, Ezekiel tells us "*In a dispute they shall take their stand to judge; they shall judge it according to My ordinances. They shall also keep My laws and My statutes in all My appointed feasts and sanctify My Sabbaths*" (Ez 44:24). Not only Israel, but everyone in the world will be keeping Torah in those days. It's called a Theonomy, which simply means society is governed by God's law (Torah).

The Torah, according to Yeshua Himself, is also how God defines love. If we look at the Ten Commandments, the first four deal with how we treat God, and the last six concern how we treat each other. In fact, all 613 *mitzvot* (commandments) describe how we are to love God and each other. The *V'havata* (and you shall love) from Deuteronomy 6:5 is called so because the first words of this verse are "*and you shall love the Lord your God with all of your heart, all of your soul and all of your might.*" The rest of that passage tells how we can do that: by keeping God's Word wherever we go and in everything we do. He says that we love Him by obeying His words. Yeshua affirms this in Matthew 22. When asked by a Pharisee what is the greatest commandment of the Torah, He responds with "*And He said to him, 'You shall love the Lord your God with all your heart, and with all your soul, and with all your mind.' This is the great and foremost commandment. The second is like it, 'You shall love your neighbor as yourself.' On these two commandments depend the whole Law and the Prophets*" (vv. 37–40). In other words, God's definition of love is defined by the commandments of Torah. The entire purpose of the Hebrew scriptures, or the Old Covenant, is to help us understand how God defines love. Yeshua affirms this in John 14:15 by telling us "*If you love Me, you will keep my commandments.*"

Do you see what we've done? By saying that we don't need the commandments of God anymore, we've made the definition of love subjective. We define it ourselves, and each of us will define it differently because we filter it through our individual lens and feelings. A pastor once said, "Your feelings will lie to you every day about what you need." The rock band Foreigner had a hit song in 1984 called "I Want to Know What Love Is." Without God's commandments, we will never find out.

On top of not being able to define love without the Torah, we can't understand what sin is either. To most people, sin means committing a moral wrong, but that's an oversimplification. In the Hebrew, there are actually three different words for sin, all having different nuances. עָוֹן (avon—Strong's Concordance 5771) infers iniquity, guilt, or even punishment for iniquity. It's a wrong committed, but the motivation isn't clear. These are the things we've done that are wrong but not necessarily with premeditated intent. פֶּשַׁע (pesha—6588) is the much stronger term "rebellion." Here the motivation is very clear: to shake one's fist at God, like Joseph Stalin did right before he died. Isaiah 57:4 even implies that *pesha* can be an entity that bears offspring: "*Against whom do you jest? Against whom do you open wide your mouth and stick out your tongue? Are you not children of rebellion* (pesha), *offspring of deceit?*" As we can see, *pesha* is a much more forceful term.

Lastly, חָטָא (chata—2398) means to actually miss the mark. It's an archery term, and the implication is that there was at least an attempt to do right, although the words can be used interchangeably. Moses uses *chata* in Exodus 32:31 as he describes to God how Israel sinned by making the golden calf. It's obvious that this sin was intentional, but despite it being outright rebellion of the worst kind against God, Moses chose not to use *pesha*.

Psalm 32:5 uses all three words as David describes his sin with Bathsheba:

"*I acknowledged my sin* (chata) *to You,*

And my iniquity (avon) *I did not hide;*

I said, 'I will confess my transgressions (pesha) *to the Lord';*

And You forgave the guilt of my sin (chata).*"

Exodus 34:7 also uses all three words: "*who keeps loving kindness for thousands, who forgives iniquity* (avon), *transgression* (pesha) *and sin* (chata); *yet He will by no means leave the guilty unpunished, visiting the iniquity of fathers on the children and on the grandchildren to the third and fourth generations."* Each of the words has a different inference, so a simple definition of sin might not suffice.

The Greek word for sin, *hamartia* (Strongs 266), like *chata*, also means to miss the mark in an ethical sense. Sin isn't necessarily defined by moral wrongness or transgressing some set of rules, but it's doing anything that takes our focus off God (the target) and onto ourselves, thinking we are the be-all and end-all. Thomas Aquinas said, "Sin is nothing else than to neglect eternal things, and seek after temporal things."[8]

Now that we've got a more accurate understanding of sin and can see its several shades or degrees, how can we define and recognize sin without the Torah? If both the Hebrew and Greek say that sin means "missing the mark," what mark are we aiming for in our pursuit of righteousness? Unless God defines that mark, we're shooting blindly, and one need look no further than the fruit we're bearing within Christianity today to know that we are missing badly. The divorce rate, even amongst pastors (many of whom continue in the pulpit), is higher than ever. Immorality, addiction to pornography, and young people sleeping together and even living together before marriage are more common within the Body today than ever before. Many denominations, once staunch defenders of the true faith, today affirm these things. Some support the homosexual lifestyle, performing gay marriages and even ordaining openly-gay ministers. Tithing and faithfulness to God with our finances continues to go down every year. During the Great Depression, believers tithed 3.3 per cent of their income, while today, after the greatest economic expansion in history, giving is down to 2.5 per cent, and thirty-seven per cent of regular church attendees and Evangelicals don't give any money to the church at all.[9] How can we be so far off track? Simple. We've forsaken the commandments of God and established our own righteousness, the very same thing Paul accuses the Jewish community of in Romans 10:4. By declaring that the commandments are no longer applicable to us, believers are defining right and wrong themselves, which none of us have the authority to do.

Much of the issue over the law being a form of bondage comes from a misunderstanding of Paul's words. Some believers worship at the feet of Paul and even suggest his writings supersede those of Yeshua Himself. Scott McKnight wrote:

"I grew up with, on, through, and in the apostle Paul. His letters were the heart of our Bible. From the time I began paying attention to my pastor's sermons, I can only recall sermons on 1 Corinthians—the whole book verse by verse, week by week—and Ephesians. I don't recall a series on any of the Gospels or on Jesus ... We were Pauline Christians and not one bit worried about it. I learned to think and believe and live in a Pauline fashion. Everything was filtered through Paul's theology. Justification was the lens for the gospel, and 'life in the Spirit,' the lens for Christian living.'"[10]

On the other hand, there's a whole movement within the Body that suggests Paul's writings aren't even inspired.

"Hence, Paul's own writing proves he was self-aware that he was often writing without inspiration. This is also clear from how Paul would give commands, and cautions his reader that Paul is not writing under inspiration."[11]

When Paul said *"But to the rest I say, not the Lord,"* (1 Cor 9:12) he was simply differentiating between quoting directly from the words Yeshua spoke Himself and what Paul had gotten in the way of revelation. He was not saying his words were not inspired. Obviously, this person doesn't understand rabbinic thought or that Peter was talking about Paul in 2 Peter 3:15–16 when he said, *"and regard the patience of our Lord as salvation; just as also our beloved brother Paul, according to the wisdom given him, wrote to you, as also in all his letters, speaking in them of these things, in which there are some things that are hard to understand, which the untaught and unstable distort, as they do also the rest of the scriptures, to their own destruction."* Paul might not have thought (according to the above quote) that his writings were inspired, but Peter certainly did, and for Peter to say that took a lot of *chutzpah* because nobody gets to add to the Word of God unless He ordains it Himself.

Assuming that Paul's writings are inspired (and if we don't, we have a whole set of other problems), what does he actually say about the Torah? Do his words suggest that he didn't need to be concerned about it anymore? Did he only appear to keep it *"so that he may by all means save some"* (1 Cor 9:22)? In Romans 7, as he's talking about the conflict between the old and new nature, he says the Torah brought sin to life and killed him (now he was rightfully judged). He then states in verse 12, *"So then, the Law is holy, and the commandment is holy and righteous and good."* In Acts 21:24, he submits to James' authority and the command to pay for some men's vow so *"everyone will know that there is nothing to what they have been told about you, but that you yourself also conform, keeping the Law."* Would someone opposed to the Law, or who thought it was no longer necessary, go to such great lengths just to keep peace? Perhaps someone else might, but Paul also called people out publicly when he felt they were in error, so we know he wasn't much for keeping up appearances.

Paul kept the Shabbat and the feasts, and even instructed the Corinthian believers to do so likewise (1 Cor 5:8). He taught from the Torah: *"When they had set a day for Paul, people came to him at his lodging in large numbers; and he was explaining to them by solemnly testifying about the kingdom of God and trying to persuade them concerning Yeshua, from both the Law of Moses and from the Prophets, from morning until evening"* (Acts 28:23). He confirmed to Felix that he believed everything in the Torah and the prophets (Act 24:14), joyfully agreed with the Torah (Rom 7:22), and told us that by faith we establish it (Rom 3:31). Tough to make a case for Paul in any way preaching against it or saying we don't need to worry about it. Paul loved the Word of God, and after Messiah was revealed to him on the Damascus Road, he understood that it was all about Yeshua. If Yeshua is the Word that became flesh, how can Paul, or any of us, just dismiss it as being irrelevant now?

No Longer Under the Law

When Paul says he's not under law but under grace, we have to ask what he really means by it. Basic hermeneutics (study of the interpretation of scripture) tells us there are some steps we have to go through before we conclude what the passage is saying. Dr. Michael Lake, in his book *The Kingdom Priesthood*, tells us:

"Hermeneutics is the science of biblical interpretation. This interpretive science has principles and techniques that serve as safeguards for the biblical researcher. Although there are many laws and methods, there are five essential elements to a proper hermeneutical application …

- Context
- History
- Culture
- Geography
- Language

When the Bible student takes the time to understand all five of these elements regarding any section of scripture, the Word comes alive with meaning, and his interpretation maintains its biblical integrity (i.e., sound doctrine)."[12]

Many of our problems with interpreting scripture come from our attempts to filter the passages through our own biases, whether they be cultural or linguistic. A hundred years ago if you said someone was gay, everyone would know you were talking about being happy. Even as recently as the 1960s, songs like "Twistin' the Night Away" by Sam Cooke where he sings about the people being so gay or the "Great Pretender" by the Platters that references being gay like a clown. Ask someone today what gay means and you'll get a completely different definition, and that's only after fifty years. In scripture, the most recent letters, the epistles of John, were written over 1,900 years ago, and the book of Job is estimated to be the oldest book in the Bible, written 4,000 years ago.[13] A lot has changed with the world and language in 4,000 years. Not only that, but most people reading this book read their Bibles in English, which means the scriptures have been translated from other languages. You also have cultural nuances that, unless you've studied in-depth, you're likely to miss in your readings. Reading the Bible isn't as simple as some believe it is. Yes, we can all understand the basic message of salvation, but after that, a little elbow grease is required to understand what the authors were trying to convey.

The other issue, and the first one that Dr. Lake lists in proper hermeneutics, is context. The Bible is really easy to manipulate by simply taking a verse, line, phrase, or even a word, and developing a whole theology around it. An entire book could be written on that subject alone, (which is sort of the point of this book, come to think of it). John made a statement in Revelation 1 that he was in the Spirit on the Lord's Day, and presto! Suddenly Saturday worship was switched to Sunday (more on this topic later). Except for one problem—there's no mention of Sunday and the

Lord's Day anywhere else in the Bible. But this is what's been drilled into our heads over the centuries, and everyone just accepts it as fact. It brings to mind the phrase *Carthago dalenda est* (Carthage must be destroyed). It was reputed to have been said in every speech Cato the Elder made in the Roman senate.[14] Despite Rome having won the first of the two Punic Wars, and Carthage no longer being a major power, the Roman senator's continual exhortation to annihilate it eventually led to the third war, and Carthage was destroyed. No explanation was given. He just said it so many times that it was believed to be true and was carried out.

Simply saying we're no longer under the Law to infer that we don't have to keep the Torah anymore takes the passage out of context and out of its cultural milieu. The thought Paul is articulating starts in Romans 6:12. The full paragraph reads:

"Therefore sin is not to reign in your mortal body so that you obey its lusts, and do not go on presenting the parts of your body to sin as instruments of unrighteousness; but present yourselves to God as those who are alive from the dead, and your body's parts as instruments of righteousness for God. For sin shall not be master over you, for you are not under the Law but under grace."

Romans 6 focuses entirely on not sinning anymore. Want proof? The very next line in verse fifteen says:

"What then? Are we to sin because we are not under the Law but under grace? Far from it! Do you not know that the one to whom you present yourselves as slaves for obedience, you are slaves of that same one whom you obey, either of sin resulting in death, or of obedience resulting in righteousness?"

He's saying that now we have been delivered from the power of sin, so don't keep doing it. He tells us we've died to sin but are alive to God now. We've been reborn spiritually, so we're not to go back and do the same things that got us killed in the first place (i.e., sin). How does scripture define sin? *"Everyone who practices sin also practices lawlessness; and sin is lawlessness"* (1 Jn 3:4). According to Romans 7:9, once the commandment was given, my behaviour was condemned and I died. Now that we have Yeshua, we've been freed from sin; therefore, nothing condemns us anymore (Rom 8:1).

Being under the Law meant being judged by it. The Torah's purpose was to contrast God's holiness and our failure to live up to its standards. Paul says in Romans 3:23 that everyone has sinned and fallen short of God's glory. If Paul were talking about not having to keep Torah anymore, that would only apply to Jews. The Gentiles were never given the Torah, so if all are condemned for sinning, how can they suddenly be released from something they never had to begin with? Everyone in the world is judged by Torah, but only Israel knew what it was to keep it. Furthermore, how silly would it be for Paul to take these pagan Gentiles who worshipped all kinds of things and committed every kind of immorality, bring them into the kingdom so that they could be holy, and then turn right around and say, "Ahh, don't worry about it!" You wouldn't apply this kind of thinking to any other part of your life, yet when it comes to people's spirituality, we tend to park logic and sound judgement at the door.

Put another way, because Yeshua paid the price and received our penalty for sin by becoming sin for us and being judged in our place, we are no longer held guilty for breaking the Torah. Joel Stucki says:

"The only problem is, Jesus didn't come to free us from the Law. He came to free us from sin. He didn't need to free us from the Law because the Law never enslaved us in the first place. Sin enslaves. Our freedom in Christ is freedom from sin, not freedom to ignore the holiness of God."[15]

For a believer to say they're not obligated to keep the commands of Torah violates so many scripture passages, many of which we've already dealt with, that it makes you want to shake your head (or slap it). To think so many believe they're free from walking in God's own definition of holiness. The question then further begs: Which commands are we freed from? All of them? The ones I don't want to keep? The ones my pastor says are no longer applicable? I've heard all kinds of reasoning about the civil and ceremonial laws not being applicable while the moral ones are. I've yet to find a passage in the Bible that makes those distinctions. I've found many that say the Law is one unit. Break one and you're guilty of the whole thing.

"But if you show partiality, you are committing sin and are convicted by the Law as violators. For whoever keeps the whole Law, yet stumbles in one point, has become guilty of all. For He who said, 'Do not commit adultery,' also

said, 'Do not murder.' Now if you do not commit adultery, but do murder, you have become a violator of the Law" (Jas 2:9–10).

There's no parsing the Torah into various commands we have to keep now and some that have been done away with. Nowhere in scripture is that allowed. Many passages are taken out of context to justify this view, some of which we'll deal with in later chapters. Suffice to say, between Yeshua telling us not one jot or tittle of the Law will pass away until heaven and earth do, and James saying if we break one command, we've broken them all, it's clear that not keeping Torah is not something God wants or has permitted for His children. To say one has to keep the commands regarding sexual relationships but not the ones regarding what's permissible to eat violates God's Word. Pick-and-choodiasm is another religion. As AJ Jacobs says, "Their point is, the religious moderates are inconsistent. They're just making the Bible conform to their own values."[16]

What about Ephesians 2:14–16? you might ask.

"For He Himself is our peace, who made both groups into one and broke down the barrier of the dividing wall, <u>by abolishing in His flesh the hostility, which is the Law composed of commandments expressed in ordinances</u>, so that in Himself He might make the two one new person, in this way establishing peace; and that He might reconcile them both in one body to God through the cross, by it having put to death the hostility" (emphasis mine).

This verse, along with Hebrews 7, seems to say explicitly that when Yeshua died, He abolished the Law—at least that's what I've heard from several aspiring theologians. However, if we look at the passage again, we see that Paul is speaking not about the entire Torah but the commandments separating Jew and Gentile. In this passage, he only references the enmity (ἔχθρα–echthran, Strong's #2189, meaning hostility, alienation)[17] contained in ordinances that separated Jew and Gentile that were abolished. The context (there's that word again) of the thought is the one new man and that the dividing wall has been broken down. Gentiles who were once far off from God are now brought near because of His death and resurrection.

Now you might say the passage is not talking about reconciliation of Gentile to Jew but the reconciliation of Jew and Gentile to God since it was the Law that condemned all of us, and you would be correct. However, in v. 11, Paul says it was the Gentiles who were far off from God, not Israel. Messiah has always been in their midst through the covenants He made with them, even if they haven't recognized Him and believed.

Furthermore, Christians tend to make this one new man that God is forming us into as something esoteric and unknowable, much like many people's concept of God. In reality, we already know what that new man looks like. It's the Messiah who was the word that became flesh and walked amongst us. The ideal human is a Jewish man who kept the Torah perfectly and we, both Jew and Gentile are being conformed to His image. (Rom 8:29). Through the Torah, the nation of Israel has always known what perfection looked like but could never attain it on their own efforts. The Gentiles on the other hand had no concept of this and had to be, as Paul says "brought near." Paul's mission was to take the gospel to the Gentiles to help them understand that they too could have salvation through Messiah. Before Yeshua, Gentiles were only permitted in a section of the outer court of the Temple, called the Court of the Gentiles. In fact, there was a sign in three languages stating that if a Gentile were to go beyond the barrier, they would be instantly killed. A tablet with this inscription was found in 1871, written in Greek.

NO FOREIGNER
IS TO GO BEYOND THE BALUSTRADE
AND THE PLAZA OF THE TEMPLE ZONE
WHOEVER IS CAUGHT DOING SO
WILL HAVE HIMSELF TO BLAME
FOR HIS DEATH
WHICH WILL FOLLOW[18]

This is what caused the riot in the Temple in Acts 21:27. Peter tells Cornelius in Acts 10 that he knows how *unlawful* it is for a Jew to associate with a foreigner or even visit him, but he was not to call any man unclean, as God was now introducing salvation to the nations. After Yeshua's death, the Gentiles were now allowed into the very Holy of Holies because we all became the Temple of God (1 Cor 6:19), and all people are part of that, Jew or Gentile.

Paul isn't saying here that all the commandments are done away with—just the ones separating Jews and Gentiles. Does this mean God changed His mind? Of course not. All through the Tanakh (Hebrew scriptures, or Old Covenant) is the promise that there are other nations besides Israel that God will bring to Himself. Amos 9:12 speaks of *"all the nations who are called by My Name declares the Lord who does this."* God tells Abraham in Genesis 12:3 that through him, all the families of the earth will be blessed. God has always had a plan for all of humanity to come to faith, but He had to separate out one nation to show how He wanted people to approach Him. It took 1,500 years of God dealing with Israel and the writing of the Hebrew scriptures, before the world was ready for Messiah and the nations coming in to God's family. Galatians 4:4 says, *"But when the fullness of time came, God sent His Son, born of a woman, born under the Law."* Think about it this way, the scriptures speak of the Kingdom of Heaven as leaven that spreads through the whole lump of dough (Mt 13:33). The Torah, God's standard of righteousness, and all of the Tanakh, which was the revelation of who God is, took 1,500 years to spread through the world to prepare for the coming of the Word made flesh. Any sooner would have been before the fullness of time. Some commandments are progressive in nature. They lead us to something greater. Hebrews 10:4 says the blood of animal sacrifices was never sufficient to remove sin. It was only a *kippur*, or a covering. That doesn't invalidate the animal sacrifices, because God ordained it. It just means it wasn't the final means to deal with sin, just an intermediary one.

The same applies to the ordinances separating Israel and the rest of the nations. In order to understand holiness (from the Hebrew "qodesh," which means "apartness, sacredness," or "separateness," showing that God is altogether holy, sacred, set apart or separate from His creation,")[19] it's important to grasp that the commands for Israel not to intermarry or adopt other nations' practices wasn't racist as God loves all people. He just didn't want His people becoming defiled by sin. Once a foreigner adopted the worship of God, they were to be accepted without distinction, which happened en masse after the Holy Spirit was given. In Hebrews 7:12, speaking about change in the Law, the author refers to the new priesthood according to the Melchizedekian order. The Levitical priest's main job was to intercede for people through the sacrificial system. Once Yeshua became our High Priest and replaced the sacrifices with that of His own blood, the former became unnecessary. When the Temple was destroyed, the sacrificial system was completed. It had been replaced with the once-and-for-all sacrifice of Yeshua. Besides, the Levitical system never took away sin (Heb 10:4) but only provided a *kippur*, or atonement, a covering. That's why they kept doing them over and over. Once Yeshua died, the Levitical priesthood was no longer necessary, but it took another thirty-seven years before the Temple was destroyed, making it official.

The Torah is a living document containing overriding spiritual principles that are timeless and apply to every circumstance in life. Because of that, it also adapts with the world. To understand how Torah works is to understand the nature of God: He's immutable (unchanging) yet always relevant. The plan of salvation was always designed to weave through time and intersect with every moment in history. Whether it was the antediluvian (pre-flood) age with the Nephilim where God found Noah; when He created a nation out of Abraham; rescued that nation out of Egypt; dealt with Israel under the era of the kings; dealt with them during and after exile; sent the Messiah to dwell among them; established the Body of Messiah during the apostolic era; kept a remnant after the Catholic Church was established where for several hundred years, even reading the Bible was illegal and punishable by death, which was referred to as the Dark Ages; or ministers today in the twenty-first century, God has always been working out a plan so that humanity might be saved and people have a relationship with their Creator. Because the Word is God Himself (*"and the Word became flesh and dwelt among us"*—John 1:14), it's not a static thing but a living one. That's why aspects of it can change without the nature of God changing. Certain commands were for a specific purpose but have been replaced by better commands without affecting the meaning or purpose of the other ones. It may seem like I'm belabouring this point, but it must be understood to rectify how God's people have gotten so far off track. People's thinking is too linear—a Greco-Roman mindset. We want everything categorized and neatly placed in the right file, yet neither the physical nor the spiritual world are like that. It's quite unrealistic for anyone to believe that in a sin-fallen reality anything is going to be simple and straightforward. Proverbs 3:5–6 says to "*Trust in the Lord with all your heart and do not lean on your own understanding. In all your ways acknowledge Him, and He will make your paths straight.*" Why would He have to straighten our paths unless they're crooked to begin with? Other than the gospel message of believing in Yeshua for salvation, very little else is so clear cut. Again, rightly dividing the word of truth takes effort and study.

Salvation vs. Obedience

The third chapter of Galatians is another "surefire proof" used by many to say that we don't need to keep God's commandments. Paul even gets a little uppity about it:

"You foolish Galatians, who has bewitched you, before whose eyes Jesus Christ was publicly portrayed as crucified? This is the only thing I want to find out from you: did you receive the Spirit by works of the Law, or by hearing with faith? Are you so foolish? Having begun by the Spirit, are you now being perfected by the flesh? Did you suffer so many things in vain—if indeed it was in vain? So then, does He who provides you with the Spirit and works miracles among you, do it by works of the Law, or by hearing with faith?" (Gal 3:1–5).

Paul basically calls them a bunch of half-witted knuckleheads for believing that keeping the Law is the key to a right relationship with God. Case closed, right? Not quite. What was that really important hermeneutical point we discussed earlier? Oh yes … context. What is the focus of the book of Galatians? Legalism. And what is legalism?

"In Christianity, legalism is the excessive and improper use of the law (Ten Commandments, holiness laws, etc.). This legalism can take different forms. The first is where a person attempts to keep the Law in order to attain salvation. The second is where a person keeps the law in order to maintain his salvation. The third is when Christians judge other Christians for not keeping certain codes of conduct that they think is needed to obey, but in reality is not."[20]

So legalism is the "improper use of the law." Paul writes in 1 Timothy 1:8: *"But we know that the Law is good, if one uses it lawfully."* The Galatians had an improper view of the purpose of the Torah, much like many in the Torah community today who, once they discover the beauty of keeping God's commandments, become imbalanced about it and go to extremes. Paul addresses their error in chapter 5: *"You have been severed from Messiah, you who are seeking to be justified by the Law; you have fallen from grace*" (Gal 5:4). Paul isn't saying the Galatians were wrong in wanting to be obedient to the commandments. He's correcting their belief that they were saved by keeping them and being circumcised. Cecil Maranville puts it eloquently:

"Trying to understand Paul's teaching on law and grace by starting with the book of Galatians is a little like trying to grasp the plot of a complex movie by starting to watch it in the final half hour.

"The reader of Galatians first needs to know the background—the unusual circumstances that caused Paul to write this epistle (letter) to several congregations in the region of Asia. Otherwise the reader is likely to fall into a trap of misassumptions taught by people who do not correctly understand the biblical doctrine of law and grace.

"Frankly, the doctrine of law and grace is one that many in today's Christianity misunderstand. The common problem one encounters today is an antinomian (anti-law) prejudice. Antinomian teachers argue that Paul—and, indeed, the entire New Testament—taught believers that it is impossible to keep God's 10 Commandments and that it is evil to say that God requires the believer to keep the 10 Commandments. Most of their anti-law arguments make use of this book of Galatians.[21]"

You can search thousands of articles on this same subject. It's rampant within Christian circles today. Maranville further says:

"Paul's thinking on the law is in complete harmony with that of our Savior and that God expects believers to live by His Commandments. That truth fits hand in hand with grace—God's benevolent kindness that is given based upon His goodness without regard to the worthiness of the recipient. God stands ready to extend grace to all who repent (turn away from breaking the law). The irrepressible truth of scripture is that it is law and grace, not law or grace.

"That the letter of Galatians was written to deal with serious problems is evident from its beginning: 'I marvel that you are turning away so soon from Him who called you in the grace of Christ, to a different gospel, which is not another; but there are some who trouble you and want to pervert the gospel of Christ' (Galatians 1:6-7).

"This is not a gentle pastoral letter of encouragement; it is obviously dealing with a doctrinal issue—a heretical teaching!

"The error infiltrated the Church over several decades through Jewish members who rejected the Church's policy to allow gentiles to become members of the Church without undergoing physical circumcision. Even after the Church had formally adopted this policy, these Jewish trouble-makers were agitating for the Church to reverse its approach. The agitators possessed a truly legalistic mentality, urging the Church to model itself after Judaism instead of accepting Christ's leadership.

"The fact that it was necessary for the apostle Paul to write this forceful letter demonstrates that those pushing the heresy had achieved a foothold in Galatia.

"Their argument centered upon circumcision, which is evident from this emphatic statement: 'I could wish that those who trouble you would even cut themselves off!' (Galatians 5:12). The original language is quite graphic, sarcastically implying that those who are so insistent on circumci-sion might as well go all the way and emasculate (or mutilate) themselves (*Theological Dictionary of the New Testament* by Geoffrey W. Bromiley and Word Biblical Commentary, 'Galatians' by Richard Longenecker). Lest anyone miss the double meaning, circumcision involves surgical cutting. Paul is saying he wishes that these people who are so obsessed with that kind of cutting would cut themselves off of the Body of Christ entirely because their thinking has no place in the Church of God!

"Therefore, the book of Galatians counters the mistaken thinking that salvation could be earned through some legalistic formula. It was not an argument against whether a believer was required to keep God's law.

"There is a world of difference between thinking that salvation can be earned by keeping a set of rules, and the fact that those who receive sal-vation must live by God's rules. This distinction is repeated throughout the book.

"Many religious teachers today reflect the widespread antinomian preju-dice (opposition to any teaching that a believer must keep the law of God) when they comment on Galatians. They overlook the reason or writing the letter, which was to counter the heresy being promoted by the pro-circumcision Judaizers.

"Some religious teachers today write or speak as if modern Christianity were in danger of believing that the way to salvation was through physical circumcision and other regulations. The idea is somewhat preposterous. Christianity isn't in danger of being taken over by promoters of circumcision!

"Many today believe that the heresy of Galatians was that God required His Church to keep the law. They fail to see the difference between legalism and being law-abiding. Paul argued with equal force against legalism and for being law-abiding."[22]

Again, if Paul were arguing that keeping the Law made you foolish, he would be contradicting himself in many other places. Paul argued vociferously against keeping the law just to be justified or saved. As a Pharisee and member of the Sanhedrin, he believed the Torah was the way to be right with God. He knew it inside and out. Who better to argue that it wasn't the commandments that save but belief in the Messiah and accepting God's gift of grace?

What about Paul when he speaks of everything being lawful?

"All things are lawful for me, but not all things are helpful; all things are lawful for me, but not all things edify. Let no one seek his own, but each one the other's well-being" (1 Cor 10:23, NKJV).

Many have said that now we are under grace, so nothing is prohibited. Is that so? By that reasoning, murder, adultery, and stealing are all permissible, yet no true follower of Yeshua would agree with this statement. Paul obviously can't be saying that everything under the sun is ok to do. Once again, we have to look at context. In the next verse he speaks of meat sold in the marketplace. What he's addressing is food sacrificed to idols. Is that permissible? It is, because he says in 1 Corinthians 8 that we know there's no such thing as an idol, but if it's going to cause a weaker brother to stumble or ruin our witness with an unbeliever, we're not to do it. Same thing with drinking alcohol. It's ok for a believer to drink (but not to get drunk—Ephesians 5:18), but if you're in the presence of people who believe that alcohol is not allowed for believers, or who struggle with alcoholism, you're not to flaunt your liberties.

There are two ways we can interpret what "all things are lawful" means. The first—and I believe correct—interpretation is that Paul is dealing with things permitted under Torah. Clean meat can be cleansed, even if offered to idols, because we have authority over the demons behind the idols. Whatever Torah permits, I am allowed to partake of. We have liberty to do whatever Torah allows. It's not edifying, though, if it causes someone else to struggle. What isn't lawful is anything outside of God's commandments.

The other way of looking at it is that everything in the world is covered under Torah. Some actions are allowed, while others are prohibited, and if we do them we will suffer the consequences. Sin is covered under the Torah. It is addressed. It doesn't mean we should do it, though.

You might be asking, "Why make such a big deal about this? If it's not a salvation issue, why focus so much on it?" Because disobedience has consequences. Leviticus 26 and Deuteronomy 28 explain in painful detail the consequences of not keeping God's commandments. Deuteronomy 28:1–14 details the blessings of obedience. You won't be able to outrun them, even if you try. The last fifty-four verses speak about the consequences of not keeping the commandments, and they are severe to the point of death, hopelessness, and even famine. They're so harsh that people would resort to cannibalism, which did happen in the northern kingdom of Israel. Most of the thirty-nine books of the Old Covenant deal with the Torah, Israel's unwillingness to keep it, the call of the prophets to return to it, and the judgements that kept coming because they wouldn't. In fact, Israel's 1,500-year history until Yeshua came can be described as the cycle of disobedience, judgement, repentance, forgiveness, rinse, and repeat.

Spiritually, the reason why Satan (the adversary) has permission to attack us is because of sin. Adam's disobedience started all of this to begin with. "*The wages of sin is death*" Paul tell us in Romans 6:23. You sin, you die. Yeshua came to defeat death, but if we go on sinning, we open up the door for the devil to go after us again. In John 5, Yeshua heals a man. He leaves him but meets him again later:

"Afterward, Yeshua found him in the temple and said to him, 'Behold, you have become well; do not sin anymore, so that nothing worse happens to you'" (John 5:14).

Sin is what apparently made him sick to begin with, and now that he's been delivered, sin will make him even sicker the next time around if he continues in it. We have to remember that the spiritual realm is governed by rules, and God's Torah defines those rules. Yeshua is our advocate, our defense attorney. When the accuser comes to God and points out our transgressions, if we haven't repented and been covered by Yeshua's blood, the kingdom of darkness has a legal right to attack us. We wonder why the church is so powerless today, why there's so much sickness, poverty, and a lack of signs and wonders, miracles, and healings. We shouldn't wonder. God told us what would happen when we didn't obey, no matter what theological gymnastics one does in order to say differently.

The Lord said to Isaiah that *"The Lord was pleased for His righteousness' sake to make the Law great and glorious."* (Isa 42:21) He gave the Torah to us for righteousness and made it great and glorious, yet today, many of His followers disdain it. Once believers renounce the satanic belief that we don't have to keep God's commandments anymore and embrace the Torah as a delight, their walk changes dramatically and invites the blessings of God to begin pouring into their lives.

"Now it shall be, if you diligently obey the Lord your God, being careful to do all His commandments which I am commanding you today, that the Lord your God will put you high above all the nations of the earth. And all these blessings will come to you and reach you if you obey the Lord your God" (Dt 28:1–2).

I would recommend anyone test the Lord to see if He will be true to His Word and bless us beyond all that we ask or can think of if we obey His commandments. You can be confident that it's a low-risk gamble.

Chapter 2—Manmade Traditions

"Here in Anatevka we have traditions for everything, how to sleep, how to eat, how to work, how to wear clothes. For instance, we always keep our heads covered and always wear a little prayer shawl. It shows our constant devotion to God.

You may ask how did this tradition get started. I'll tell you. I don't know. But it's a tradition. And because of our traditions, every one of us knows who he is and what God expects him to do.

Traditions, traditions. Without our traditions, our lives would be as shaky as, as a fiddler on the roof."

Tevye from *Fiddler on the Roof*

Traditions. They're wonderful things. They bring continuity to our lives and even define culture. Many traditions go back thousands of years. Most people will accept the traditions of their religion or nation without questioning where they come from or what they mean, and that can be dangerous, especially when dealing with spiritual things. In my life as a believer and one who is called to the ministry, I've come to realize that there is nothing we do physically that doesn't have some spiritual consequence, whether good or bad. Yeshua told us that whatever we bind on earth will be bound in heaven, and whatever we loose on earth will already have been done likewise in heaven (Mt 18:18). If we remember that we are spiritual beings having a physical experience, we become more sensitive to the spiritual realm and the fact that everything we do has a reaction there. Since both the kingdom of darkness and the Kingdom of Heaven are spiritual realms, we are serving either one or the other, and sometimes the reactions are very subtle without our understanding.

"The word tradition comes from the Latin traditionem, acc. of traditio, which means 'handing over, passing on,' and is used in a number of ways in the English language:

1. Beliefs or customs taught by one generation to the next, often orally.
2. A set of customs or practices.
3. A broad religious movement made up of religious denominations or church bodies that have a common history, customs, culture, and, to some extent, body of teachings."[23]

"A tradition is a practice, custom, or story that is memorized and passed down from generation to generation, originally without the need for a writing system. Tools to aid this process include poetic devices such as rhyme and alliteration. The stories thus preserved are also referred to as tradition, or as part of an oral tradition."[24]

There are two types of traditions. There are secular ones, such as wedding anniversaries, bowling night (my mother played mahjong on Wednesday nights for over twenty years), or anything that's done on a regular basis. Major League Baseball had a tradition that the first pitch of the season would always occur in Cincinnati. I always try to wear my red maple leaf tie on the Shabbat closest to Canada Day when I'm delivering a message. These are all examples of traditions that are followed because they're enjoyable and bring us a little happiness. Nothing too sacred about these activities.

The other type of traditions are the religious or spiritual ones. They can be further divided between biblical and unbiblical ones. Biblical traditions are those within the commandments that help us to keep them. Paul commends the Corinthians for *"adhering to the traditions which I gave you"* (1 Cor 11:1). These traditions help us to be obedient to the Word of God. For example, there are many ways to celebrate Passover. I have been to and conducted countless Seders over the years, and every one had a different flavour to it, different things we talked about, songs we sang, or different scriptures we read throughout the ceremony. The point is to celebrate it every year because God has commanded us to.

Regarding the copying of the books of the Bible, there was no specific command on how the scriptures were to be transcribed. Yet a process was developed by the scribes after the Babylonian exile that included the following steps:

1. They could only use clean animal skins, both to write on and even to bind manuscripts.
2. Each column of writing could have no less than forty-eight, and no more than sixty, lines.
3. The ink had to be black and of a special recipe.
4. They had to verbalize each word aloud while they were writing.
5. They had to wipe the pen and wash their entire bodies before writing the word "Adonai" every time they wrote it.
6. There had to be a review within thirty days, and if as many as three pages required corrections, the entire manuscript had to be redone.
7. The letters, words, and paragraphs had to be counted, and the document became invalid if two letters touched each other. The middle paragraph, word, and letter had to correspond to those of the original document.
8. The documents could be stored only in sacred places, such as synagogues.
9. As no document containing God's Word could be destroyed, the rejected ones were stored, or buried, in a genizah—a Hebrew term meaning "hiding place." These were usually kept in a synagogue or sometimes in a Jewish cemetery. [25]

We often take for granted the accuracy of the Bible and speak of it as if it somehow magically happened. Were it not for the traditions developed by these men who so revered God's Word, we might not be able to quote 2 Timothy 3:16 so confidently: *all scripture is inspired by God.* This is a wonderful illustration of how beneficial traditions can be to us.

Other biblical traditions enable us to keep the commandments, such as the ones that welcome in and conclude the Shabbat. scripture is quite spartan in what we actually have to do to keep the Sabbath day holy, other than not working and not lighting a fire (Ex 35:3—which was hard work back then, not like turning on the stove or BBQ today). All we're really commanded to do is to rest on it. However, the tradition of welcoming the Shabbat with a meal, lighting the candles, and blessing the bread and the wine, one that stems from Abraham's meeting with Melchizedek (Gen 14:8), are all added to our practices. Furthermore, the Havdalah (separation) service to end off Shabbat is practised by the lighting of a special candle and smelling a special mix of spices. These two traditions are bookends that help define the Shabbat and keep it separate from the rest of the week.

The practice of parading the Torah scroll around the sanctuary at the synagogue and kissing the tallit (prayer shall), the siddur (prayer book), or the Bible and then touching the Torah scroll with them helps us to honour the Word of God and to remember David's exhortation to us in Psalm 34:8 to *"Taste and see that the Lord is good."*

Weddings involve many different traditions that have changed over the millennia and from country to country. I see no reference anywhere in the Bible to having the bride and groom lifted up on chairs and paraded around the dance floor (I can't picture the monkeys doing that for Adam and Eve in the garden), but it sure is fun to participate in that at Jewish weddings today. The cutting of the cake together and standing under the chuppah (canopy) while performing the ceremony (ours was custom made for us as a quilt) are all beautiful traditions to help us confirm the covenant of joining man and wife together in marriage.

Tradition even helps define our very cultural identity:

"Cultural traditions are important because they transmit shared values, stories and goals from one generation to the next. Traditions encourage groups of people to create and share a collective identity, which in turn serves to shape individual identities."[26]

Our cultural traditions give us an identity. In the case of Israel, their entire identity was based on their devotion to God. In fact, it was the very reason that God chose a nation as His own—to reveal Himself to the world. Phillip Schaff tells us "The Jewish Christians, at least in Palestine,

conformed as closely as possible to the venerable forms of the cultus (traditions) of their fathers, which in truth were divinely ordained."[27] Israel's
main job as God's covenant nation was to keep His commandments, be
blessed because of it, and, as a result, draw all other nations unto Him.
They were supposed to contrast what happens when a people worship the
one true God as opposed to all the other nations who worshipped idols,
which did nothing for them except stare back. Their entire identity was to
be formed around their relationship with YHWH (pronounced Yehovah
with the vowels) ELOHIM. Their traditions were, as Schaff said, "divinely
ordained." For instance, at the time of Yeshua, it was common practice for
all boys to have memorized the entire Torah by the time they were thirteen
years old, the age we have bar mitzvahs today. How much different would
our society be if children were still required to do that today? The problem
Israel always ran into was when their customs and practices deviated from
what God instructed them to do. They would start adopting other religions' traditions, which always led to judgement, as God is a jealous God
(His Name is even Jealous—Exodus 34:14) and will not tolerate rituals that
give honour to any other god but Him. This should start to turn on a few
lightbulbs for the reader as to what has happened to God's people today,
both Jews and Christians.

As we can see, some secular traditions and the religious ones that help
us keep the commandments all enrich our lives. They're either benign or
pleasing to God, as they draw us closer to Him. It's the traditions that are
anti-biblical that get us into trouble. Secular ones can be bad if they lead
us to do things that are wrong, but it's the religious ones that take us away
from the things of God that have the most serious consequences because
they deceive us into thinking we're doing the right thing when, in fact, it's
offensive to the Father.

Yeshua constantly battled the religious leaders of the day on how they
interpreted scripture and when they got after Him because His disciples
did "*not walk in accordance with the tradition of the elders, but eat their
bread with unholy hands*" He retorted:

"Rightly did Isaiah prophesy about you hypocrites, as it is written:

'This people honor Me with their lips,
But their heart is far away from Me.
And in vain do they worship Me,
Teaching as doctrines the commandments of men.'"

"Neglecting the commandment of God, you hold to the tradition of men"
(Mark 7:6-8) emphasis mine)

With our traditions, we can easily nullify God's loving instruction to us and make religion a burdensome thing. There were no commandments in the Torah about how to wash your hands, but there's nothing a religious spirit loves more than to come up with its own rules, make them into traditions, and then insist everyone else do them the same way. Makes us feel important and more spiritual, and it enables us to put ourselves above others when they don't do things the right way. The Pharisees were arrogant about their religiosity. Yeshua says they put burdens on others they themselves weren't willing to carry (Mt 23:4). A religious spirit specializes in making things difficult for people, which will eventually cause them to reject God's purpose for their lives as following Him becomes dreary, devoid of joy, and a burden. Remember, God's commandments were given to a free people, not those in slavery. The commandments of Torah are instructions for how a free people live. The commandments themselves give freedom. When Paul says in Romans 6:18 that after being freed from the bondage of sin, we *"became slaves to righteousness,"* it seems in our Western, anti-authoritarian mindset that we just went to being slaves to something else. But what Paul is actually saying is paradoxical. When we are slaves to righteousness, we're actually free because being a slave to righteousness is a choice. God isn't forcing us to obey. He's inviting us to submit ourselves to His authority, and in return He gives us freedom through the commandments of Torah. I can't emphasize this enough: the commandments of Torah do not put us in bondage; they free us. John says so in 1 John 5:3:

"For this is the love of God, that we keep His commandments; and His commandments are not burdensome."

If the Apostle Paul tells us the commandments are freedom, and so does the Apostle John, perhaps if we still think being obedient to what God tells us is bondage then maybe we need to rethink our paradigms. But how does being a slave to righteousness make us free? The very word "slave" means bondage, but Paul is showing us that when we willingly submit ourselves as slaves to God, He makes us free:

"For when you were slaves of sin, you were free in relation to righteousness. Therefore what benefit were you then deriving from the things of which you are now ashamed? For the outcome of those things is death. But now having been freed from sin and enslaved to God, you derive your benefit, resulting in sanctification, and the outcome, eternal life. For the wages of sin is death, but the gracious gift of God is eternal life in Messiah Yeshua our Lord" (Rom 6:20–23).

Becoming slaves to righteousness sanctifies us, or separates us from the world that brings death.

"There is no absolute independence. All of us obey something or someone. People may not want to admit it, but we all serve something or someone. We each have things that control our lives … Paul made an interesting statement in this passage. He wrote, 'You are slaves of the one whom you obey.'"[28]

The difference between being a slave to tradition and to God is that God's commandments bring us joy and freedom, while being a slave to sin or human traditions brings us into bondage. No matter how noble or righteous it may sound, if we submit ourselves to anything but God's perfect, loving instruction for our lives, it becomes a snare to us, trapping us. Only God can give commandments and instructions, rules to follow that actually make us free. That shows His wisdom. Isaiah 55:8–9 says:

"For My thoughts are not your thoughts, nor are your ways My ways," declares the Lord. *"For as the heavens are higher than the earth, So are My ways higher than your ways And My thoughts than your thoughts."*

When you have all knowledge and wisdom, you can do the impossible. Only through God's infinite wisdom can regulations and restrictions bring freedom. Anyone else who tries it fails. That's why Paul warns us in Colossians 2:8:

"See to it that there is no one who takes you captive through philosophy and empty deception in accordance with human tradition, in accordance with the elementary principles of the world, rather than in accordance with Messiah."

He highlights the fact that philosophy (love of wisdom) and human tradition are empty deception. The world and its god (Satan) offer bondage, while God offers freedom through Messiah. I believe that in our own understanding, it's impossible to grasp this concept, so we must accept it on faith. The point here is that we must be oh so careful of what traditions we follow and, more importantly, what we try to insist others do as well. We could very well be setting ourselves in opposition to God by our best intentions.

We do have some examples in everyday life of restrictions bringing freedom. Telling a child not to touch the stove is a restriction, but it results in freedom or sanctification (separation) from pain and injury. Not smoking helps keep us free from cancer and heart disease. Having a specific bedtime keeps us free from being tired and non-productive the next day. (Every student knows the consequences of this one.) My son recently broke his arm (running recklessly on the street after some friends). After six weeks, the doctor removed the cast and told my son he needed to be careful about what he did for the next few weeks until the bone fully healed. When my son suggested using his hoverboard (wheels but no handles), the doctor immediately told him no. Why? Because if he fell and broke the same bone again, he would need surgery with metal rod implants to fix it. Not having surgery and the pain and inconvenience that would go along with it is a matter of freedom, isn't it? So when we're slaves to righteousness through obedience to His commandments, God is keeping us safe and away from the hurt and pain the devil will certainly hit us with if we step outside of God's loving protection in those commandments. The commandments of God are guardrails, not barriers. They don't restrict us from the good things in life. They protect us from the bad things.

Traditions can be wonderful. They help forge and keep our identity. They give us consistency and some measure of familiarity in an ever-changing world full of uncertainty. They help us keep the commandments of God and honour Him if they are done with the right intent. However, they can also accomplish the exact opposite. Traditions can take us away from God, can turn our worship into rote customs without ever having a change of heart. They can make us arrogant by giving us a superiority complex. They can even invite evil spirits in to start manipulating our thoughts and cause us to look down on others. In the prayer of the Pharisee in the Temple (Luke 18:9), he was thanking God that he was not like the despised tax collector in the back of the sanctuary, who was actually repenting and asking for mercy. This man was so full of religiosity and self-righteousness that he had the gall to stand in the very presence of God and tell the Lord how wonderful he was and how wretched the other guy was. If that's not a classic definition of how a religious spirit works then I don't know what is, and I've had to deal with many of them over the years. Peter and James both tell us that God resists the proud but gives grace to the humble. We must constantly analyze our traditions to make sure they're not making us proud or self-sufficient because that is a snare the enemy will use to bring us back into the bondage that Yeshua died to bring us out of.

Chapter 3—Christmas

"We have no superstitious regard for times and seasons. Certainly we do not believe in the present ecclesiastical arrangement called Christmas: first, because we do not believe in the mass at all, but abhor it, whether it be said or sung in Latin or in English; and, secondly, because we find no Scriptural warrant whatever for observing any day as the birthday of the Savior; and, consequently, its observance is a superstition, because not of divine authority."

(Charles Spurgeon, Sermon on December 24, 1871).

In 1984, the world responded to the famine that was ravaging Ethiopia with a music festival called Live Aid, headed by Bob Geldof. The UK, Canada, and the US assembled their music stars to produce songs to raise money for the crisis. The UK group, called Band Aid, began its platinum-selling song, "Do They Know It's Christmas" by telling us that because it was Christmastime, there was no need to be afraid.

It's a quaint notion, but is the statement true? Is there really no reason to be afraid? On the surface, the question seems preposterous. Christmas is many people's favourite holiday, whether they be Christian or secular. Family gatherings, fireplaces warming the house, food, gifts, and themes of world peace, universal love, and goodwill toward men give us a nostalgic feeling about this time of year. Children spend months sharpening their lists, and parents and grandparents try hard to surprise them. Countless famous movies have been made invoking the Christmas spirit, and songs like "White Christmas" and "Rudolph the Red-Nosed Reindeer" bring back fond memories of our childhood. What could be wrong with it?

Well, nothing if we're going to take a me-centric view of things. However, if the point of religious holidays is the worship of God, then the main question we need to ask is "What does God say about it?" If the purpose of our gathering is to give honour and glory to Yeshua, our view matters little.

Several years ago, I debated a pastor on whether Christians should celebrate Christmas. He took the "for" argument, and most of his presentation was on how Christmas made him feel. In my presentation, I asked four questions.

1. Should believers celebrate the birth of the Messiah?
2. Should we celebrate on December 25 and in the manner we do?
3. Even if the origins are pagan, what if that's not what it means to me?
4. Won't the Father redeem or sanctify it?

Understanding God's heart will answer these questions.

Should believers celebrate the birth of Messiah?

There's a difference between commemorating and celebrating. Since the nativity story is biblically documented, studying it and giving thanks for Yeshua's birth doesn't violate any biblical command. God brought the Messiah into the world, and we are grateful to Him for doing so. Having a birthday celebration in the manner we are accustomed to today, though, is a different story. When we look at the origins of birthday celebrations, we find some disturbing things.

"Originally the idea [of birthday greetings and wishes for happiness] was rooted in magic. The working of spells for good and evil is the chief usage of witchcraft. One is especially susceptible to such spells on his birthday, as one's personal spirits are about at that time. Dreams dreamed on the birthday eve should be remembered, for they are predictions of the future brought by the guardian spirits which hover over one's bed on the birthday eve. Birthday greetings have power for good or ill because one is closer to the spirit world on this day. Good wishes bring good fortune, but the reverse is also true, so one should avoid enemies on one's birthday and be surrounded only by well-wishers. 'Happy birthday' and 'Many (more) happy returns of the day' are the traditional greetings [The Lore of Birthdays, Linton, p. 20] …

"The giving of birthday gifts is a custom associated with the offering of sacrifices to pagan gods on their birthdays. Certainly the custom was linked with the same superstitions that formed the background for birthday greetings. The exchange of presents is associated with the importance of ingratiating good and evil fairies on their or our birthdays.

"The traditional birthday cake and candles also have their origin in ancient pagan idol worship. The ancients believed that the fire of candles had magical properties. They offered prayers and made wishes to be carried to the gods on the flames of the candles. Thus we still have the widely practiced birthday custom of making a wish, then blowing out the candles. The Greeks celebrated the birthday of their moon goddess, Artemis, with cakes adorned with lighted candles …"[29]

Then there's this:

"The highest of all holidays in the Satanic religion is the date of one's own birthday. This is in direct contradiction to the holy of holy days of other religions, which deify a particular god who has been created in an anthropomorphic form of their own image, thereby showing that the ego is not really buried. The Satanist feels: 'Why not really be honest and if you are going to create a god in your image, why not create that god as yourself.' Every man is a god if he chooses to recognize himself as one. So, the Satanist celebrates his own birthday as the most important holiday of the year. After all, aren't you happier about the fact that you were born than you are about the birth of someone you have never even met? Or for that matter, aside from religious holidays, why pay higher tribute to the birthday of a president or to a date in history than we do to the day we were brought into this greatest of all worlds? Despite the fact that some of us may not have been wanted, or at least were not particularly planned, we're glad, even if no one else is, that we're here! You should give yourself a pat on the back, buy yourself whatever you want, treat yourself like the king (or god) that you are, and generally celebrate your birthday with as much pomp and ceremony as possible" (From the Satanic Bible).[30]

All of a sudden, these exciting celebrations where kids get presents and play games, and we hop them up on sugar and toxic ingredients before sending them home all hyper with loot bags, isn't so innocent anymore, is it? The previous paragraph from the Satanic Bible really tells what birthdays are all about: me. Have you ever noticed how children (in small or bigger bodies, as some never really grow up) behave on their birthdays? The attitude of entitlement is over-the-top. On birthdays, I often wish someone a "happy pagan, self-worship day," (tongue in cheek, of course!). I know of people who have birthday weekends and even weeks. I know someone who takes off work for their birthday every year. Why? Because it's my birthday. Reminds me of the scene in *The Return of the King* of the Lord of the Rings trilogy where Sméagol (Gollum) and his friend Déagol are fishing and Deagol finds the Ring of Power at the bottom of the river. Sméagol tells Déagol to give the ring to him, and when Déagol asks why, he responds, "Because it's my birthday and I wants it." Attitude of entitlement. They end up in a fight, and Sméagol kills his friend to get the ring.

Now granted, there are many altruistic people who do things for others on their birthdays like raising money for charity or going to serve food at a soup kitchen. On my fiftieth birthday (I know, you can't tell by looking at the lines on my face), I invited family and friends to go axe throwing to raise money for an orphanage we support in Africa. It was an excuse to get my family, who all lived out of town, together and support a good cause. However, this is more of an exception to the prevailing attitude and does not negate the spiritual origins of the practice, which are evident when we look at the traditions we have with the celebration.

In churches I'll ask why we celebrate birthdays anyway. What did you do to come in to the world? When my son was born, he was five days late. My wife was in labour for twenty-four hours, and he arrived at 3:30 a.m. As we were all deliriously tired by then, my wife had to push so hard she could have knocked down a brick wall at that point. My son cried when he finally came out, and ever since then he has eaten, slept, and made a lot of senseless noises and many messes. In other words, he did nothing to be born. I personally think we should celebrate people's mothers on their birthdays because they did all the work, but trying to get a new tradition started like that would just take too much time and resources. Goes over well when I preach it, though.

The point is that in witchcraft and satanism, if a birthday is all about you and has pagan traditions invoking luck from the gods, should we be participating in such things? The answer is obviously no. I am thankful for my family being born, and we do try to have a special dinner, but we don't make a big deal about it and certainly don't have all the trappings of paganism.

Ecclesiastes 7:1 says, *"And the day of one's death is better than one's birth."* The three times birthdays were celebrated in scripture—Job's children, Pharaoh, and Herod—someone dies.

Origen of Alexandria, writing over two centuries after the death of Jesus, followed this same line when he recorded a diatribe against the memories of birthdays, indicating that at the time of his writing, a day to remember the birth of Jesus was not part of the church calendar. In his Homilies on Leviticus, speaking on the aspect of birth, Origen states:

"... not one from all the saints is found to have celebrated a festive day or a great feast on the day of his birth. No one is found to have had joy on the day of the birth of his son or daughter. Only sinners rejoice over this kind of birthday. For indeed we find in the Old Testament Pharaoh, king of Egypt, celebrating the day of his birth with a festival, and in the New Testament, Herod. However both of them stained the festival of his birth by shedding human blood ... But the saints not only do not celebrate a festival on their birth days, but, filled with the Holy Spirit, they curse that day (after the example of Job, Jeremiah and David)"[31]

At birth we've done nothing. Our death is when our legacy on earth is sealed. Even Yeshua did nothing at His birth other than fulfil prophecy. I told this to the head of a denomination one day at a coffee shop while I was explaining why believers shouldn't be celebrating Christmas, and he just about fell off his chair in shock. But it's true. Yeshua had done no miracles, preached no sermons, or done anything. And where was our salvation purchased? Not in the manger but at the cross. And when was that? Not at

Christmas but at the biblical feast of Passover. On our tombstones, there are two dates: when we were born and when we die. In between is a dash. We have control over what that dash means. That dash is when Yeshua fulfilled his mission of being an example to us and then dying to defeat the works of the devil and death, hell and the grave. Then He rose again to show that the last date on the tombstone really isn't the end. That's quite a dash! Birthdays are really meaningless other than to make us feel good, and if they're attached to witchcraft and self-worship, then I personally don't want to be involved with that. I'd rather celebrate someone's accomplishment, like wedding anniversaries. Celebrate joyously for that occasion, because every year that you stay married is a testimony to hard work, sacrifice, and perseverance ... and you get to thumb your nose at all the demons who have been trying to work at breaking your marriage down. Birthdays? Not so much.

Should we celebrate on December 25 and in the manner we do?

Even if celebrating a birthday were harmless and not tied into the occult, if having a day to celebrate Yeshua's birthday was ok, should believers do it on December 25 and with all the rituals associated with it: Santa Claus and wreaths, pinecones and flying reindeer, elves and mistletoe, nativity scenes under Christmas trees? (I won't even bother trying to explain fruitcake because I'm not sure any explanation would suffice for something that awful.) Again we need to do some checking into the background of these traditions.

While it has an extremely convoluted history, the story, as with most occultic practices, seems to find its origin with Nimrod. Nimrod was the great-grandson of Noah, who came through the line of Ham. God sent the flood to destroy the works of the Watchers (rebellious angels) who fell and made a pact to breed with humans. Although there is scant detail in the Bible, Genesis 6 does allude to it and the gaps can be filled in through extra-biblical sources, such as the books of Enoch and Jasher. Although it's not my intention to get into the details of this, as many have done a much more thorough job than I could, it's important that we understand that these fallen spirit beings (Revelation 12 says Satan took a third of them with him, which means there are a lot of them) are the main source of the evil and havoc we see in the world today.

"And all the others together with them took unto themselves wives, and each chose for himself one, and they began to go in unto them and to defile themselves with them, and they taught them charms and enchantments, and the cutting of roots, and made them acquainted with plants. And they became pregnant, and they bare great giants, whose height was three thousand ells: Who consumed all the acquisitions of men. And when men could no longer sustain them, the giants turned against them and devoured mankind. And they began to sin against birds, and beasts, and reptiles, and fish, and to devour one another's flesh, and drink the blood. Then the earth laid accusation against the lawless ones.

"And Azazel taught men to make swords, and knives, and shields, and breastplates, and made known to them the metals of the earth and the art of working them, and bracelets, and ornaments, and the use of antimony, and the beautifying of the eyelids, and all kinds of costly stones, and all colouring tinctures. And there arose much godlessness, and they committed fornication, and they were led astray, and became corrupt in all their ways. Semjaza taught enchantments, and root-cuttings, Armaros the resolving of enchantments, Baraqijal [taught] astrology, Kokabel the constellations, Ezeqeel the knowledge of the clouds, Araqiel the signs of the earth, Shamsiel the signs of the sun, and Sariel the course of the moon. And as men perished, they cried, and their cry went up to heaven …"[32]

Unlike what many in the church believe, it wasn't Adam and Eve who brought the unbelievable onslaught of evil upon us with their original rebellion in the garden. They only opened the door. It was the fallen angels that taught mankind about witchcraft, the zodiac, and astrology; the making of poisons and weapons of war; and sexual perversion and cannibalism. When it says in Genesis 6:5 that *"The wickedness of mankind was great on the earth, and that every intent of the thoughts of their hearts was only evil continually,"* it was no exaggeration. The half-human, half-angel beings called the Nephilim inherited the wholly evil nature of their rebellious fathers who, as Jude said in verse 5 of his epistle, *"left their proper dwelling place.*" Evil had proliferated on the earth to unimaginable levels, and God's decision to destroy them in the flood produced what we know as demons. Demons are not fallen angels. They are the dispossessed spirits of the Nephilim, the children of these angels. Because they were neither fully human nor fully angel, they remain in limbo today until the final judgement, when all wicked spirits, human, angel and in between, will be cast into the lake of fire.

"The origin of demons is not commonly known in our time. However, in ancient times it was well understood that demons are the disembodied spirits of the Nephilim ... The Nephilim were the offspring of the fallen angels and the 'daughters of men.' According to numerous ancient rabbinic and Early Church texts, when the Nephilim died their spirits became disembodied and roamed the earth, harassing mankind and seeking embodiment! This is most evident in the Book of Enoch ... According to the Book of Enoch and other ancient rabbinic writings, the 'Watchers' were a specific group of angels that God had placed to watch over the earth. According to the Book of Enoch, 200 of these Watchers lusted and fell into sin when they married the 'daughters of men.' The result of this ungodly union was the birth of the unnatural offspring, the Nephilim. The destiny of the spirits of the Nephilim is described in chapter 15 of the Book of Enoch.

"'Now the giants [Nephilim], who have been born of spirit and of flesh, shall be called upon earth evil spirits, and on earth shall be their habitation. Evil spirits shall proceed from their flesh, because they were created from above from the holy Watchers was their beginning and primary foundation. Evil spirits shall they be upon earth and the spirits of the wicked shall they be called. The habitation of the spirits of heaven shall be in heaven, but upon earth shall be the habitation of terrestrial spirits, who were born on earth. The spirits of the giants [Nephilim], shall be like clouds, which oppress, corrupt, fall, contend and bruise those upon earth.'

"In this remarkable text we learn that evil spirits (a common Biblical synonym for demons) appear to proceed from the flesh of the Nephilim."[33]

We have fallen angels and their hideous offspring, the Nephilim, that are constantly opposing us. They are also responsible for the knowledge we received on how to sin. God destroyed them in the flood but, according the Genesis 9, the evil nature and knowledge they passed on seems to have continued after the flood through Noah's youngest son, Ham. (Anyone named after unclean meat obviously can't be trusted, right?)

Why is it important to know all of this, and what does this have to do with Christmas? Well, everything. In fact, if we don't understand this, we're in a battle and don't even understand who our enemy is or how to fight him. The spirit behind our quaint little family celebration every year on December 25 is connected to these events within history, and it's vital to know what spiritual doors we're opening. Christianity has been weakened and is largely ineffective in transforming society today because it has come into agreement with so many of Satan's practices, which drains and dilutes our spiritual power.

Genesis 10 tells us that Ham fathered Cush, and Cush bore Nimrod, who was a "mighty hunter before the Lord." Many volumes have been written on who Nimrod was. Dr. Michael Lake, in his book *The Shinar Directive*, says "under Nimrod the original false religious system was successfully implemented."[34] Dr. Tom Horn tells us that Nimrod was "the giant 'mighty hunter' before the Lord—a fantastic personality who in later mythology was also called Osiris and Apollo."[35] According to the historian Josephus, he told people to ascribe their happiness to him instead of God:

"Josephus ... says: 'Nimrod persuaded mankind not to ascribe their happiness to God, but to think that his own excellency was the source of it. And he soon changed things into a tyranny, thinking there was no other way to wean men from the fear of God, than by making them rely upon his own power.'"

The Jerusalem Targum says: "He was powerful in hunting and in wickedness before the Lord, for he was a hunter of the sons of men, and he said to them, 'Depart from the judgment of the Lord, and adhere to the judgment of Nimrod!' Therefore is it said: 'As Nimrod [is] the strong one, strong in hunting, and in wickedness before the Lord.'"[36]

Even his name tells us his character. Nimrod comes from the Hebrew word *marad*, which means to rebel. Everything ever written about this man shows that he is the prototype to the coming son of perdition who will speak blasphemies against God.

"First, what does the name Nimrod mean? It comes from the Hebrew verb marad, meaning 'rebel.' Adding an 'n' before the 'm' it becomes an infinitive construct, 'Nimrod' (see Kautzsch 1910: 137 2b, also BDB 1962: 597). The meaning then is 'The Rebel.' Thus 'Nimrod' may not be the character's name at all. It is more likely a derisive term of a type, a representative, of a system that is epitomized in rebellion against the Creator, the one true God. Rebellion began soon after the Flood as civilizations were restored. At that time this person became very prominent."[37]

Gen 10:8 says הוּא הֵחֵל, לִהְיוֹת גִּבֹּר (hu he-hel liyot gibbor—he began to be a mighty one). Although God destroyed the world and the abomination that was the Nephilim, the Hebrew saying that Nimrod began to be a mighty one infers that he somehow figured out how to become a giant. He actually transformed himself by altering his DNA. All occult and secret society activity ever since has been trying to replicate Nimrod's extraordinary feat. In order to do this, he must have had contact with and knowledge from the Watchers (the fallen angels), even though according to the book of 1 Enoch, they had been imprisoned by God at the time of the flood. In fact, the entire purpose of Satanism and all its related organizations is to get knowledge and power from these beings and use it to rule over others as well as achieve immortality, the serpent's original promise to Eve in the garden.

"*You certainly will not die! For God knows that on the day you eat from it your eyes will be opened, and you will become like God, knowing good and evil*" (Gn 3:4–5, emphasis mine).

They're trying to figure out what Nimrod did so they can do the same thing. Transhumanism, artificial intelligence, genetic modification, and other related practices are all designed to help the elite become what Nimrod had become.

"Nimrod achieved something that only the Watchers of old had accomplished, yet he took it to a whole new level. In fact, no one has been able to reproduce this highly revered occult achievement. This cutting-edge breakthrough of Nimrod has been the goal of all secret societies, alchemists, wizards, sorcerers, warlocks, and Illuminati elite throughout the millennia ... You see, he was a fully grown man who was able to become a *gibborim* (another type of Nephilim)—he was not born that way. It would appear Nimrod took the arcane knowledge of his family line and pushed it beyond what the Watchers themselves could do. He was able to alter his DNA and become a Nephilim."[38]

The ancient Mesopotamian story, the "Epic of Gilgamesh," describes a man remarkably similar to Nimrod. Gilgamesh was king of Uruk in southern Mesopotamia. He was a giant (eighteen feet tall), a tyrant, a tremendous builder and hunter, and was described as two-thirds god and one-third man. Sounds a lot like our antihero, Nimrod. In the epic, a flood is mentioned as well as many other parallels to the biblical account. It's also been reported by many sources that the tomb of Gilgamesh was found in Iraq in the early 2000s to validate what the scriptures tell us.

Another indication of whom Christmas is really about is found in how people abbreviate it. Have you ever asked why so many people shorten Christmas to Xmas? Where does the X come from, and what does it have to do with the Messiah? In her book the *Curse of Canaan*, author Eustace Mullins says:

"The legendary symbol for Nimrod is 'X.' The use of this symbol always denotes witchcraft. When 'X' is used as a shortened form meaning Christmas, it actually means 'to celebrate the feast of Nimrod.' A double X, which has always meant to double-cross or betray, in its fundamental meaning indicates one's betrayal into the hands of Satan. When American corporations use the 'X' in their logo, such as 'Exxon,' the historic Rockefeller firm of Standard Oil of New Jersey, there can be little doubt of this hidden meaning."[39]

So it has nothing to do with Messiah and everything to do with His human archenemy, Nimrod. Is it just mere coincidence that people use the letter X to shorten it? Mullins talks about X and double X. How about three of them, as in XXX, the universal symbol for pornography, which is ubiquitous in our culture today? While most people are oblivious to these things, the spirit realm is fully aware of the power of these symbols.

Despite this fantastic knowledge that he had and the extraordinary power he wielded (he created the first world empire), it didn't help him in the end. Nimrod was killed, and there are generally two theories as to how. Josephus says that Shem, Noah's eldest son, killed him, chopped him up into twelve pieces, and distributed them throughout the empire. This forced all the wicked practices to become occult (from the Latin *occultus*, meaning "hidden, clandestine, or secret").[40] The Book of Jasher, however, says that Esau killed Nimrod. Either way, he died, and this is where things get interesting.

Nimrod married Semirimas, and after he died, he was worshipped as a god (more on this as we discuss other holidays). He achieved this through apotheosis, or the raising to godlike status. Many scholars believe that Nimrod became the sun god, also called Ba'al Hadad, the chief deity of the Canaanites and Yehovah's primary competition in Israel before the exile. On the rotunda of the Capitol Building in Washington, D.C. is a painting of the apotheosis of George Washington, where he is elevated to a deity, which is a Masonic belief. Again, it's the original lie of Satan that when we eat from the tree of the knowledge of good and evil, we will become like God.

Nimrod was known by various names in various cultures. In Egypt, he was known as Osiris, Ra, and Horus. In Greece he was known as Helios and Apollo, and in Persia he was known as Mithra. All pagan cultures worshipped the sun as the largest object in the sky and the source of life on earth. The key point is that Nimrod, and all of the other names by which he was known and worshipped, was believed to have been born on December 25. The reason for that date was that it was believed to be the winter solstice, or the shortest day of the year, and the sun was "reborn." The "Ahas" are deafening right now.

When my wife first became a believer, she was in church for a Christmas service because that's what you did as a Christian. The pastor very matter-of-factly told the congregation that most people knew that Yeshua wasn't born on December 25, but it was the day the church had chosen to celebrate His birth. My wife's immediate reaction was to question why they were there, and she wondered why they didn't want to know the right day.

Everyone has special days that we desire our loved ones to remember. Can you imagine if your family just randomly decided to choose a date to celebrate your birthday? What meaning would it have? Most people would be very upset. But what if the date wasn't so random? What if it was actually someone else's birthday? What if that someone was your rival? December 25 in Rome was the Feast of Saturnalia (Saturn). It was a celebration of Mithras (the Persian sun god, one of Nimrod's aliases). Now how does this celebration compare? If you're a woman, imagine that your husband has trouble remembering your birthday but clearly remembers the date of his high school sweetheart's, so he chooses to celebrate you then. Furthermore, he takes you to his ex's favourite restaurant. Now how are you feeling? He's sharing blankets with the dog tonight is how you feel. That's how God feels when you attempt to "worship" Him on the day the pagans used to celebrate their gods.

It makes sense to assume that God would feel that way, but is there any scriptural evidence to support this?

"When the Lord your God cuts off from you the nations which you are going in to dispossess, and you dispossess them and live in their land, be careful that you are not ensnared to follow them, after they are destroyed from your presence, and that you do not inquire about their gods, saying, 'How do these nations serve their gods, that I also may do likewise?' You shall not behave this way toward the Lord your God, because every abominable act which the Lord hates, they have done for their gods; for they even burn their sons and daughters in the fire for their gods" (Dt 12:29–31).

Just before Israel enters the land of Canaan, Moses warns them not to take the ways of the nations, the previous tenants that God was about to evict from said land, and worship Him with them. Note that He doesn't say not to worship those gods but not to worship Him the way they worshipped their gods, because their practices were abominable, especially child sacrifice. It was the same sin as occurred at Mt. Sinai, where they built the golden calf and said that it was the Lord who had brought them out of Egypt. Yehovah Elohim has no interest in the practices of the false gods He will one day destroy. He's already made it clear as to how He wants to be approached through His Word. No guessing needed, and we most certainly don't need to change anything either. That's actually forbidden. Right after He says not to approach Him with their ways, God says "*Whatever I command you, you shall be careful to do; you shall not add to nor take anything away from it*" (Dt 12:32).

One year I got an email from the denomination I served with in which they went to great lengths to explain why, even though it's not mentioned anywhere in scripture, it was ok to celebrate Christmas. They included links to several articles. The articles went through all the usual arguments (cue Charlie Brown's teacher). I replied to the gentlemen who'd sent the email and asked why they were spending so much time trying to justify doing something that God hadn't told us to do, while not doing what He had told us to do (the Feasts of Leviticus 23). I got quite a snarky response that didn't answer my question. So much for "Christian love." If we're having to justify doing something, that's usually a good sign we shouldn't be doing it. If our practices come from the very people and faiths that God has destroyed in the past (anyone go to a Mithras service lately, where the worshipper stands underneath a live bull and slits its stomach to drench himself in its blood?), we can safely assume He doesn't want us doing the same thing, and He has expressly told us so.

Symbols and Traditions of Christmas

"The word 'symbol' is derived from the ancient Greek *symballein*, meaning to throw together. Its figurative use originated in the custom of breaking a clay tablet to mark the conclusion of a contract or agreement: each party to the agreement would be given one of the broken pieces, so that when they reconvened the pieces could be fitted together like a jigsaw. The pieces, each of which identified one of the people involved, were known as symbola, so that a symbol not only represents something else but also hints at a missing 'something,' an invisible part that is needed to achieve completion of wholeness. Whether consciously or unconsciously, the symbol carries the sense of joining things together to create a whole greater than the sum of its parts, as shades of meaning accrue to produce a complex idea."[41]

Symbols represent other things. While having most likely always been part of society, they became especially prevalent after the Tower of Babel, when people could no longer speak the same language and needed another way of communicating. They are widely used within secret societies in order to obscure what they are doing while at the same time letting members know what's happening.

Symbols are incredibly powerful. Confucius is reputed to have said, "Signs and symbols rule the world, not words nor laws." While the Bible may take issue with that statement, as Solomon declares in Proverbs 18:21 that "*death and life are in the power of the tongue*" (emphasis mine), there is no doubt that symbols have power. Take, for example, the obelisk. These monuments are placed strategically all over the world, including across from the Capitol Building in Washington, DC and in St. Peter's Square in the Vatican, with very few knowing what they represent. Symbolizing the phallus of Nimrod, the god of Free Masonry (Lucifer) is primarily all about sex. The one-eyed sign on the apron of Masons' covers? You guessed it. By putting these huge stone symbols all over the world, for those in the know, they tell you: a) who's in charge (I don't get to just put a monument of my choosing in a public place at my pleasure) and b) what they stand for.

Every aspect of society has symbols. Someone who wears a religious symbol as jewellery declares to everyone who can see it what he or she believes. Wearing a team logo on your shirt declares who you cheer for. On the other hand, wearing something with a red circle and line through it instantly communicates what you are not in favour of or don't believe in. No words need be said.

Symbols within our religious celebrations are especially potent, as they have spiritual power behind them, both good and bad. The occult world is all about symbolism, and practitioners go to great lengths to make sure they use them in the prescribed manner to maximize their access to dark powers. A book on witchcraft or Masonic rituals is meticulous in the details. God is pretty specific too in what He accepts in His ceremonies and practices. That's why there's so much detail, especially in the guidelines regarding sacrifices or purification rites in the Bible. Everything points toward Yeshua, and it must be exact in its meaning.

The Lord went to great lengths to warn us about adopting pagan symbols in our worship because mixing the holy with the profane invites the evil one into our worship of God. In Acts 7, when Stephen is committed to death by the Sanhedrin, he reminds the leadership of Israel's unfaithfulness to Yehovah by worshipping Molech and Rompha. Stephen quotes the prophet Amos, who said:

"Did you present Me with sacrifices and grain offerings in the wilderness for forty years, house of Israel? You also carried along Sikkuth your king and Kiyyun, your images, the star of your gods which you made for yourselves. Therefore I will make you go into exile beyond Damascus," says the Lord, whose name is the God of armies" (Amos 5:25–27).

According to Wikipedia, *Kiyyun* is a different pronunciation of the ancient Persian word *Kayvan*, meaning "Saturn,"[42] who is Lucifer. Tying Rompha in with Molech means both involved the practice of child sacrifice. God was infuriated with Israel's idolatry and made specific mention of their symbols. And the star of Rompha? The hexagram, the six-pointed star that we commonly refer to today as the Star of David, placed squarely on Israel's flag! The treason goes deep and continues to this day.

Why all this background? Because it's impossible to overestimate or exaggerate the importance of symbols and the power they wield. The power of the spirit world is unlocked through the symbols we use, *whether knowingly or otherwise.*

Back to Christmas. How many customs and symbols associated with this holiday are borrowed from the pagans? Have we ever explored what they represent? It would be wise to do so.

Most of the symbols and even some of the practices we commonly use at Christmastime were actually part of fertility rights and celebrate a lack of restraint. Christmas caroling is looked upon with warm affection as people in their scarves and toques knock at your door and sing about the birth of Jesus. Who were the original carolers, though, and what did they do?

"Much like today's Mardi Gras, the all-day/all-night party was marked with rampant overeating and drunkenness. Bands of naked carolers roamed the streets, serenading other revelers with their bawdy songs. Gambling for nuts and coins was also permitted, the one time of the year such activities were allowed, even encouraged."[43]

Remember, God sees the past, present, and future at the same time, and when He looks at what we do now, He sees what was happening when the practice originated. It reminds Him of it. We cannot separate a practice's past from its current intention (discussed further in question 3 of this chapter).

Mistletoe is a parasitic plant that latches on to trees, sucking the life from them. It's highly poisonous. It was used in fertility rites, often by being hung over the newlyweds' bed on their wedding night. Orgies were also performed underneath it during Saturnalia. Yes, these morphed into more innocuous practices, but where they came from matters. Mistletoe is also associated with magic rituals.[44] Evergreen trees are a symbol of fertility because they never lose their leaves. They're also associated with Nimrod's deification. Semiramis claimed that after her husband died, a full-grown evergreen tree sprung out of a dead stump, symbolizing his life-giving force from the sun working on earth. The wreaths that we hang on our door represent the circle of life and also the female genitalia. Ivy and holly are associated together and symbolize death and rebirth but also the male and female who were burnt together in the pagan festival of Beltane.[45]

Pinecones are another common symbol of Christmas. Not only are they symbols of fertility (almost everything in paganism seems to go back to this and the shedding of blood), but they also represent the pineal gland (shaped like a pinecone) or the opening of the third eye. The all-seeing eye of Free Masonry depicts illumination, or secret knowledge, given by Lucifer. Ever notice the ubiquitous nature of the one-eyed symbolism within pop culture and entertainment? Countless magazine covers show celebrities hiding one eye—all telling us who controls them. Many of the pagan gods had a pinecone on their staff, including Osiris, Assyrian and Mexican deities, Bacchus (Greece), and Dionysus (Rome), who was the god of debauchery, revelry, wine, and war. Another person revered highly today is the pope, who has a pinecone on his staff. In fact, the Fontana della Pigna (Fountain of the Pinecone) in the Vatican courtyard contains a four-metre-high bronze pinecone that Dante compares to Nimrod's head.

"In his physical description of Nimrod, Dante reinforces the association of the Giants with the ruinous consequences of pride: 1) comparing the size of Nimrod's face to the pine cone at St. Peter's in Rome (Inf. 31.58–60)."[46]

The Christmas Tree

O Christmas tree, o Christmas tree,
Such pleasure do you bring me,
For every year this Christmas tree
Brings to us such joy and glee.

Of all the symbols of Christmas, the tree is the most pervasive. Countless pine trees give up their lives every year to be put in living rooms around the world for a few days to weeks, be covered with messy tinsel, have coloured balls hung on them, be crowned with a star and angels, have presents and nativity scenes put underneath them, and then be cast to the curb for garbage pickup after the season is done. Some have taken to plastic trees (the first ones produced by the same machinery that was used to make toilet brushes) to avoid the mess, which spares us the senseless slaughter of innocent trees. But again, where does this tradition originate?

As mentioned, pagans have always revered the evergreen tree as a symbol of eternal life and fertility, since in cold climes it's about the only thing in nature that doesn't die. The Christmas tree tradition is said to have originated with St. Boniface, an eighth-century Catholic missionary to what is now Germany, who saw the pagans worshipping at Donar's (another name for Thor) Oak, some say with a human sacrifice. He chopped the tree down and pointed to a small evergreen tree behind it, proclaiming to the heathen that:

"This little tree, a young child of the forest, shall be your holy tree tonight. It is the wood of peace … It is the sign of an endless life, for its leaves are ever green. See how it points upward to heaven. Let this be called the tree of the Christ-child; gather about it, not in the wild wood, but in your own homes; there it will shelter no deeds of blood, but loving gifts and rites of kindness."[47]

So this German bishop cuts down a pagan symbol of a pagan god and proceeds to introduce another pagan symbol to replace it as a representative of the one true God. Have you ever asked what cutting down a tree and killing it to decorate it in your home has to do with the living Messiah of Israel, where no evergreens grew? Even scripture addresses this one specifically:

"Hear the word which the Lord speaks to you, house of Israel. This is what the Lord says: 'Do not learn the way of the nations, and do not be terrified by the signs of the heavens, although the nations are terrified by them; For the customs of the peoples are futile; For it is wood cut from the forest, the work of the hands of a craftsman with a cutting tool. They decorate the idol with silver and gold; They fasten it with nails and hammers So that it will not totter. They are like a scarecrow in a cucumber field, and they cannot speak; They must be carried, because they cannot walk! Do not fear them, for they can do no harm, nor can they do any good'" (Jer 10:1–5).

Jeremiah specifically warns the people not to take a tree and decorate it with gold or silver as the pagans do. The response I often get is that this passage is talking about them worshipping the tree, and Christians don't worship the Christmas tree. That may be debatable if you see how frantic some people get about putting it up every year, but the point is that the people from whom the tradition came (the Druids) certainly did. As we've mentioned a hundred-and-eleventeen times already, a tradition's origins are critical to what kind of spirituality it will open you up to.

The star that many people put on top of the tree is most often five-pointed, and the pentacle is universally accepted as a major power symbol within satanism and witchcraft. There's nothing biblical about these things. They are totally pagan. One year, I was at a pastor's Christmas party at the house of one of the leaders of the denomination we served with at the time. During the evening I had a very animated discussion with one of the ladies who worked in head office about the Christmas tree right in front of us. She said, "You seem to have a real problem with it." I replied, "I think God has a real problem with it." My personal preferences are irrelevant, and that's where we've strayed so far from the narrow path Yeshua talks about. People evaluate their practices based on what they mean to them, not God.

Santa Claus

The star of the Christmas show every year is Santa Claus. Children eagerly anticipate this day for months. Trying to get them to wake up for school can be like trying to raise the dead, but come Christmas morning they're up at the crack of dawn, if they were able to sleep at all. They dash to the room where the Christmas tree is and under it presents galore. Where did they come from? Good ol' St. Nick or Santa Claus. Somehow he managed to traverse the entire world with his sleigh and eight flying reindeer to drop gifts off at every house by coming down the chimney. Watching the delight on children's faces as they open their gifts is always heartwarming. (Does anyone feel sorry for the poor puppy that had to be stuffed inside the box, though?) We do like to spread joy around, but once again—not to be the killjoy here—where does all this originate from and what's the meaning behind it all?

While giving gifts to ones we love can be a good thing, this practice of self-indulgence can breed issues of entitlement, which the world definitely does not need more of these days. Secondly, if we're celebrating Yeshua's birth, why are *we* getting presents? I posed this question to a young lady one time and her response was classic: "Why not?" Tough to argue with that. However, as we've already discovered, the giving of gifts on birthdays was a form of worship. The Christmas tradition of gift giving comes from the wise men. (Why does everyone say there were three? It never says how many there were. It only mentions the three gifts they gave, and we don't know if there were any more of those either. Three men travelling alone all the way from Babylon to Israel would have been very risky.) They were worshipping Yeshua and paying homage to the king when they came to see Him. Buying gifts for one another in the "spirit of the season" has nothing to do with Yeshua, and the commercial frenzy is as worldly as you can get. People feel pressure to buy gifts, and millions of people end up in a debt that takes months or all year to get out of. How is this honouring to

God again? Yeshua came to set the captives free, not put them further into bondage in their celebrations of Him.

Next we have the whole issue of lying. How many children have been traumatized when they found out Santa wasn't real? (Sorry if this is news to you.) There was a story posted online about a woman who walked away from faith in Yeshua because she said if her parents lied to her about Santa, they probably lied to her about God too, since she never saw either of them. Never lie to your children. Ever. The eighth commandment says not to bear false witness. There's no such thing as a little white lie. Satan is the father of lies, so any lie comes from him. Telling kids about tooth fairies and other mythical creatures is not healthy, even in fun. Lying breaks trust, and who knows what seeds of doubt have been planted because of this.

Lastly is the tradition of Santa Claus. The jolly big guy we've become so familiar with is a rather late edition to this centuries-old legend. Coca Cola commissioned artist Haddon Sundblom of the D'Arcy Advertising Agency to draw the overweight man with the red suit and hat (Coke's colour) in 1931 to encourage people to drink Coke.[48] For a while, children were encouraged to put a bottle of Coke on the table instead of milk with cookies because sugar and caffeine were needed in large amounts to make sure he got to every house throughout the night. Didn't hurt Coke's bottom line either.

So while we can thank American capitalism for our current image of Santa, the origins go back to old Norse legends. The god Odin (or Woden, for which our weekday Wednesday is named, meaning "inspired one") was the deity for intoxicating drink, ecstasy, and death, wisdom, occult, and magic. He travelled around the world on a white horse with eight legs. Odin used to travel around with a Krampus (from the German *krampen*, or claw), a dark one who used to scare and punish naughty children, put them in a sack, and take them to the underworld. Half-man and half-goat, these scary little demons eventually became our modern-day elves. Nothing like an image makeover.

"Krampus's name is derived from the German word krampen, meaning claw, and is said to be the son of Hel in Norse mythology. The legendary beast also shares characteristics with other scary, demonic creatures in Greek mythology, including satyrs and fauns."[49]

Today in Austria, Germany, and the Czech Republic, they have a Krampus Night and people (often drunk) dress up in hideous costumes and parade around the streets scaring children. The Bulgarians have a similar festival, called Kukeri. The Dutch created a version of him similar to Odin, called Sinterklaas. Part of his uniform was the crozier, which was an early pagan instrument with the symbol of the serpent built into it. Every pope has a crozier (or since Pope Paul IV, the bent cross, another satanic symbol)[50] as part of his uniform, and some of them are pretty hideous. Sinterklaas also travelled with a dark elf called Zwart Piet, or Black Pete. How godly or honouring to Yeshua is any of this?

Many will argue that St. Nicholas was reputed to be a fourth-century Turkish bishop who gave gifts to the poor, especially dowries to young women so that they wouldn't have to become prostitutes. Therefore, our Christmas traditions actually honour him. The Second Vatican Council of 1962 revoked his sainthood, claiming there is no evidence he existed. Even if he did, though, what people today associate with Christmas has very little to do with him and a lot more in common with all the pagan things we have covered. The devil was even called Old Nick in England during the Middle Ages.

Have you ever seen the look on some children's faces when they go to the mall during the Christmas season to wait in line for long periods of time to sit on Santa's lap and tell him what they want for Christmas? My wife has a picture of herself when she was only four or five and did this. She was terrified of this bearded stranger, and many children are. They have more discernment sometimes than adults.

It's clear that since God didn't put the date of Yeshua's birth in scripture, He didn't intend for us to commemorate it. We know December 25 can't be the right date even if we were supposed to celebrate it because no sheep are in the fields in Bethlehem and Jerusalem, which are up in the mountains, at that time of year because it's too cold. We also know December 25 is associated with the birthdays of Nimrod and many pagan gods, and all of the traditions associated with Christmas have pagan and occultic origins. Knowing all of this, it's safe to conclude that the way we celebrate Christmas violates God's commandment from Deuteronomy 12:29 to not worship Him as the pagans did their gods.

Even if the origins are pagan, what if that's not what it means to me?

When it comes to music, poetry, any kind of art, or even day-to-day conversations in which one person says something and someone else receives it in a way that wasn't intended, personal interpretation is fine. However, when it comes to religious practices, that argument doesn't apply for one simple reason: we are not the ones being worshipped. We might have the best of intentions, but if we're doing something for God that He prohibited, we need to understand that it's not honouring to Him, no matter how we feel about it. Our feelings are irrelevant. Why is so much of Christianity today about how we feel? God doesn't care how we feel about His commandments. He knows what's best for us and expects us to trust Him.

If I don't like salmon (I do) and romance movies (is there a car chase involved and things blowing up?), and my family decides to celebrate Father's Day with grilled salmon and watching *The Notebook* because my wife likes them, and my gift is a shirt for the New York Yankees because my son likes them, how do you think I'll feel? But they had the best of intentions, right? They honoured me on my day. Or did they? If I liked those things, we have no issues. But if they know that I don't and they still celebrate my special day with those things, then who are they really serving? God detests anything devoted to another god because: a) they're not real gods but created spirits receiving worship only meant for Him and b) they had abhorrent practices associated with their worship, especially human sacrifice. The Feast of Saturnalia involved public drunkenness and debauchery, cessation of all civil law for seven days, and the offering up of more than a few people to whatever god they were honouring. Just because we don't know its history doesn't mean a celebration is any less offensive to God when the foundation is based on evil things.

The greatest problem with human nature is that once Adam and Eve partook of the fruit of the knowledge of good and evil, they became me-focused. Everything in their lives and every person's life since then was primarily about themselves. Even our good deeds are like filthy rags (Is 64:6) if they are about bringing glory to ourselves instead of Him. When Yeshua established His *ekklesia* (Assembly), it was supposed to be different, but our modern-day church has become so much like the world by adopting its values, it has the same problem: it's still all about me. Our praise music today focuses a lot on the worshipper. Have you ever studied the words of contemporary Christian music? Most of it is about feelings and precious little about what God has done or what we actually do in response. In contrast, look at the words of the old hymns or Messianic praise (which is most often scripture put to music). The emphasis is on God and His works, faithfulness, power, glory, and what we do in response to that.

Celebrating holidays once devoted to other gods is not pleasing to the Lord. Since they are supposedly about honouring and worshipping Him, how we feel about them is irrelevant. How He feels about them ought to be our only concern.

Won't the Father redeem or sanctify it?

Since God is in the redemption and sanctification business, even if Christmas was once dedicated to another god, Yehovah Elohim owns everything. so can He not redeem this holiday for His glory? If we now dedicate it to Him, will it not erase the old meanings? I've heard this a lot, and theologically it's a fair question, but to properly answer it we have to understand what redemption and sanctification mean biblically.

The word redeem from Strong's in the Hebrew is גָּאַל (*gaal*), and some of the definitions for this are "buying back, claiming or to avenge."[51] The key here is the buying or bringing *back*. It had to have belonged to someone to begin with and then was lost. Hosea redeemed his wife Gomer when she went astray from him and ended up as a literal slave to another man. He paid money to get her back. She was his wife originally. You can't redeem something that didn't belong to you first. You then either just purchase, borrow, or steal it.

The word "jealous" is usually viewed as a negative emotion. Claim someone is jealous and the image one gets is irrational possessiveness, or the chest-beating, controlling man who rages at his girl in an abusive manner if he suspects she's done anything without his approval. How then can God be a jealous God and His name even be "Jealous" (Ex 34:14) if jealousy is bad? How can jealousy be a sin? It isn't. Jealousy and envy or coveting aren't the same thing. Jealousy is desiring what belongs to you. Coveting is wanting what is someone else's. The tenth commandment of the Decalogue is to not desire what belongs to your neighbour, whether it be his wife, his livestock, or his new Mustang convertible. God hasn't given you those things. He gave you what you have. Being protective (but not possessive) about them is perfectly legitimate and even healthy in God's eyes. He desires our worship, our devotion, and our love, which are *rightfully His*. They belong to Him, so when we go after other gods, He's hurt. It's just as my love, affection, and attention belong to my wife and not the bikini that walks by on the beach or an image on the computer screen. If what belongs to someone is given elsewhere, God has programmed jealousy within our souls to protect those things. There's even a test for a woman whose husband is overtaken by a spirit of jealousy to determine if his jealousy is *warranted* and to see if she *went astray* (Nm 5:11–31). We are jealous for our children's wellbeing, which is why we'll put ourselves in harm's way to defend it, even at the cost of our own lives. Didn't Yeshua do that on the cross for us? He redeemed us by buying us back from Satan with His blood. That is redemption. Redemption is not taking what belongs to someone else (a holiday devoted to worship) and making it your own. You can't redeem it (buy it back) if it never belonged to you to begin with.

What about sanctifying it? Sanctify (Strong's #6942) is קָדַשׁ (*qadash*) and is defined as "to be set apart or consecrated."[52] It's the same in the Greek. Being holy isn't being good, although that's an element of it. It's being separated from the world and its system, which is entirely corrupt. When the Father sanctifies something, He sets it apart for His own use, pleasure, and glory. When Leviticus 19:2 says we are to be holy, for He is holy, it means we are no longer part of the corruption that is creation. Arthur Weigall in his book *The Paganism in Our Christianity* said:

"… for it was a definite Christian policy to take over the pagan festivals endeared to the people by tradition and give them a Christian significance."[53]

So can God not sanctify something that was once profaned and make it holy? Can't we claim it for His glory by using our authority and cleanse it by Yeshua's blood? Doesn't 1 Timothy 4:4–5 tell us, *"For everything created by God is good, and nothing is to be rejected if it is received with gratitude;*

for it is <u>sanctified</u> by means of the word of God and prayer" (emphasis mine). He can and does. It depends on what it is, though.

In reading through the entire Bible, I only see one thing that God sanctifies: us. Nothing else is ever made holy that starts off as unholy, whether it be meat (we'll deal with clean and unclean animals in a later chapter), objects, days, and times, and most importantly for us with this topic, practices. In Acts 10, Peter is told not to call anything unclean that the Lord has cleansed. Christianity, for the most part, has interpreted that to say, "Great! Spiral ham and shrimp cocktail for supper tonight!" However, Peter himself tells us in verse 28 that "*You yourselves know that it is forbidden for a Jewish man to associate with or visit a foreigner; and yet God has shown me that I am not to call any <u>person</u> unholy or unclean*" (emphasis mine). If God was telling Peter that He was nullifying the food commands, why would Peter feel the need to interpret it and Luke record that interpretation for us by saying God was talking about people? Furthermore, what has what they eat got to do with the context of the rest of the passage? The point of Peter's mission to Cornelius's house was that God was about to bring the message of salvation to the Gentiles. He was going to call those who were not His people to be His people (Hos 2:23). Peter declares that God was cleansing the rest of humanity, and that was the only thing He was doing there. Reading anything else into the passage is nothing more than conjecture. Other than human beings, God doesn't cleanse anything that is defiled to begin with. If it starts unclean, it remains that way.

There is biblical precedent for this. In Haggai 2:11–14, the Lord tells Haggai to go get a ruling from the priests. This is official business, and He's going to tie in the physical commands with our spiritual walk.

"*The Lord of armies says this: 'Now ask the priests for a ruling: If someone carries holy meat in the fold of his garment, and touches bread with this fold, or touches cooked food, wine, oil, or any other food, will it become holy?' And the priests answered, 'No.' Then Haggai said, 'If one who is unclean from a corpse touches any of these things, will the latter become unclean?' And the priests answered, 'It will become unclean.' Then Haggai responded and said, "So is this people. And so is this nation before Me," declares the Lord, "and so is every work of their hands; and what they offer there is unclean."'*"

The principle here is that the holy cannot sanctify the unclean, but the unclean will defile the holy. Why do you think James tells us that pure religion is doing good deeds *and* keeping yourself away from the world? Because the world will defile you. You will not purify the world, meaning its system. Paul says in 1 Corinthians 15:33: "*Do not be deceived: 'Bad company corrupts good morals.'*" The only thing we can change through the power of the *Ruach Ha Kodesh* (Holy Spirit) is seeing people saved by preaching the gospel to them. Pagan holidays start off defiled; therefore, God will not receive them from us as holy and honouring to Him, no matter what our intentions. He gave us perfectly good festivals, which we will address in detail later, but those are holy and will remain so. One well-known radio preacher whose work I tremendously admire would spend about the last two months of every year railing about how "Jesus is the reason for the season" and the need to get the "Christ back into Christmas." Well, he was never there to begin with, so that's tantamount to chasing windmills. No matter how hard we try, we cannot make Christmas about Yeshua. They lament about the commercialization of Christmas and it's all about presents. It's mocked in pop culture. Have you ever seen the feasts of the Lord, such as Passover and Tabernacles, made fun of on TV or radio? Do they have models dressing up in lingerie, or nothing at all, for Pentecost like they do for Advent calendars? Never, because God protects what is His. He keeps those days holy (separate or set apart). Christmas is not protected by God because it's not His gift to His people to come and fellowship with Him. Personally, I think we should give the devil his holiday back and stop having anything to do with it.

Chapter 4—Other Holidays

"At Easter, popular customs reflect many ancient pagan survivals—in this instance, connected with spring fertility rites, such as the symbols of the Easter egg and the Easter hare or rabbit."

Encyclopedia Britannica

Although Christmas is the most celebrated of holidays that God says we shouldn't observe, others are equally egregious to the Lord and violate the Deuteronomy 12:29 command or have nothing to do with God at all. But Christians still participate in them anyway. Again, the danger with these holidays with pagan origins is that they open up spiritual doors for the enemy to afflict us, regardless of our intentions or what they mean to us, and we want to avoid that as much as is possible.

Easter

Perhaps even more offensive and certainly more insidious than Christmas is Easter. It's the time of year when Christians commemorate the death, burial, and resurrection of the Messiah, except they do it all in an unbiblical manner.

First is Good Friday. Everyone assumes that He died on Friday, was buried, and rose again sometime early Sunday morning, before dawn. The problem is that Yeshua tells us in Matthew 12:40 that, just like Jonah was in the fish, He would be in the earth three days *and three nights.* Now I know math has changed a lot since I was in school, but no matter how you do your calculations, you cannot get three nights between Friday and Sunday. There's an obvious contradiction here.

The error comes from the interpretation of Mark 15:42, where we're told that Yeshua died and was gathered by Joseph of Arimathea for burial on the day before the Sabbath. It's assumed that meant Friday because the Sabbath is on the seventh day, or Saturday. However, the weekly day of rest isn't the only Sabbath in God's calendar. This will come as a shock to many Christians, but there are actually other Sabbaths in scripture. This is one of the perils of not knowing the Hebrew scriptures or not looking at the Bible through the lens of a first-century Jewish believer. It's interesting to note that in the celebration of Good Friday, the Catholic and the Protestant churches acknowledge that the Sabbath was on the seventh day. At least that understanding is still intact.

Leviticus 23 speaks of God's appointed times. In addition to the weekly Sabbath, there are seven annual ones, which we'll cover more extensively in another chapter. Within these seven yearly celebrations are seven days where Israel is told they cannot work—the definition of a Sabbath. John even helps us here in his Gospel:

"Now then, since it was the day of preparation, to prevent the bodies from remaining on the cross on the Sabbath (for that Sabbath was a high day), the Jews requested of Pilate that their legs be broken, and the bodies be taken away" (John 19:31).

The denoting of a high Sabbath indicates it was one of the annual ones and not the weekly one. Since the first day of Unleavened Bread was a Sabbath, and it always occurs on the fifteenth of Aviv/Nisan (the first month in the Hebrew calendar), it can fall on any day of the week. Therefore, the Passover Yeshua ate with His disciples was on Wednesday night. He was betrayed later on, appeared before Pilate in the early hours of Thursday morning, and was crucified and buried that day. Now you can have your three days and nights. It's Interesting that the holiest day on the Christian calendar isn't even on the right day. Of course, God judges the heart, and if we come to Him with the right attitude, even if we get some of the details wrong, including the day, He will accept it. But if we can know the right day, why hold on to tradition?

Easter Sunday is as full of pagan rituals and symbols as any holiday on the Christian calendar. Going to churches and seeing pictures or figurines of bunnies in the sanctuary, as I have, is very disturbing. Giving kids chocolate eggs to celebrate the resurrection of Messiah, the key event in history for humanity's hope, is perplexing to say the least. Many have asked what one has to do with the other, but most, even when they can't answer or, worse, know the answer, continue to participate in the practice anyway. I questioned a pastor one year at a conference when he boldly proclaimed to a few of us that his new church had just done a huge Easter egg hunt for a community outreach. I asked why he would do that, knowing the practice was pagan. His response was quite dismissive: "Where do we draw the line?" That's a pretty major line we're talking about here, not some insignificant issue. Where did we get the *chutzpah* (audacity) to believe that no matter what we bring before God, He'll accept because He's just so delighted that we came to Him? Here's a news flash for a lot of Christians— God doesn't need us. He was complete in Himself before He ever created anything. He created us not out of need but a desire for family and fellowship, but it's only pleasing to Him if we do it His way. I adore my son beyond what I knew I could feel before we had him, but if he's disobedient, I'm not feeling so great about him. Still love him, but any experiences of warmth and fuzziness are definitely absent at that point, which he certainly is aware of. It's the same with God. He loves us unconditionally but isn't happy with us all the time, and He will let us know. The theology of the all-loving God who's got a perma-grin is not biblical. That is a god people have created in their own image. God hates pagan things, and as we begin to understand where the symbols and practices of Easter come from, we'll better appreciate how detestable they really are to Him and should be to us.

It should be no surprise at this point to know that all of the traditions at Easter go back to our old friend Nimrod. The name Easter comes from the Eostre, who was the Anglo-Saxon goddess of the dawn spring, renewal, fertility, the moon, etc. The only reference we have for this is from the eighth-century monk Venerable Bede,[54] but knowing how paganism spread, the small details don't really matter too much. They all originate from the same place. Eostre is also associated with Ishtar, who was the Babylonian goddess of fertility as well. (They're really the same god. They just change names from country to country.) Ishtar is actually the deification of Semiramis, Nimrod's wife. After Nimrod died, Semiramis became pregnant and claimed that it was by the light of the sun, which was Nimrod. Tammuz was then worshipped as the reincarnated Nimrod, and now Semiramis was the mother goddess[55] you had to pray through to get to Baal. Tammuz becomes a mighty hunter, but at forty years old, he's killed by a wild boar (ok, maybe not so mighty). Semiramis then claims that some of his blood fell on the stump of an evergreen tree and immediately sprang up as a new tree. Semiramis then called for a forty-day fast, one day for every one of Tammuz's years, where no meat was to be eaten. It culminated with a feast where they ate a pig in revenge for killing their god. They would also make cakes with the sign of a cross, or a T, on them in worship of Tammuz (the Phoenician and Hebrew letter *tav* is where we get our letter T from). Semiramis eventually dies, and legend has it that Baal sent her back to earth in the form of a giant egg that landed in the Euphrates River. The fish pushed the egg to the shore where it hatched, producing a rabbit. Tammuz is worshipped at sunrise on Easter morning because he is now with his father, Nimrod/Baal, ruling in heaven.

Now when worshippers go to an Easter sunrise service, do you still believe it's all about Yeshua? Do the eggs they colour really represent His and our new life? Is it really Yeshua's forty-day fast in the desert before being tempted by the devil that we are commemorating with Lent? There's literally nothing about these practices that have anything to do with Yeshua's death, burial, and resurrection. As we've previously discussed, it doesn't matter what we want them to mean. We can't just slap a little Jesus jam over them and, voila, it's now a Christian holiday.

Lent comes from the Anglo word *lencten*, which means spring. Easter is always the first Sunday after the first full moon that follows the vernal or spring equinox. The equinox is important in paganism because it's when the days become longer than the nights. It's also when the plants begin to grow again. It goes back to the worship of the gods of nature. The Hebrew calendar is based on the lunar cycle. That's why Easter and Passover can either be on the same day or up to a month apart.

The forty days of fasting are said to be about identifying with Yeshua's temptation. The Catechism of the Catholic Church says

"'For we have not a high priest who is unable to sympathize with our weaknesses, but one who in every respect has been tested as we are, yet without sinning' [Heb 4:15]. By the solemn forty days of Lent the Church unites herself each year to the mystery of Jesus in the desert." [56]

However, this practice predates the Catholic Church and Christianity by centuries. What does the Lord say to Ezekiel about this?

"Then He brought me to the entrance of the gate of the Lord's house which was toward the north; and behold, women were sitting there <u>*weeping for Tammuz*</u>*. And He said to me, 'Do you see this, son of man? Yet you will see still greater abominations than these!' Then He brought me into the inner courtyard of the Lord's house. And behold, at the entrance to the temple of the Lord, between the porch and the altar, were about twenty-five men with their backs to the temple of the Lord while their faces were toward the east; and they were* <u>*prostrating themselves eastward toward the sun*</u>*. And He said to me, 'Do you see this, son of man? Is it a trivial thing for the house of Judah to commit the abominations which they have committed here, that they have filled the land with violence and provoked Me to anger repeatedly? Yet behold, they are putting the twig to their nose! Therefore, I indeed will deal in wrath. My eye will have no pity nor will I spare; and though they cry out in My ears with a loud voice, yet I will not listen to them'"* (Ez 8:14–18, emphasis mine).

The weeping for Tammuz and worshipping the sun (Baal/Nimrod) in the Temple were big reasons why God destroyed Jerusalem and the Temple in 586 BCE. He said He would not pity or spare them because of this abomination, and now we show up on Ishtar Sunday morning at sunrise, facing the east. We finish our service with a chocolate egg hunt that's associated with Semiramis, the wicked wife of Nimrod, who not only defied her husband but herself and her illegitimate child. Incidentally, the Statue of Liberty (made by French Free Masons) and the Columbia Pictures icon (holding the torch representing the sun god) are both modelled after her. We eat cakes dedicated to Tammuz, even having his initial put on them. Jeremiah also condemned the Israelites for making cakes to Semiramis:

"The children gather wood, the fathers kindle the fire, and the women knead dough to make sacrificial cakes for the queen of heaven; and they pour out drink offerings to other gods in order to provoke Me to anger" (Jer 7:18).

"'And,' said the women, 'when we were burning sacrifices to the queen of heaven and pouring out drink offerings to her, was it without our husbands that we made for her sacrificial cakes in her image, and poured out drink offerings to her?'" (Jer 44:19).

The Catholic Church just replaced Semiramis with Mary as the Queen of Heaven.

Then we finish off our worship services by coming home and having an Easter ham. Has anyone ever considered the irony of honouring the Jewish Messiah by eating ham? It just boggles the mind how much we put aside reason and common sense to continue in our customs and traditions, never once bothering to ask how God feels about it. No wonder I see a picture of Him with a red mark on His forehead!

If we're going to honour God in a way that's pleasing and acceptable to Him, the obvious source of our information is His Word to us. The Bible tells us in Leviticus 23 which times and in what manner He wants us to commemorate what He has done for us. The symbols in those feasts are consistent with His character and provide types and shadows of the Messiah who was to come. We have no need to borrow from the pagans and practise theological gymnastics to make it work. Again, I say leave the devil's holidays to him and celebrate how God has already told us to. That's when He is truly honoured, and peace and blessing will be our reward.

Valentine's Day

Valentine's Day is the one universal day of the year when every man is impressed upon to be romantic to his wife or girlfriend. Chocolate and flower vendors drool as February 14 approaches, and Hallmark also does brisk sales on this day for love. It's estimated that over a billion dollars in business is done on this day.[57] Without getting into too much detail, let's look at a bit of the history of this holiday and the all-important symbolism.

The holiday was originally called Lupercalia. Lupercus was a hunter, and this festival was celebrated once again as a fertility right.

"The pagan fertility celebration of Lupercalia took place February 13th, 14th, and 15th. Men sacrificed goats and dogs, stripped their hides, and then ran through the city square in the nude, literally whipping women, all in celebration of fertility. Many women would actually line up and volunteer for the lashing, believing it a fertility blessing.

"Even after Christianity's legalization in Rome, the pagan holiday remained for a century and a half, too popular with the populace to be abandoned. Pope Gelasius eventually did shut down Lupercalia for its pagan origins … but soon after, many historians believe, the Catholic Church rebranded Lupercalia as a new, Christian holiday by declaring an annual feast for Saint Valentine on February 14th."[58]

Valentinus was a Christian who performed illegal marriages under Emperor Claudius II, who banned them to prevent men getting married to escape the draft.[59] Valentinus was executed in the year 269.

Lupercus was called Pan by the Greeks, the chimera who was half-man, half-goat. Pan was known as Baal in Babylon and Canaan. These holidays always trace back to the unholy trinity of Nimrod, Semiramis, and Tammuz. It seems a little more than a coincidence that Lupercus was also a great hunter in the tradition of Nimrod, who Genesis 10:9 tells us " … *was a mighty hunter before the Lord; therefore it is said, 'Like Nimrod a mighty hunter before the Lord.'*"

The symbol most associated with Valentine's Day is the heart. It is ubiquitous in society, whether in drawings, on cards, and even as emojis. But have you ever noticed that the two curves meeting together symmetrically bear no resemblance whatsoever to the organ in our bodies that pumps our blood? Several theories have been presented as to where that symbol originates from. Many have suggested it comes from the ancient herb silphium (which no longer exists), which had a similar shape. It was used as a spice but also as a type of birth control because it was known to abort the fetus when taken. When you see two swans together nuzzling, their necks and heads make the heart shape. However, closer to the theme of the holiday, it has been suggested that it represents various parts of the woman's anatomy, including her breasts, genitalia, or, most likely, her buttocks when she is bent over.[60] This can also be seen in Disney's *The Lion King*, where on one official poster, Simba's nose is clearly a woman's bikini-clad bottom.

Cupid is the hero of this holiday. His job is to run around getting people to fall in love. He does so by shooting them in the heart with his arrows. Sounds great. Got a crush on the popular girl in tenth grade who doesn't even know you exist? Pray and make an offering to Cupid to shoot her and she falls in love with you. You both live happily ever after. Sounds no different than going to a witch or a shaman to cast a spell. How many obnoxious romance movies (that I won't have to watch on Father's Day) have been loosely based on this theme?

First of all, the whole idea of falling in love is a Hollywood (magic) thing. The wood of a holly tree is what magic wands were made of. In real life, you don't "fall" in love, because falling into something usually denotes getting wet or hurt. We decide to love. The hormone that makes you "feel" love, oxytocin, eventually dissipates after a certain amount of time. What happens when the hormone has gone out of your system? If you fall in love, by the same logic you can also fall out of love, which is why people switch partners so often and the divorce rate is so high, even in the church. Falling is precarious business. We are following the world's concept of love instead of God's.

Secondly, this whole idea of being shot with something to suddenly love someone sounds quite dangerous. When hearing the lyrics of Sam Cooke's 1961 song "Cupid" or Bon Jovi's 1986 "You Give Love A Bad Name" about people getting shot through the heart with Cupid's arrows, one doesn't get a picture of a happily-ever-after scenario. In real life, if you get shot through the heart, you die. This is nothing more than sorcery. It's love by coercion, forcing someone against their will. In some depictions, Cupid is even shown as being blindfolded, demonstrating that love is blind.[61] Contrast that with the biblical picture of courting someone and winning their affections through noble character, such as Jacob working seven years for Rachael's hand in marriage. The two couldn't be farther apart.

According to Alexander Hislop in his famous work *The Two Babylons*:

"Speaking of a statue of Cupid, it is a fair, full, fleshly, round boy, in fine and sportive action, tossing back a heart. Thus the boy-god came to be regarded as the 'god of the heart,' in other words, as Cupid, or the god of love. To identify this infant divinity, with his father 'the mighty hunter' [Nimrod], he was equipped with 'bow and arrows.' He was the woman's seed. Venus and her son Cupid, (Semiramis and Tammuz) were none other than the Madonna and the child (bearing the sacred heart).

"The worship of the 'Sacred Heart' was introduced into Rome. It was so in ancient Babylon, as is evident from the Babylonian system as it appeared in Egypt. There also a 'Sacred Heart' was venerated. The 'Heart' was one of the sacred symbols of Osiris when he was born again, and appeared as Harpocrates, or the infant divinity, borne in the arms of his mother Isis. Therefore, the fruit of the Egyptian Persea was peculiarly sacred to him, from its resemblance to the 'HUMAN HEART.' Hence this infant divinity was frequently represented with a heart, or the heart-shaped fruit of the Persea, in one of his hands."[62]

Cupid (Roman), or Eros (Greek), is associated with different stories about his origins, but the idea of this cute little cherub flying around naked or with a diaper on is insulting to every cherub God created. Cherubim are warrior spirits who were greatly feared in scripture. One killed 185,000 Assyrians in one night as they were about to attack Jerusalem under King Hezekiah's rule. That's not someone whose cheek you want to pinch. In Roman mythology, Cupid is the son of Venus (Semiramis), who is the goddess of love and sexuality. She lusted after him, and it has even been suggested that Semiramis married her own son, Tammuz, which would explain the origins of that story. The Greek name Eros is where we get our word erotic from, and it implies lust, not love. The word for God's unconditional love is ἀγάπη, (agapé), which denotes unconditional love and is completely separate from feelings or emotions. God decides to love us, and we decide to love someone else. Agapé was actually disdained in the ancient Greek world. Not much different than the world we live in today.

Valentine's Day is one day devoted to love, based on a story involving witchcraft and coercing someone to love you by casting a spell on them, and it's dedicated to a god who was involved in incest and celebrating with men running naked through the streets and whipping women. God joins people together because they share similar goals and values and make a covenant (an agreement binding until death) to share life together and grow together. We struggle through difficulties and decide to treasure one another regardless of how we feel at the time—and this is every day, not just one a year. Once again, here is a holiday that followers of Yeshua should be avoiding completely.

Halloween

Of all the celebrations believers participate in, nothing makes me shake my head in disbelief more than Halloween. Christmas and Easter have a Christian veneer on them, and Valentine's Day is at least supposedly about love and romance, but Halloween is laid out in all of its satanic glory of who and what it really represents. Making some flimsy excuse that it's about honouring the Saints and calling it All Hallows Eve, the night before All Saints' Day on November 1, like the Catholic Church has done, is absurd. Halloween is about evil spirits, full stop. There's nothing remotely associated with the God of creation in it. It has everything to do with Satan and the kingdom of darkness. There's not even a pretense that it has anything to do with Messiah, yet believers by the millions participate in it. I was at a pastors' conference a few years back in November, and while sitting a table with other couples and feeling somewhat frisky, I declared to them that I didn't understand how Christians, especially pastors, could allow their kids to participate in Halloween, knowing that it was an overtly satanic holiday about death. I did this because I wanted to see their reaction (I've been known to do that periodically). Sure enough, the younger pastor and his wife, who had young children, were both very quiet. By the look on their faces, I knew they had done just that. Another pastor's wife and children within the same denomination celebrated Trunk or Treat one year and posted the photos on Facebook. This is where people line up their cars and give children treats out of their trunks, instead of having them knock on doors. The pastor's wife and son were dressed as pirates, and they had a mock coffin complete with skeleton in their trunk. She boldly proclaimed they were doing this as an outreach into the community to celebrate Jesus and promote their church. When my wife called her out on Facebook and asked her why she was attempting to represent the Lord using symbols of death, she responded by snapping back, "What's your problem?" and proceeded to unfriend her. Another stellar example of Christian love.

Halloween is a druidic holiday. The druids were the priestly class of the Celts, a lovely bunch of people who worshipped nature and were quite fond of human sacrifice. Remember the Christmas tree story in which St. Boniface interrupted an offering that was about to commence? Halloween was originally called Samhain (pronounced Saw-win in Gaelic). Samhain is the Celtic lord of the dead, and this festival was known as the feast of the dead. It was a harvest festival to usher in the "dark half of the year."[63] Samhain is the most important pagan festival of the year, the second being Beltane, which is May 1. Both are high sabbats (witches' holidays) and involve human sacrifice. Wiccan High Priestess Doreen Valiente said:

"Halloween is one of the four Great Sabbats of the witches that everyone has heard about. To witches, Halloween is a serious occasion, however merrily celebrated. It is the old Celtic Eve of Samhain."[64]

Anton LaVey, founder of the Church of Satan and author of the Satanic Bible, states:

"After one's own birthday, the two major Satanic holidays are Walpurgisnacht (May 1st) and Halloween."[65]

It was believed that at on October 31, time stood still and the barrier between the physical and spiritual worlds was the thinnest, so spirits could easily breach the barrier; therefore, they had to be placated as they roamed about looking to either bless or torment people. Food was left outside for these spirits so they wouldn't harass the families. This is where the origins of "trick or treat" came from. If the offering wasn't sufficient, the spirits would ruin their future crops. Bonfires were lit, and who doesn't love a good bonfire? Except they were offered to the sun in hopes it would come back. Originally, they were called "bone fires" because they contained the bones of either animals or children that had been sacrificed. Yellow ribbons were tied around oak trees (which were worshipped by the Druids) by families in the hopes their children would be spared. Gives a whole new significance to the 1973 song by Tony Orlando and Dawn, "Tie a Yellow Ribbon 'Round the Old Oak Tree." Apparently it wasn't just a song about the guy needing a sign from his girlfriend as to whether she still wanted him or not. Paganism and the occult are everywhere in our culture.

Jack-o'-lanterns stemmed from a legend involving a wretch named Stingy Jack, who outsmarted the devil twice. After he died, he wasn't allowed into heaven or hell, so he was condemned to roam the earth forever as a spirit. He did ask the devil for an ember from hell to light his way, and he put that into a carved-out pumpkin so that when people saw strange lights they would say it was "jack of the lantern."[66] The tradition would be to carve out a pumpkin or gourd and use the fat from the sacrifices of animals or children as fuel. It's appropriate that the face on a carved pumpkin looks demonic.

Bobbing for apples is another fun event people usually do at fall country fairs, and it's often associated with Halloween. The tradition started when the Druids would fill a cauldron full of boiling oil and make prisoners bob for apples. Many died in the process, but if you happen to survive with horrendous pain, you were then put into a giant man made of wicker with all the other survivors and lit on fire to complete the sacrifice. The Burning Man Festival, a nine-day occult-themed celebration of art that occurs in the Nevada desert every August, gets its inspiration from this horrendous practice. The highlight of the entire affair is the giant statue that has a different pagan or esoteric theme every year that is lit on fire at the end of the festival. In 2017, a man ran into the flames of the burning statue and died, thus bringing the tradition back to its origins.

Halloween is one of the two highest days of the satanic year and therefore requires a human sacrifice. Hundreds, even thousands, of children and animals disappear every year leading up to October 31. Nothing infuriates God more than the offering up of the most defenseless members of society as a sacrifice to Satan and his demonic army. God tells Moses in Deuteronomy 18:10:

"There shall not be found among you anyone who makes his son or his daughter pass through the fire, one who uses divination, a soothsayer, one who interprets omens, or a sorcerer, or one who casts a spell, or a medium, or a spiritist, or one who consults the dead. For whoever does these things is detestable to the Lord; and because of these detestable things the Lord your God is going to drive them out before you. You are to be blameless before the Lord your God. For these nations, which you are going to dispossess, listen to soothsayers and diviners, but as for you, the Lord your God has not allowed you to do so."

The worship of Molech involved a huge statue of a half-bull, half-man (a minotaur, another chimera) with arms stretched out. Babies were placed into its hands and would then roll into the blazing furnace of its chest. The drum beats had to be loud enough to drown out the screams of the burning children. The sacrifice of children today through either abortion or after birth is the highest crime one can commit against God, and Halloween is one of the bloodiest days of the year.

No matter what we call it, or how cutesy the costumes might be, Halloween is the outright worship of Satan. When I was about thirteen or fourteen and going out trick or treating for one of my last Halloweens before I was too old, I intentionally dressed up as a vampire because I wanted to go as something that represented the true spirit of the holiday. I understood what Halloween was about and wanted to make it authentic. As with any other pagan holiday, not matter how you dress it up (pun intended), it doesn't change what it's about. Any participation in it violates God's commands not to be involved in these things in any way. Nothing can justify it. One young mother replied to my wife several years ago when she questioned her for handing out candy to trick or treaters by saying that she wouldn't be demonstrating God's love if she didn't open the door for them. That is outright foolishness. Perhaps having a prayer meeting that night, or even fasting that day for the protection of the children, might be a little more loving. If you have participated in Halloween in the past, know that we've all made our mistakes, but repenting of it and committing to having nothing do with it again would be what God desires of you.

Holidays are wonderful things, as they are a celebration of something. God's festivals given to us in Leviticus 23 are rich in meaning and intended for us to meet with Him and rejoice in His faithfulness. However, through outright disobedience, the Body of Messiah has forsaken these appointed times by God and instead adopted ones that are putrid to Him. They were originally dedicated to other gods and involved every kind of abhorrent practice, especially human sacrifice. No amount of good intentions or warm feelings from memories can change that. If we're going to be holy because He is holy, believers need to keep away from what is defiled in the world, and that includes religious holidays not ordained by God.

Chapter 5—Gentiles Don't Have To

"Before God, from a spiritual perspective, all humanity is the same!
The requirements one must meet in order to be allowed in God's
presence are the same!"

Rishoka

While many in the Body claim the commandments are completely done away with for everyone, an erroneous idea we thoroughly dealt with in chapter 1, many others say the commandments only apply to the Jews and not the Gentiles. After my wife's first Christmas service, where the pastor said that everyone knew Yeshua wasn't born on December 25, she went home and decided to look into the scriptures to find out when the right day was. Even though she was told to focus on the New Testament, she rebelled and decided to start from the beginning. When she got to Leviticus 23, lo and behold there was God's calendar. Excitedly, she ran back to her pastor to show him her wonderful find, telling him we didn't need to guess when to come worship God because He already told us with His appointed feast days. His response was "Those are for the Jews." Undaunted, my wife replied to him, "They're in my Bible, and God wants me to do them, so I guess I'm going to the Jews." I am ever grateful for that conversation because I ended up with a wife out of the deal. Thank you, Pastor.

I am always befuddled as to how people will set aside reason and plain sense when it comes to their spiritual lives. They will accept things when it comes to their relationship with God that they would never accept in any other aspect of their lives. So many theological positions in the church today are contradictory. They wouldn't be accepted if they were written in a business or legal contract. Parents don't accept them in their homes. Governments and law enforcement agencies don't accept them in society, yet so many believe God is perfectly fine with them.

Many years ago, I was at a Pentecostal church where I'd spoken several times. I was up on stage, and a prayer meeting got started. It was like a rodeo broke out. One woman, who had to be in her sixties, walked down from the choir benches, got down on her hands and knees on the stage, and started crawling around, banging her hand on the floor while everyone was screaming and carrying on in the rest of the sanctuary. This went on for about half an hour.

After the service, the pastor and I went out for lunch, and I said to him, "Bishop, I want to ask you a question. If a successful businessman had walked into the back of the church when all that was going on, would he have been provoked to jealousy?" He responded no. "So why do you allow it?" I pressed him. That lady would not have behaved that way before the prime minister of Canada, the president of the United States, the queen of England, the pope, or her fifth-grade teacher, so why did she think it was ok to do it before the King of the universe? What do we think of God when we believe He's ok with us acting like complete fools in a worship service? Does anyone truly think that in the Millennial reign of Yeshua on earth that we'll be doing that before Him as he sits on the throne? I rather suspect not.

The same goes for this different-commandments-for-Jews-and-Gentiles stuff. Every time I hear this, I ask if they think parents (especially if the ones I'm addressing are parents themselves) have different rules for their kids. One has to do homework; the other doesn't. One has to show up for dinner at a certain time or do chores or has a curfew, while the other is exempt. They all say no. So why would God be this way? If it's the same God we worship, then doesn't it stand to *reason* that all of God's children have to abide by the same rules?

"Or is He the God of the Jews only? Is He not also the God of the Gentiles? Yes, of the Gentiles also" (Rom 3:28).

This isn't to say that all commandments apply to every person. There are commandments for women only (Leviticus 12, dealing with childbirth). Every male has always been exempt from those. Some of the commandments apply only to the priests when they're serving in the Temple. We have no standing temple now, so they don't apply. Others apply to the king only. But the ones that say to show up on a specific day aren't just for one believer and not another. If it says don't eat certain things, it's not just unhealthy for one and not the other. What about mixed marriages? The Jewish spouse has to obey and the Gentile one doesn't? How about the children who are half and half? Which half has to keep the Sabbath and which half keeps Sunday? Can you see the absurdity in this position? Even before we get to the theological proof that this isn't true, from a pure reasoning point of view, it doesn't even make sense. I believe a whole lot of doctrinal errors would grow wings and just fly away if, as Josh McDowell and Bob Hostetler say in their best-selling book, you *Don't Check Your Brains at the Door.*

Scripturally, everything God does is for the sake of unity within His family. Yeshua says in John 17:20–21:

"I am not asking on behalf of these alone, but also for those who believe in Me through their word, that they may all be one; just as You, Father, are in Me and I in You, that they also may be in Us, so that the world may believe that You sent Me."

Yeshua prayed to the Father that we would be one. Tough to do if we're following different rules, days, and practices. How is the world supposed to know we worship the same God if He's got a split personality? One of the major impediments to the spread of the gospel message is the division within the Body. If we have all this infighting, what does the world need Yeshua for? They've already got division in their lives, and by our witness, coming to faith won't change that.

During His Millennial reign, everyone will be worshipping the same way. Zechariah 14:9 says, *"And the Lord will be King over all the earth; on that day the Lord will be one, and His name one."* Furthermore, in verses 16–19, we're told:

"Then it will come about that any who are left of all the nations that came against Jerusalem will go up from year to year to worship the King, the Lord of armies, and to celebrate the Feast of Booths. And it will be that whichever of the families of the earth does not go up to Jerusalem to worship the King, the Lord of armies, there will be no rain on them. And if the family of Egypt does not go up or enter, then no rain will fall on them; it will be the plague with which the Lord strikes the nations that do not go up to celebrate the Feast of Booths. This will be the punishment of Egypt, and the punishment of all the nations that do not go up to celebrate the Feast of Booths."

Not only will every nation have to go up to worship at the Feast of Sukkot, or Tabernacles, but every family will. If they don't, they'll experience famine because of drought. All of God's children had to keep the feasts before Yeshua came to earth as a man, and everyone in the world will have to do it when He returns. But right now God isn't concerned about it? Because of grace, we can come whenever we want by whatever means we want? I ask again, would that illogic apply anywhere else in our lives?

The final nine chapters in the book of Ezekiel deal with the Millennial Kingdom as well. God clearly tells the prophet how things are going to run during His reign. Speaking of the Levites, who will serve in the Millennial temple, He has him write:

"Moreover, they shall teach My people the difference between the holy and the common, and teach them to distinguish between the unclean and the clean. In a dispute they shall take their stand to judge; they shall judge it according to My ordinances. They shall also keep My laws and My statutes in all My appointed feasts, and sanctify My Sabbaths" (Ez 44:23–24).

All the ordinances, laws, statutes, appointed feasts, and Sabbaths will be observed by everyone in the world, and it's going to be the Levites who will teach the world these things. Gentiles don't get a pass like they think they do now. So if God is going to have everyone in the world keeping all of Torah when He returns, which will be the world's constitution, would it not make sense that He wants us to do it now, if for nothing else than at least to practice? I say this tongue in cheek, but how can we read these passages and still maintain that some believers are excused from God's instructions today? It doesn't make sense, and in order to buy into it, you have to suspend logic. Isaiah 1:18 tells us to "*Come let us reason together,*" but we disdain that for convenient but well-worn theological contradictions that satisfy our flesh's desire to not obey God. If you can spiritualize it, then you can sleep at night thinking you're still a good Christian. Many will come to me in that day and say "Lord, Lord … "

At some point in time, almost every one of the conversations I've had on this topic eventually comes around to Acts 15 and the Council in Jerusalem. James very clearly says that the apostles should not bother the Gentiles with anything else but four simple rules to follow: three had to do with food and one with sexual purity.

"*Therefore, it is my judgment that we do not cause trouble for those from the Gentiles who are turning to God, but that we write to them that they abstain from things contaminated by idols, from acts of sexual immorality, from what has been strangled, and from blood*" (Acts 15:19–20).

It would appear once again that the Bible itself confirms that the Gentiles don't gotta do Torah, and once again we need to reiterate: Context, my dear Watson. We don't start in verse 19. We start at the beginning of the story. And what was the issue?

"*Some men came down from Judea and began teaching the brothers, 'Unless you are circumcised according to the custom of Moses, you cannot be <u>saved</u>*'" (Acts 15:1, emphasis mine).

The issue was whether the Gentiles had to be circumcised to be saved. You don't have to do anything to be saved but believe and confess. It's amazing that when the Bible talks about being obedient to the commandments as a life that is pleasing to God, Christians right away switch the topic and say that you don't have to keep them to be saved. The Bible does agree with them on that but then they say it proves that we don't have to keep the commandments at all, even after we're saved. That's called circular reasoning.

If we're going to take this argument literally and agree with James that Gentiles only have to keep the four he mentioned, why do so many churches insist Christians have to keep Sunday as a day of worship? That's not mentioned among the four. It doesn't say anything about honouring our parents, murdering, stealing, lying, or coveting either. Well, that's in the Ten Commandments. Ahhh, I see. So those four aren't the only standard for believers, are they? Then what is the whole issue the council was meeting over?

In order to answer that question, we have to understand the milieu of the day. Judaism had a system of proselytization or converting, which circumcision was part of. Being circumcised was a term that meant going through the complete conversion process, which involved keeping all of Torah. We have examples of this in the Dead Sea Scrolls, which were found at Qumran. In her paper, "Community Structures in the Dead Sea Scrolls: Admission, Organization, Disciplinary Procedures," Charlotte Hempel said:

"The admission of new members in 1QS 6 (the scroll number) is characterized by several stages involving periods of probation and examinations so that full membership is only acquired after a process lasting several years."[67]

In order to convert to Judaism, one had to get circumcised and then go on probation for up to several years before being welcomed into the community as a full-fledged member. Yeshua turned that whole system upside down with the Great Commission, which was to make disciples, immerse (baptize) them and make a public confession, and *then* teach them the ways of walking with God. New believers were welcomed into the community before having all of their ducks lined up in a row. The gospel message is Yeshua saying to us "You catch them, and I'll clean them up." What we see here with the Jerusalem Council was the exact same thing. Get them saved and then teach them how to walk in holiness, not the other way around.

The reason they even had to have this council was because they had to answer a burning question: What do we do with the Gentiles? That was the biggest issue in the first-century assembly. One of the biggest questions we have today in the twenty-first-century church is what to do with the Jews. How things have changed. The council was necessary because Gentiles getting saved and filled with the Spirt caught everyone off guard (which it shouldn't have, since God foretold it many times through the prophets). It was easy when the believers were all Jews. They already knew Torah. The

Gentiles coming into the community were called growing pains ... a nice problem to have.

The four commands from James were the basic elements of behaviour for joining the community for Gentiles with no tradition of righteous living by God's standards. Have you ever wondered why it was those four commandments? There are over six hundred of them, yet the Council chose only four that addressed food and sexual purity. Peter said in Acts 10 that it was unlawful for a Jew to enter into the house of a Gentile, but God told him not to call men unclean. Why were Jews not allowed into a Gentile's house? Because of what they ate (unclean meat), what they did with that meat (offered it to idols, which might have even been in the house), and their sexual practices, which were also part of religious rites to those idols. That's why God used the illustration of the blanket—it was one of the primary reasons a Jew considered a Gentile unclean. The blanket came down three times. Any guess as to how many men from Cornelius's house showed up? While we don't have to be perfect in order to come to faith, there are basic standards we're expected to adhere to, even at the beginning of our walk. How different is that from any other organization we belong to, whether it be family, a club, or a faith community? Violate those standards and you're out.

But that doesn't mean the Gentiles weren't to grow in holiness. Again, if that was the case, there'd be no expectation to keep most of the Ten Commandments or any of the other things the church preaches today. If Yeshua is the end (goal or objective) of the law to all those who believe (Rom 10:4), and we are being conformed to His image (Rom 8:29), we're all on that journey to be more like the living Torah. Does scripture affirm this? How about the very next verse?

"For from ancient generations Moses has those who preach him in every city, since he is read in the synagogues every Sabbath" (Act 15:21).

I've asked numerous people, especially pastors, why this verse is there, and no one has given me an answer. It's like they've never seen it before. It's very simple, though. There was only one place a *Goy Tzadik* (righteous Gentile) could worship the one true God at this time, and that was at the synagogue. House churches hadn't taken off yet, and the hostilities between the Messianic and unbelieving communities didn't really begin in earnest until after the Temple was destroyed in 70 CE, when going to the synagogue became increasingly difficult. Based on this verse, it was assumed a Gentile convert would go to the synagogue on the Shabbat. And what would he learn there? Moses, or the Torah. They would learn the rest of the commandments by going through the Torah week by week. How do you think Cornelius was called a devout man and knew what the hours of prayer were? (He saw the angel at the ninth hour, or 3:00, while he would have been praying.) He would have learned it at the synagogue where he worshipped every week. He kept the commandments.

If we look again at Yeshua being the end of the Torah, picture a conveyor belt that all believers are on. We're all headed toward perfection as the Ruach HaKodesh (Holy Spirit) sanctifies us as we submit to God's will for our lives. Each of us is on a different point on that conveyor belt, but we're all on it, all heading in the same direction. If the vast majority of Messiah's disciples never have to get on that conveyor belt, how do they grow in holiness?

Torah

Many in the Church believe the Torah is exclusively for the Jewish people. They think that while the Ten Commandments are good to follow, the Torah doesn't address Gentiles directly. As we look closely, though, we see God letting His future sheep know what behaviour He expected from them as well.

Right as they were leaving Egypt, the Lord addresses the non-Hebrews by saying:

"But if a stranger resides with you and celebrates the Passover to the Lord, all of his males are to be circumcised, and then he shall come near to celebrate it; and he shall be like a native of the land. But no uncircumcised male may eat it. The same law shall apply to the native as to the stranger who resides among you" (Ex 12:48–49, emphasis mine).

The Hebrew word for stranger is גֵּר (*gare*), and it means "sojourner" or one who's passing through.[68] When someone is called a stranger in reference to

Israel, it means they are aligning themselves with Israel, dwelling in their midst, and living as one of them. When Israel left Egypt, many who were not one of the twelve tribes came with them, as they saw the power of God in dealing with Pharaoh. A stranger might not permanently become part of the community, but while they were there, there were rules they had to follow, *and they were the same ones the Israelites did.* The principle is that if you worship Israel's God, you have to worship Him in the way He instructed His people through the Torah. You don't come with your own customs or ideas. This passage deals with the Passover, so it might be argued that it doesn't apply in every situation with every command. Notice how Moses tells us *he shall be like a native of the land* and *the same law shall apply.* With regards to behaviour, you shouldn't be able to easily distinguish a Jew from a non-Jew because they both follow the same Law (Torah). That means all of Torah, not just the parts we like or agree with.

Regarding the divisions within Law (civil, ceremonial, and moral), Yeshua doesn't say He didn't come to destroy the moral law, but the ceremonial law is done away with. Paul never tells the Gentile congregations that the civil law was abolished so don't worry about those things. Anytime Torah is spoken about, it's referred to as *The Law of Moses.* One law. James tells us, *"For whoever keeps the whole Law, yet stumbles in one point, has become guilty of all"* (Jas 2:10). There's no divvying it up into convenient little categories that I can dismiss so that I don't have to bother with them. Picture the Torah as a ball with 613 pins. If you pull one pin out, the whole ball deflates. That's what Torah is like. You break one command, you've sinned. You're guilty of all the whole thing.

The stranger in the midst of Israel, whether temporarily or permanently, had to approach God through His commandments if they wanted to worship Him. Just in case you thought that command was a one off:

Exodus 12:19 — *"For seven days there shall be no dough with yeast found in your houses; for whoever eats anything with yeast, that person shall be cut off from the congregation of Israel, <u>whether he is a stranger or a native of the land</u>."*

Leviticus 16:29—*"This shall be a permanent statute for you: in the seventh month, on the tenth day of the month, you shall humble yourselves and not do any work, <u>whether the native, or the stranger who resides among you</u> ..."*

Leviticus 17:15—*"And any person who eats an animal which dies or is torn by animals, <u>whether he is a native or a stranger</u>, shall wash his clothes and bathe in water, and remain unclean until evening; then he will become clean."*

Leviticus 18:26—*"But as for you, you are to keep My statutes and My judgments, and you shall not do any of these abominations, <u>neither the native, nor the stranger who resides among you.</u>"*

Leviticus 24:16—*"Moreover, the one who blasphemes the name of the Lord must be put to death; all the congregation shall certainly stone him. <u>The stranger as well as the native</u>, when he blasphemes the Name, shall be put to death."*

Leviticus 24:22—*"There shall be one standard for you; <u>it shall be for the stranger as well as the native</u>, for I am the LORD your God."*

Numbers 9:14—*"You shall have one statute, <u>both for the alien and for the native of the land</u>."*

Numbers 15:15–16—*"As for the assembly, <u>there shall be one statute for you and for the alien who sojourns with you</u>, a perpetual statute throughout your generations; as you are, so shall the alien be before the Lord. <u>There is to be one law and one ordinance for you and for the alien who sojourns with you</u>."*

Numbers 15:29–30—*"You shall have one law for him who does anything unintentionally, <u>for him who is native among the sons of Israel and for the alien who sojourns among them</u>. But the person who does wrong defiantly, <u>whether he is a native or a stranger</u>, that one is blaspheming the Lord; and that person shall be cut off from among his people."*

Deuteronomy 31:22—*"Assemble the people, the men, the women, the children, <u>and the stranger who is in your town</u>, so that they may hear and learn and fear the Lord your God, and be careful to follow all the words of this Law."*

All emphasis in the above has been added by the author.

How many times does it have to be repeated? If a Gentile wanted to be part of the faith community in Israel, there was only path of approach to worship the one true God, and that was through His Torah. Paul says in Galatians 3:28 that in Messiah, there's no Jew or Gentile. We don't keep our earthly distinctions in our standing before God. In the Millennial Kingdom, there won't be separate worship services. The Jews aren't going to be required to show up early to get all of the sacrifices and ceremonial cleansing rituals out of the way so that the Gentiles can then show up and just raise hands and sing a bunch of hallelujahs. Yet that's what this theology postulates.

When Israel entered the land and went to Mount Gerizim and Mount Ebal to pronounce blessings and curses as Moses commanded them, we see the Gentiles right there.

"*And all Israel with their elders, officers, and their judges were standing on both sides of the ark before the Levitical priests who carried the ark of the covenant of the Lord, the stranger as well as the native*" (Jo 8:33, emphasis mine).

Notice where the people were standing: on both sides of the ark of the covenant, where the Law was. The *gare*, or stranger, was not to be a stranger from God if he knew and kept His commandments, just like Israel.

Circumcision

One of the most divisive issues in the Messianic/Torah/Hebrew roots community is the issue of circumcision. Much is spoken about it in the scriptures, especially the *Brit Chadasha* (New Covenant), because the religious leaders honestly had no idea how to integrate non-Jews into the community, which again was the purpose of the council. Phillip Schaff expounds upon this:

"The question of circumcision, or of the terms of admission of the Gentiles to the Christian Church, was a burning question of the apostolic age. It involved the wider question of the binding of authority of the Mosaic law, yea, the whole relation of Christianity to Judaism. For circumcision was in the synagogue what baptism is in the church, a divinely appointed sign and seal of the covenant of man with God, with all its privileges and responsibilities, and bound the circumcised person to obey the whole law on pain of forfeiting the blessing promised. Upon the decision of this question depended the peace of the church within, and the success of the gospel without. With circumcision as a necessary condition of church membership, Christianity would forever have been confined to the Jewish race with a small minority of proselytes of the gate, or half-Christians; while the abrogation of circumcision and the declaration of the supremacy and sufficiency of faith in Christ ensured the conversion of the heathen and the catholicity of Christianity. The progress of Paul's mission among the Gentiles forced the question to a solution and resulted in a grand act of emancipation, yea not without great struggle and temporary reactions."[69]

Schaff continues to explain regarding the apostles and first Jewish converts:

"They indeed regarded Jesus as the Saviour of Gentiles as well as Jews; but they thought Judaism the necessary introduction to Christianity, circumcision and the observance of the whole Mosaic law the sole condition of an interest in the Messianic salvation. And, offensive as Judaism was, rather than attractive, to the heathen, this principle would have utterly precluded the conversation of the mass of the Gentile world. The apostles themselves were at first trammelled by this Judaistic prejudice, till taught better by the special revelation to Peter before the conversation of Cornelius.

"But even after the baptism of the uncircumcised centurion, and Peter's defence of it before the church of Jerusalem, the old leaven still wrought in some Jewish Christians who had formerly belonged to the rigid and exclusive sect of the Pharisees. They came from Judea to Antioch, and taught the converts of Paul and Barnabas: 'Except ye be circumcised after the manner of Moses, ye cannot be saved.' They no doubt appealed to the Pentateuch, the universal Jewish tradition, the circumcision of Christ, and the practice of the Jewish apostles, and created a serious disturbance. These ex-Pharisees were the same whom Paul, in the heat of controversy, more severely calls 'false brethren insidiously or stealthily foisted in,' who intruded themselves into the Christian brotherhood as spies and enemies of the apostle, but also from the great majority of the brethren in Judea who sincerely rejoiced in his conversion and glorified God for it. They were a small, but very active and zealous minority, and full of intrigue. The compassed sea and land to make one proselyte. They were baptized with water, but not with the Holy Spirit. They were Christians in name, but narrow-minded and narrow-hearted Jews in fact. They were scrupulous, pedantic, slavish formalists, ritualists, and traditionalists of the malignant type. Circumcision of the flesh was to them of more importance than circumcision of the heart, or at all events of indispensable condition of salvation. Such men could, of course, not understand and appreciate Paul, but hated and feared him as a dangerous radical and rebel. Envy and jealousy mixed with their religious prejudice. They got alarmed at the rapid progress of the gospel among the unclean Gentiles who threatened to soil the purity of the church ...

"The agitation of these Judaizing partisans and zealots brough the Christian church, twenty years after its founding, to the brink of a split which would have seriously impeded its progress and endangered its final success."[70]

Schaff also quotes Ernest Renan (translated from French), who said:

"Circumcision was, for adults a painful ceremony, one not without danger, and disagreeable to the last degree. It was one of the reasons which prevented the Jews from moving freely about among other people, and set them apart as a caste by themselves. At the baths and gymnasiums, those important parts of the ancient cities, circumcision exposed the Jew to all sorts of affronts. Every time that the attention of the Greeks and Romans was directed to this subject, outbursts of jestings followed."[71]

This was a major issue, and the insistence on circumcising the Gentiles would have made the new faith, called "The Way," dead on arrival. As barbaric as some of these other religions were, trying to convince a full-grown male that the one true God insisted on him maiming himself in his most sensitive parts to come into the community of faith would make anyone run away. Cut the arm or chest, no big deal. Get anywhere near the nether regions and you can forget about it. Circumcision isn't a big deal for an eight-day old baby. When my son had his bris (or brit, meaning covenant, of circumcision), the doctor froze him a little, cut the skin, and he started to cry. Then my father dipped his finger in wine, put it in my son's mouth, and there was instant quiet. Medical studies have shown that healing occurs quickest for a boy who gets the procedure done on the eighth day. God apparently knows what He's doing. On the other hand, for an adult, as Renan said, it was painful and dangerous. Remember Shechem and Hamor in Genesis 34? Simeon and Levi wiped out an entire city because all the men were in pain from being circumcised. It was the same with the Israelites when they crossed the Jordan to conquer the land of Canaan, starting at Jericho. They had to be circumcised before they took the land, and the Bible says they had to convalesce first.

While the issues of appeal and physical discomfort are certainly pertinent in the discussion, the main issue is: Do the scriptures require it? Based on the apostles' teaching in the New Covenant, the answer is obviously no. But what about the Torah? Is circumcision not required? Is it not a command? Leviticus 12:3 clearly says that after a boy is born, " ... *on the eighth day the flesh of his foreskin shall be circumcised.*" As we saw in Exodus 12:48, a Gentile wanting to celebrate the Passover had to be physically circumcised, just as the Israelite was. Why did God change His mind once the New Covenant was established? Because circumcision was never for the Gentiles. Although commanded in Torah, it wasn't established in Torah but rather with Abraham:

"'I will make you exceedingly fruitful, and I will make nations of you, and kings will come from you. I will establish My covenant between Me and you and your descendants after you throughout their generations as an everlasting covenant, to be God to you and to your descendants after you. And I will give to you and to your descendants after you the land where you live as a stranger, all the land of Canaan, as an everlasting possession; and I will be their God.' God said further to Abraham, 'Now as for you, you shall keep My covenant, you and your descendants after you throughout their generations. This is My covenant, which you shall keep, between Me and you and your descendants after you: every male among you shall be circumcised. And you shall be circumcised in the flesh of your foreskin, and it shall be the sign of the covenant between Me and you. And every male among you who is eight days

old shall be circumcised throughout your generations, including a slave who
is born in the house or who is bought with money from any foreigner, who is
not of your descendants. A slave who is born in your house or who is bought
with your money shall certainly be circumcised; so My covenant shall be in
your flesh as an everlasting covenant. But as for an uncircumcised male, one
who is not circumcised in the flesh of his foreskin, that person shall be cut off
from his people; he has broken My covenant" (Gn 17:6–14).

The covenant of circumcision was with Abraham and his *physical descen-*
dants for the *physical land of Israel*. It had nothing to do with the Gentiles.
Only a Jew needs to be physically circumcised to show covenant with
God. The Mosaic Covenant was the one dealing with righteousness. The
Abrahamic Covenant was about God's unconditional promise to Abraham
to give him many descendants and land to live in. Whether a Gentile got
snipped or not, he still had no part in this.

The problem is that the Jewish people began mixing covenants. When
the Jews said to Yeshua in John 8:39 that *"Abraham is our father,"* they were
banking on that to be right with God. They were counting on the wrong
covenant. It was Moses who told them what their standing was before the
Lord, and just in case you think that was a problem only in Yeshua's day,
Jeremiah warns the people of Israel:

"Do not trust in deceptive words, saying, 'This is the temple of the Lord, the
temple of the Lord, the temple of the Lord'" (Jer 7:4).

It seems that they were actually quoting a chorus they sang in Temple. They
believed that God's promise to give them the land would go on forever,
regardless of their behaviour. Nebuchadnezzar took care of that idea. The
main error is that the Jews were prideful of their racial heritage, thinking
that being chosen by God made their conduct beyond reproach. It didn't
matter what they did; God was still going to bless them. Romans 2 is Paul's
polemic against this idea:

"For indeed circumcision is of value if you practice the Law; but if you are
a violator of the Law, your circumcision has turned into uncircumcision"
(Rom 2:25).

Right there the apostle sorts the whole matter out. Circumcision was supposed to be an outward sign of being in covenant with God and keeping the Torah. If you didn't, you became just as a pagan unbeliever.

The difference between the Old and New Covenants is in how they operated.

"The difference is not that one covenant has a law and the other does not. The difference is the Old Covenant forms people in holiness from the outside in, and the New Covenant forms them from the inside out."[72]

That was the Pharisees' problem. Everything was external for them. They were meticulous about keeping the commandments but were full of pride and contempt for others who weren't like them. When God gave the New Covenant, it was for everyone, and He was doing an inside-out job. He had to change our hearts. Physical circumcision had nothing to do with that, and since the Gentiles weren't the beneficiaries of that promise anyway, it would have served no purpose in making it a requirement for becoming part of the faith community.

So are Gentiles getting circumcised against God's will? It depends. (I know how much you love when I say that.) What do we always have to go back to? Motivation. If it's to make them more spiritual, then it's offensive. Paul addresses this issue with the Corinthians:

"Only, as the Lord has assigned to each one, as God has called each, in this way let him walk. And so I direct in all the churches. Was any man called when he was already circumcised? He is not to become uncircumcised. Has anyone been called in uncircumcision? He is not to be circumcised. Circumcision is nothing, and uncircumcision is nothing, but what matters is the keeping of the commandments of God. Each person is to remain in that state in which he was called" (1 Cor 7:17–20).

Circumcision has nothing to do with salvation. Requiring it would have given the wrong message. However, if a Gentile *chooses* to be circumcised out of a desire to identify with the Jewish people, it's not displeasing to God, as many in the church declare today. They will even quote Paul in Galatians 5:11–12 to verify this:

"And I, brethren, if I still preach circumcision, why do I still suffer persecution? Then the offense of the cross has ceased. I could wish that those who trouble you would even cut themselves off [mutilate themselves]*!" (NKJV).*

If that was the case, why would God require Gentiles coming out of Egypt to be circumcised if it was counter to His will? That would be contradictory, which God never is. Paul speaks a lot against circumcision but only when it comes to the issue of getting saved or keeping our salvation. Insisting Gentiles get circumcised is not how God saves them. If they get circumcised because they believe it makes them more spiritual, then it will be of no benefit to them. If they willingly do so because they believe it pleases the Lord for them to do it (and not to impose it on anyone else), it's a decision between them and God and for no one else to judge.

What about the Millennial Kingdom? What are the requirements there for the other nations? If the Lord was against circumcision in principle for Gentiles, there should be either no mention of it, since the apostles dealt with it (and the Holy Spirit agreed—*"For it seemed good to the Holy Spirit and to us"*— Acts 15:28), or it would be condemned in the age to come.

"Now say to the rebellious, to the house of Israel, Thus says the Lord God: 'O house of Israel, let Us have no more of all your abominations. When you brought in foreigners, uncircumcised in heart and uncircumcised in flesh, to be in My sanctuary to defile it—My house—and when you offered My food, the fat and the blood, then they broke My covenant because of all your abominations. And you have not kept charge of My holy things, but you have set others to keep charge of My sanctuary for you.' Thus says the Lord God: 'No foreigner, uncircumcised in heart <u>or uncircumcised in flesh, shall enter My sanctuary, including any foreigner who is among the children of Israel'"</u> (Ez 44:6–9, NKJV, emphasis mine).

This will come as a shocker to most believers, but when the Messiah is reigning from His throne in Jerusalem, anybody wanting to come and worship Him up close will need physical proof of their circumcised heart. Once again, just as it was when they left Egypt, the Gentiles will have to come to God in all the ways He has commanded Israel, or they will not have access to Him. Before His return, though, Paul exhorts us not to be concerned about it. As you were called, so remain, unless the Lord lays it on your heart to do otherwise.

The issue of circumcision isn't really as complex as it has been made out to be, once we look at God's will for it. It is mandatory for the Jews as a sign of His covenant with Abraham regarding the promise of the land. For Gentiles, it's completely optional and shouldn't be enforced, but neither should it be condemned. I've known many Gentile believers who truly felt it was God's will for their lives to be circumcised. Remember, Paul tells the Philippians that *"everyone must work out his own salvation in fear and trembling"* (Phil 2:12), and it's not for anyone else to contradict what they feel the Lord is saying to them unless it goes against His written Word.

The belief that Gentiles are excluded from keeping the commands of Torah cannot be supported biblically. God's desire is for all of His children to walk in holiness and love, and that can only be achieved through being obedient to Him by keeping the commands of Torah. If we remove the whole salvation argument, it's not such a contentious issue anymore. Much of our theology today comes from the Church fathers,, who were extremely hostile to the Jews (which we'll deal with in a later chapter). If we remove this bias against the Jews and, therefore, Israel's practices, we wouldn't have such an issue with just doing what God said to do. The theology of "different commands for different people groups" is irrational, and if it applies to Jews and Gentiles, the same argument can be made for Blacks and Whites, French and English, Latino and Asian, left-handed and right-handed, curly or straight hair, etc. We are all one before Almighty God. Christians are fond of saying, "God is not a respecter of persons." If that's true, then everyone, regardless of race, colour, gender, or any other category, has to adhere to the same standard of conduct. The path of approach to God is through His commandments. Remember, when you were saved, they were written on your heart. Rejecting them is denying your new identity.

Chapter 6—The Sabbath

"Interestingly, even though God's instruction concerning Shabbat is widely ignored and misunderstood by Christians, it is a blessing desperately needed by all of us in our modern world."

Dr. Robert Heidler

The 1964 musical and 1971 film adaptation of Sholom Aleichem's story, *Fiddler on the Roof*, told the tale of Tevye, a poor Jewish milkman who lived in in the fictional town of Anetevka in 1905. One of the most successful Broadway productions in history, *Fiddler* depicts the life of Jewish people in Tzarist Russia at the turn of the twentieth century. In one scene, Tevye, his wife, and five daughters hurry home for Shabbat dinner and sing the song known as "The Sabbath Prayer." The song requests God's blessing on the girls for good husbands, to be good mothers and to have happiness and peace. It is a beautiful, melancholy piece and encapsulates what the Shabbat (Sabbath) is supposed to mean: God's goodness to us. The Shabbat is about God's greatest provision to humanity. He gives us rest. From Strong's # 7673, שָׁבַת means to cease, desist, rest.[73] It points toward the ultimate rest we will have from our travails in this life in the world to come.

In my over twenty years of walking with the Lord and living a Messianic lifestyle, I've found the two issues people get the most riled up about are: a) days of worship and b) food. Other theological issues can be discussed at length and disagreed on, but when talking about these two in particular, you often get a visceral reaction because now you're dealing with day-to-day life. If you and I differ on the timing of the rapture … well, we're both still here, so it's not a reality yet. If one believes that Ezekiel 28 is only speaking about the King of Tyre, while another believes it's a description of Satan operating behind the scenes, it doesn't change our bedtime or how we pray. If we worship on different days, though, one of us has to admit that we're doing it wrong, which most people have a hard time doing. Pride prevents people from being teachable. Additionally, changes now have to be made to lifestyles, which admittedly isn't easy. If you suddenly realize that the day you've been worshipping on isn't the right one, what happens if you work, or the kids have hockey or dance on the day you're now convinced is the proper one? What if that has always been your shopping day? To change the day of corporate worship means upsetting the schedule, which is an inconvenience.

Moreover, as we will discuss in a later chapter, there's more than a hint of anti-Semitism amongst the people who advocated for and worked toward changing the day the people of God gathered together. Disdain and outright hatred for the Jewish people amongst the Church fathers has shaped much of our theology today.

Thirdly, as I have witnessed personally, if people are convinced that the day they have worshipped on is the wrong one, it undermines one of the foundations of their faith. As one young man asked at a conference I was teaching at years ago when I explained that Yeshua wasn't born on December 25th in a very animated tone, "Why would they lie to us?" If the day we gather together to worship the Lord isn't His day, what other things that we've taken for granted are also not aligned with the Word and why would our spiritual leaders lead us astray? These are very real issues that help explain why people get so upset when these topics are discussed.

For those who advocate for Sunday worship there are several different positions they will choose from. Many will say the seventh-day Sabbath was for the time of the Torah but after the resurrection, any day is acceptable. Some will say the Sabbath was for the Jews but not for Gentiles which we addressed in the last chapter. Others will use various scriptures to prove the change was of God which we will examine, while still others will use extra-biblical events and sources to prove that any day or specifically Sunday is the correct day to gather with the saints.

The first thing we need to remind ourselves of is that the Sabbath was not instituted at Mt. Sinai. God gave the Shabbat long before there was ever a written Torah or the nation of Israel. God gave the Shabbat to all mankind at creation.

"And so the heavens and the earth were completed, and all their heavenly lights. By the seventh day God completed His work which He had done, and He rested on the seventh day from all His work which He had done. Then God blessed the seventh day and sanctified it, because on it He rested from all His work which God had created and made." (Gen 2:1-3)

The principle of taking a day off was because God Himself did so. Why did the Creator take a rest? Was it because He was tired? In Ex 31:17 it we're even told that that God stopped working and was refreshed. Does God need refreshing?

The word refreshed, from the root word נָפַשׁ (naphash) means passively to be breathed upon.[74] It comes from the same root as the word we get breath or spirit from. It doesn't mean He was tired but that He just stopped working, a change in activity that does not indicate any special need on His part. Secondly, Isa 40:28 says, *"Do you not know? Have you not heard? The Everlasting God, the Lord, the Creator of the ends of the earth does not become weary or tired,"* and Ps 121:4 informs us that *"Behold, He who watches over Israel will neither slumber nor sleep."* God never gets tired.

So why do we have a day of rest? For our benefit. We're the ones who need rest. That's why He took six whole days to create everything. The all-powerful God could have spoken everything into existence all at once but He chose to do it systematically through a process for our benefit and capped the whole process of with a day of rest. God's way of establishing creation was so we have a pattern to follow as unlike Him, we're not able to do everything all at once.

In the order of creation, mankind is the pinnacle. He is the only thing described as being created in His image and we are commanded to subdue creation and have dominion over it. We manage it on His behalf. But man is not the finality of creation. Rather, *"the climax of creation is the Sabbath."*[75] If the principle of the day of rest is all that mattered, then we, as Rom 14:5 appears to indicate, can choose any one we want to come to God. However, if there is something special about the seventh day, then we need to take notice.

The Number Seven

Numerology is very significant in scripture. It has led to abuses and the truly absurd in the body of Messiah (e.g., the Bible Codes craze in the 1990s). The occult of course uses numbers too, based on vibrations to determine the best times to do something or to evaluate character,[76] but numbers have very specific and important meaning to God and therefore to us. Just as the Fibonacci sequence has the formula for how the universe is structured, so the Bible has numbers that have key meaning to us.

Seven is commonly described as the number of spiritual perfection or completion. Throughout the scriptures, seven is always associated with something being fulfilled or finalized. The Gospel of John has many things in sevens, from Yeshua's "I AM" statements, His sermons, His miracles, etc. The Book of Revelation is also replete with sevens in the messages to the assemblies, the three different types of judgements (scroll, trumpet, and bowl), which are seven each, the seven-fold Spirit of God, the seven visions and the seven angels. There are also seven colours in the rainbow that God gave as a sign of the covenant He would never flood the world again. The number seven is literally everywhere in scripture, from Genesis to Revelation symbolizing perfection.

"Therefore, it expresses God's ultimate and total blessing over His complete and perfect creation"[77]

After overseeing everything that He had made and declaring it to be very good and resting on the seventh day, God then sanctifies it, meaning made it separate, set apart as holy or consecrated.

*When God introduced the Number Seven as a symbol of the completion of His Work of Creation, He also associated it with sanctification (holiness), declaring that He "blessed the seventh day, and sanctified it." Thus God laid the foundation for its application throughout the rest of scripture. It is a double symbol signifying both **completion** and **sanctification**. These ideas natural cohere because sanctification denotes the setting apart or separating of a person or thing as **wholly devoted** or **completely given over** to God, as when He separated the Levitical Priests saying "they are wholly given unto* *me" (Num 8:16), or again when Paul prayed that "the very God of peace* **sanctify you wholly"** *(1 Thes 5:23).*[78]

We even see the human body operating in a cycle that culminates on the seventh day.

"It is already known that the human body maintains its own biological clock. He has a "circadian rhythm" internal twenty-four hours that drives the increase and the reduction of many molecules. Chronobiology has documented how human beings are highly rhythmic. Most of the many tick tocks are difficult to detect; they operate just below the human consciousness. Innate and hidden in the cell structure, the mysteries of biological time have been revealed by modern computers and scientific advance. I knew about the twenty-four-hour circadian rhythm for some time, but surprisingly there is also a seven-day cycle (circaseptan rhythm) . It was detected and related to the record of geomagnetic disturbances (Kp-Index) over a time period of fifty-nine years, (Halberg 1991). Jeremy Campbell says in his book: "The circaceptan pace is one of the big surprises that emerged in modern Chronobiology. Some years ago, few scientists would have expected that biological cycles of seven days would become so widespread and established.

"The existence of such precise circaceptan endogenous rhythms (including the need to seven days excretion of 17-ketosteroids [urinary metabolites] in healthy men) suggests that all circaceptanos rhythms are endogenous actually - described as a "built-in" (genetically determined) on the exact period of seven days."[79]

Biology certainly knows to respond to God's design. Yet despite this, we see many of the Church fathers speaking about the seventh-day Sabbath as something that needed to be done away with, which we will demonstrate in a later chapter. The number seven has specific meaning for God and to us; therefore, if the seventh day is the day of completion, changing it to anything else signifies that we don't accept God's completion but rather think that we can improve upon it.

After Genesis 2, we don't hear anything about the Shabbat until Mt. Sinai, 2,500 years later. Many have interpreted this to mean that after the Fall, the Shabbat wasn't kept. Far too often, a theology is established because something *isn't* mentioned in scripture. The LGBQT movement uses that same argument to say that Yeshua was ok with homosexuality because He never spoke about it in the Gospel accounts. They believe it was Paul who had the issue. Making an argument from silence doesn't make for sound biblical interpretation. You can come to just about any conclusion with that kind of reasoning. Some reason that it wasn't mentioned because it didn't need to be addressed. Yeshua didn't have to speak about the immorality of a homosexual lifestyle because it wasn't an issue in Israel during that time. It certainly was in the pagan world, which is why Paul does deal with it. God speaks to and the Bible records the issues He feels are important at the time. He doesn't need to be redundant and cover everything He's already mentioned over and over again. Your Bible would be too big to even move if He did that.

Just because the Bible itself doesn't mention it doesn't mean it wasn't addressed, especially if we have a record of it elsewhere. In the *Sefer Hayasher* (Book of Jashar, or the Upright), a non-canonical book but one referenced twice in scriptures (Joshua 10:12 and 2 Samuel 1:18), there's a story about Moses approaching Pharaoh and asking him to allow the Israelites to observe the Shabbat. According to the book, it was granted, but after Pharaoh dies and his son replaces him, he revokes the privilege, which might have been the issue Moses and Pharaoh were debating when Moses came and asked Pharaoh to allow his people to go into the desert to worship.[80]

There was no need for God to mention the Shabbat before and after the flood because everyone from Adam to the Patriarchs who followed God understood and most likely kept it. We don't see that mentioned explicitly, but do theologians honestly think that the Lord established the Sabbath, sanctified it, and then just ignored it for two and half millennia? Then, after Israel comes out of Egypt, it all of the sudden becomes important again? Goes back to the logic issue. It doesn't make any sense. I'm pretty certain that when we get to heaven and ask Noah or Enoch or Abraham if they kept the seventh-day Shabbat, I know what the answer will be.

Another justification made for choosing any day is that when Yeshua was debating the Pharisees on their accusations that He broke the Sabbath,

He responded by saying *"For the Son of Man is Lord of the Sabbath"* (Mat 12:8). Many say that Yeshua superseded the Sabbath, so it was no longer necessary to observe. It has now been replaced by the eighth day. In the Roman Catholic Catechism, issued after the Council of Trent ended in 1563 as a response to the Protestant Reformation, it says:

"The other commandments of the Decalogue are precepts of the natural law, obligatory at all times [and for all people] and unalterable. Hence, after the abrogation of the Law of Moses, all the Commandments contained in the two tables are observed by Christians, not indeed because their observance is commanded by Moses, but because they are in conformity with nature which dictates obedience to them.

"This Commandment about the observance of the Sabbath, on the other hand, considered as to the time appointed for its fulfillment, is not fixed and unalterable, but susceptible of change and belongs not to the moral, but the ceremonial law. Neither is it a principle of the natural law; we are not instructed by nature to give external worship to God on that day, rather than on any other. And in fact the Sabbath was kept holy only from the time of the liberation of the people of Israel from the bondage of Pharaoh.

"The observance of the Sabbath was to be abrogated at the same time as the other Hebrew rites and ceremonies, that is, at the death of Christ ... Hence St. Paul, in his epistle to the Galatians, when reproving the observers of the Mosaic rites, says: "You observe days and months and times and years; I am afraid of you lest perhaps I have labored in vain amongst you' (Gal 4:10). And he writes to the same effect to the Colossians (Col. 2:16)."[81]

An entire chapter could be written on all the wrong assumptions and statements made here alone, and we've already demonstrated that the seven-day cycle is part of the law of nature, but our focus here is on the eighth day.

The Eighth Day

The whole idea of the eighth day originates in Yeshua having risen from the dead on the first day of the week, after the Sabbath. This is the primary justification for belief that the Sabbath was now done away with and replaced with a superior day.

"The number 8 was, for ancient Christianity, the symbol of the Resurrection, for it was on the day after the Sabbath, and so the eighth day, that Christ rose from the tomb. Furthermore, the seven days of the week are the image of the time of this world, and the eighth day of life everlasting [this understanding was also that of the Jews]. Sunday is the liturgical commemoration of this eighth day, and so at the same time a memorial of the Resurrection and a prophecy of the world to come. Into this eighth day, inaugurated by Christ, the Christian enters by his Baptism."[82]

It goes back to the issue of people believing Yeshua abrogated the Law, the very thing He said He did not come to do in Matthew 5:17. The Christian website Questions.org tells us:

"God gave the Sabbath to Israel as a sign of His special covenant with His chosen people. It was part of an elaborate system of sacrifices, rituals, and offerings (Exodus 31:13–17; Nehemiah 9:13–14). The Epistle to the Hebrews makes it clear, however, that the coming of the Messiah invalidated these regulations (Hebrews 10:1–18). It emphasizes that the Old Testament has been replaced by a new covenant (Hebrews 8:7–13). Paul warned the church in Galatia about legalism relating to the Mosaic law."[83]

Once again, we have to emphasize that Paul's letters against the Torah only dealt with believing that keeping the Law saved us, not doing so out of obedience and thankfulness to God once we're saved.

If the perfection of the Shabbat can be improved upon by a human tradition, can God's perfect plan regarding the nation of Israel be improved upon too? Supersessionism of the eighth day over the Shabbat is really about Replacement Theology, or the Church superseding and replacing Israel as God's covenant people. This theology has its roots in the anti-Semitism that pervaded the early Church and is responsible for much of the errors we are addressing in this book. Again, we will speak to this in greater detail in a later chapter.

The primary theme of Shabbat is redemption. Samuuele Bacchiocchi, in one of the most thorough books ever written on the subject, *From Sabbath to Sunday—A Historical Investigation of the Rise of Sunday Observance in Early Christianity*, says:

"The blessings of the Sabbath in the unfolding of the history of salvation, become associated more specifically with God's saving acts. For instance in the Exodus version of the commandments, Yahweh introduces Himself as the merciful Redeemer who liberated Israel 'out of the land of Egypt, out of the house of bondage' (Ex. 20:2). To guarantee this newly granted freedom to all the members of the Hebrew society, the Sabbath commandment enjoins that rest be granted to all, including even the animals (Ex. 20:10). In the Deuteronomic version of the decalogue, the redemption motif not only appears in the preface (Deut. 5:6) to all the commandments (as in Exodus 20:1), but also is explicitly incorporated into the Sabbath commandment itself. It was perhaps to drive home the immediate relevancy of the Sabbath commandment to the Israelites and to all ensuing generations, that in this reiteration of the commandments the Sabbath is grounded not in God's past act of creation (as in Exodus 20:11), which does not always speak to people's immediate concerns, but rather in the divine act of redemption: 'You shall remember that you were a servant in the land of Egypt and the Lord your God brought you out thence with a mighty hand and an outstretched arm: therefore the Lord your God commanded you to keep the Sabbath day' (Deut 5:15)."[84]

Bacchiocchi also ties in Yeshua's ministry with the Sabbatical Year and the Year of Jubilee, both of which are special years of rest and release and occur in multiples of seven. He says:

"Practically all commentators agree that the 'acceptable year of the Lord' (4:19) which Christ is officially ordained ('anointed') to proclaim, refers to the sabbatical year (i.e. the seventh year) or the Jubilee year (i.e. fiftieth year, after seven Sabbaths of years). After these annual institutions, the Sabbath became the liberator of the oppressed of the Hebrew society ... It is significant that Christ in His opening address announces His Messianic mission in the language of the sabbatical year."[85]

The number seven represents completion, perfection, sanctification, *and* redemption, but for some reason we think by switching the day of worship to the first day of the week, it is somehow better. This is a combination of lack of understanding about the full scope of the Shabbat and what it means to God and represents to us, combined with a healthy dose of hubris. Just like the transhumanists or companies that produce genetically modified food, humanity somehow thinks it can improve upon what God created. Yeshua came to restore Torah to its original intent, not to do away with it.

It's the same with Shabbat. The Talmud is rabbinic commentary on the commandments. It's called the Oral Torah, and Jewish tradition says it was given to Moses on Mt. Sinai, passed down over the centuries, and began to be codified or written down about 200 BCE. The Babylonian Talmud is the more extensive version and much more widely used than the Jerusalem one and has twenty-three volumes. If you're ever struggling with insomnia … An entire volume is dedicated to just what constitutes work, and there are over 1,500 rules broken down into thirty-nine categories. That is bondage, and when Yeshua rebuked the religious leaders by telling them the Shabbat was made for man and not man for the Shabbat, He was reminding them of the Shabbat's original purpose. As we've discussed, God gave the Shabbat to liberate people, and the reason why so many of Yeshua's healings came in the synagogue on that day was to contrast the binding nature of man's religion and God's freedom given through His commandments.

In order to properly address the situation, we have to understand how the early Church thought of Sunday. There are some who believe today that the Sunday *replaced* the seventh-day Sabbath and that Sunday, or the first day of the week, is the *new*, Christian Sabbath. Theologically this contradicts what scripture says about the eternality of the Shabbat, but it also doesn't line up with how most historians and the Church fathers regarded Sunday worship. They viewed Sunday as an entirely new thing, distinct from the ordinance in the Ten Commandments. Henry Sheldon tells us in *The History of the Christian Church*, Vol. 1:

"In what sense was Sunday a sacred day? Was it regarded as the Jewish sabbath transferred from the last to the first day of the week, a day coming under the positive prescription of the Fourth Commandment? By no means. All the writings of the first three centuries are destitute of any intimation of such a belief. The unmixed impression which comes from the perusal of this whole body of literature is, that the Christian sacred day was viewed as independent of the Jewish, having indeed a certain kinship with it as respects use and design, but in its origin and sanctions just as distinct from it as Christian baptism was from Jewish circumcision. Not one of the Fathers of this period so much as hints that he finds in Sunday a commemoration of God's rest from the work of creation. Not one of them betrays the least consciousness that the Fourth Commandment was to be looked upon as applying to Sunday. That which Sunday was regarded as celebrating, was no event connected with the physical creation (except the creation of light, as referred to by Justin Martyr), no event of Jewish history, but the crowning event of the ministry of redemption, the resurrection of Christ. It was the festival of the resurrection, the day of holy rejoicing, on which fasting or even kneeling in prayer was counted inappropriate. So far were the early Fathers from seeing in Sunday the old Jewish sabbath with all its sanctions, only carried over from the last to the first day of the week, that we find several of them specifying the abolition of the latter. Justin Martyr and Tertullian state expressly, that, like circumcision, the sabbath is under Christianity abolished. What could be more distinct than these words from the latter of these writers? "The precept (to keep the Sabbath) was not eternal nor spiritual, but temporal, which would one day cease … It was not with a view to its observance in perpetuity, that God formerly gave them such a law." Irenaeus also indicates that he did not consider the sabbath law of the old dispensation as having any statutory force under the new dispensation, speaking of it as being like circumcision, a type of sign of something beyond itself, a sign, namely, 'that we should continue day by day in God's service.'"[86]

Phillip Schaff says:

"The fathers did not regard the Christian Sunday as a continuation of, but as a substitute for, the Jewish sabbath, and based it not so much on the fourth commandment, and the primitive rest of God in creation, to which the commandment expressly refers, as upon the resurrection of Christ and the *apostolic tradition*. There was a disposition to disparage the Jewish law in the zeal to prove the independent originality of Christian institutions."[87]

Both Sheldon and Schaff tell us that Sunday worship was something intended to be completely different from the Shabbat, which is fine if it's added to our practices. But why did it eventually replace the Shabbat?

Schaff informs that:

"The day was transferred from the seventh to the first day of the week, not on the ground of a particular command, but by the free spirit of the gospel and by the power of certain great facts which are at the foundation of the Christian church. It was on that day that Christ rose from the dead; that he appeared to Mary, the disciples of Emmaus, and the assembled apostles; that he poured out his Spirit and founded the church; and that he revealed to his beloved disciple the mysteries of the future."[88]

Clearly the Church admits that there is no command given to worship on Sunday, but it has chosen to do so of its own free will, based on a new man-made tradition. The Methodist Church admits as such. Clovis Chappell in his book *Ten Rules for Living* exclaims:

"The reason we observe the first day instead of the seventh is based on no positive command. One will search the Scriptures in vain for authority for changing from the Seventh day to the first ... Our Christian Sabbath, therefore, is not a matter of positive command. It is a gift of the church ..."[89]

Sunday worship is a gift of the Church? Where is the returns department?! The obvious question that nobody seems to be asking is: Who gave men the authority to change the day Yehovah Elohim, from the time of creation, set aside to be worshipped on as an eternal ordinance?

"We Catholics, then, have precisely the same authority for keeping Sunday holy instead of Saturday as we have for every other article of our creed, namely, the authority of the Church. whereas you who are Protestants have really no authority for it whatever; for there is no authority for it [Sunday sacredness] in the Bible, and you will not allow that there can be authority for it anywhere else."-The Brotherhood of St. Paul, "The Clifton tracts," Volume 4, tract 4, p. 15.[90]

The Church gave itself the authority to abrogate God's Word. Although Sunday worship started out as supposedly being about Yeshua's resurrection, add the anti-Jewish attitudes of the many of the Church fathers and the paganism that Constantine brought in with his newfound faith and you now have the Pope as God's representative on earth who has the authority to define doctrine and morals as he sees fit. The Mormons also have the same belief. It's called progressive revelation, meaning the leader of the church can receive revelation from God that can even contradict earlier revelation, and it is binding. Mohammed made this a central tenet when he wrote the Koran. And the spirit behind this change of day of worship? Prophesying about the Antichrist, Daniel writes:

"And he will speak against the Most High and wear down the saints of the Highest One, and he will intend to make alterations in times and in law" (Dn 7:25, emphasis mine).

It is Satan and his offspring, the false messiah, who bring changes to God's law and His times of worship. Jeroboam did the same thing after God gave him the northern kingdom of Israel. He changed the days of worship to turn people away from worshipping God (1 Kgs 12:32). The same spirit is active today in those who proclaim it doesn't matter to God which day He said He was Lord of. He is Lord of the Sabbath and is the fulfillment of the Shabbat. A rejection of the Shabbat is a rejection of Him. Just as the Pharisees rejected His work and subsequently Him, we do the same when we take authority and change His appointed times, or anything else about His Word. He cannot be separated from His Word, for He is the Word that became flesh.

The seventh day again points to our eternal rest. There are six thousand years of toil leading up to Yeshua's return, and one thousand years of rest in His Millennial reign. If we change the day, it no longer has any meaning from God's perspective, no matter how much we try and make it so.

Scripture Verses Regarding the Shabbat

We've looked at numerous quotations from the Church about why the switch was made and also the importance of the number seven, which indirectly supports the continuation of the seventh day. But we always want to see what the scriptures explicitly say about an issue before trying to figure out how it applies to our lives. What does God's Word say specifically about the Shabbat? Genesis 2 says God instituted the Shabbat, blessed it, and sanctified it. Then what?

The next mention of the Shabbat is in the Ten Commandments. Of the ten, it's the longest and contains the most details. Interestingly enough, it starts out by saying remember to keep it. That should be a clue right there that this wasn't something being reintroduced after some long dormancy but was an existing practice being codified. We have to remember that Israel had just walked out of four hundred years of slavery and would have a struggle with the old way of life, much like we experience when we come to salvation. The old habits and ways of thinking don't just simply get a one-way, express ticket to hell. They tend to linger around, with the devil promoting them like a carnival barker, asking us to come back and enjoy his wares once again. Until Israel had become comfortable with its new identity as a free nation, the people were going to need clear instructions as to how God expected them to behave and not revert back to what they knew, namely paganism and slavery.

In the command, the Lord reiterates why He gave the Shabbat to humanity in the first place—to remind them of creation and how all creation needed to rest and cease from its labours. In slavery, you never get to do that. Only when you have freedom can you rest. As God was moving from working through individuals to working through a nation, it was clear they would need a concrete set of rules to refer back to—a constitution, as it were.

Exodus 31:12–17 speaks again of the need to keep the Shabbat:

"Now the Lord spoke to Moses, saying, 'Now as for you, speak to the sons of Israel, saying, "You must keep My Sabbaths; for this is a sign between Me and you throughout your generations, so that you may know that I am the Lord who sanctifies you. Therefore you are to keep the Sabbath, for it is holy to you. Everyone who profanes it must be put to death; for whoever does any work on it, that person shall be cut off from among his people. For six days work may be done, but on the seventh day there is a Sabbath of complete rest, holy to the Lord; whoever does any work on the Sabbath day must be put to

death. So the sons of Israel shall keep the Sabbath, to celebrate the Sabbath throughout their generations as a permanent covenant." It is a sign between Me and the sons of Israel forever; for in six days the Lord made heaven and earth, but on the seventh day He ceased from labor, and was refreshed."

This was right after He finished instructing Moses on the furniture of the Tabernacle and the last of the instructions before the two tablets with the Ten Commandments were completed. The last thing God said to Moses from his forty days on the mountain with Him was about keeping the Sabbath. Though He'd already told him this in Exodus 20, it was so important to God that He repeated Himself and added new details here. Not only does the Lord repeat that the pattern was established at Creation but that the reason Israel needs to keep the Shabbat is because the Lord sanctifies Israel and makes them holy. Twice He said anyone working on it would be put to death. If God repeats something in the same conversation, you know it's important. Then He said the thing that is key for us; it is a permanent covenant. In fact, in Leviticus 23, when God gave the commandments for His other appointed times, He said they were permanent statutes, which uses the Hebrew word עוֹלָם (*olam*—Strongs #5769), which is translated "long duration" or "antiquity,"[91] but most often means forever. That means it will never change, yet so many in the Body claim that everything changed at the cross. So not only are we changing God's ordained practices but the meaning of words too! But again, the Word of God is clear. If it says eternal, it goes on forever, regardless of what happens along the way.

Leviticus 23 introduces us to God's calendar, which we'll cover this in more detail in a later chapter. But the very first of God's appointed times is the Shabbat, and this time, in addition to saying we're to rest, He also included that we are to have a holy convocation, which means a corporate gathering.

"We can clearly understand that the word 'convocation' is firstly to practise, secondly to read and understand the laws of Elohim. In a nutshell, we can say that the term 'convocation' means to set apart an appointed time (Sabbath/Festivals) to Elohim and to read, understand His laws so that you can use His laws in your life (practise them)."[92]

Not only is a holy convocation a corporate gathering of believers, but its primary purpose is to read God's Word. So much for those who say they can keep Shabbat at home on their own. That isn't the intent of the day. It was designed for us to stop working and meet together so we can all worship God collectively and study His Word. It was really designated as a family day, for God and His children to be together.

Isaiah speaks of the Sabbath at length. In 66:23, the second last verse of his book, he writes:

"And it shall be from new moon to new moon and from Sabbath to Sabbath, all mankind will come to bow down before Me," says the Lord."

The last chapters of Isaiah speak of His Millennial reign, where we see that all humanity will worship Him on His designated days, not the ones of our choosing. He tells us when to show up. In chapter 58, God says to Israel:

"If, because of the Sabbath, you restrain your foot from doing as you wish on My holy day, and call the Sabbath a pleasure, and the holy day of the Lord honorable, and honor it, desisting from your own ways, from seeking your own pleasure and speaking your own word, then you will take delight in the Lord, and I will make you ride on the heights of the earth; and I will feed you with the heritage of Jacob your father, for the mouth of the Lord has spoken" (Is 58:13–14).

On the Shabbat, we call the Sabbath a pleasure, and we honour it. We don't do what we want but rather what He wants, not even speaking our own words but what His Word says. Then we delight in *Him*. Again, Yeshua is Lord of the Shabbat, so when we delight in it, we delight in Him. If we change it, we redefine God Himself. Strong words, but this is what He is saying, that His nature is inextricably woven in with His Word and instructions for us. If we on our own authority change God's Word, we create a new god in our own image. The Sunday honouring, Christmas celebrating, ham eating, blond hair, blue eyed Jesus that so many worship today in their Greco-Roman churches is not the Messiah of the Bible.

How about the Gentiles? Do the scriptures have any direct instruction for them regarding the Shabbat? I'm glad you asked.

"This is what the Lord says: 'Guard justice and do righteousness, for My salvation is about to come and My righteousness to be revealed. Blessed is a man who does this, and a son of man who takes hold of it; who keeps from profaning the Sabbath, and keeps his hand from doing any evil.' Let not the foreigner who has joined himself to the Lord say, 'The Lord will certainly separate me from His people.'

"Nor let the eunuch say, 'Behold, I am a dry tree.' For this is what the Lord says: 'To the eunuchs who keep My Sabbaths, and choose what pleases Me, and hold firmly to My covenant, to them I will give in My house and within My walls a memorial, and a name better than that of sons and daughters; I will give them an everlasting name which will not be eliminated. Also the foreigners who join themselves to the Lord, to attend to His service and to love the name of the Lord, to be His servants, every one who keeps the Sabbath so as not to profane it, and holds firmly to My covenant; even those I will bring to My holy mountain, and make them joyful in My house of prayer. Their burnt offerings and their sacrifices will be acceptable on My altar; for My house will be called a house of prayer for all the peoples.' The Lord God, who gathers the dispersed of Israel, declares, 'I will yet gather others to them, to those already gathered'" (Is 56:1–8, emphasis mine).

In the one-thousand-year reign of Yeshua on Earth, the Gentiles who join themselves to the Lord and keep the Shabbat will be made joyful in His temple. But it doesn't matter to Him now, so we can choose whatever day pleases us? That's not what I read in these passages. Ezekiel, describing the Millennial Temple and the role of the Levitical priests, says:

"Moreover, they shall teach My people the difference between the holy and the common and teach them to distinguish between the unclean and the clean. In a dispute they shall take their stand to judge; they shall judge it according to My ordinances. They shall also keep My laws and My statutes in all My appointed feasts and sanctify My Sabbaths" (Ez 44:23–24).

In the Millennium, the Temple is rebuilt and fully functional. The Levitical priesthood is re-established, sacrifices will be offered, and they will teach the people all of God's Torah and how to keep all the Sabbaths, including the weekly one.

Verses "Proving" Sunday Worship

When it comes to discussing what day we keep, Christians point to a few verses in scripture that they say either affirm the change to Sunday specifically or else give us the freedom to choose whatever day we want, since all days belong to God. A closer examination will help clarify what these verses say and, equally as important, what they don't say.

The first passage is 1 Corinthians 16:1–2:

"Now concerning the collection for the saints, as I directed the churches of Galatia, so you are to do as well. On the first day of every week, each of you is to put aside and save as he may prosper, so that no collections need to be made when I come."

Here we see Paul giving directives for the Corinthian congregations to take up a special offering for the Jerusalem saints who were suffering hardship. He obviously did the same in Galatia. These verses are used as proof texts that the early Assembly met on Sundays for worship instead of the Shabbat.

"Various scholars see in this text a reference to or at least an implicit indication of a regular Christian Sunday gathering. A. Robertson and A. Plummer, for instance, in their comment on this verse affirm: 'This is our earliest evidence respecting the early consecration of the first day of the week by the apostolic church.'"[93]

Many Christians look at this verse as proof that even from the first churches, Sunday worship was already an established practice. The problem with this conclusion is that there's nothing in the verse that indicates that. Paul was simply giving instructions as to when to set aside the special offering for the poor. There's no suggestion this was a worship service. In fact, he doesn't even say they were meeting at all. Even the Greek phrasing says *hekastos hymon par'heautō* which is translated each of you *by him(self)*.[94] This would suggest the giver was alone and not together with others. The word save is *thēsaurizōn,* which means to treasure or store up. That too would have been done at home. Samuele Bacchiocchi writes:

"These attempts to extrapolate from Paul's fund-raising plan a regular pattern of Sunday observance reveal inventiveness and originality, but they seem to rest more on construed arguments than on the actual information the text provides."[95]

House churches were also a fairly new concept at the time, and a regular time of worship at them had not been established. They would have varied in time and places.

Conspicuously absent from Paul's writings is the reference to Sunday as the Lord's Day and, therefore, a time of regular worship. Paul was familiar with the term The Lord's Day, as he used it to describe the communion service in 1 Corinthians 11:20 as "The Lord's Supper." Yet the first day of the week is only described as just that, with no special designation. If he were intent on reinforcing this new tradition of Sunday replacing Saturday as the corporate day of worship, it would make sense that it would be referred to as something more than the mundane term of the first day of the week.

The second verse is Acts 20:7:

"On the first day of the week, when we were gathered together to break bread, Paul began talking to them, intending to leave the next day, and he prolonged his message until midnight."

Again, we are told that they gathered together for a public worship service on Sunday morning, as was the new practice. Except that once again, there's nothing in the text to actually prove that. It just says they gathered together to break bread. We don't know by Luke's own testimony what the purpose of the meeting was, but since emphasis is put on Paul's departure the next day, we might assume it was a goodbye meeting. Furthermore, many have speculated on when the meeting took place. Did Luke, who was a Gentile, count the time as the Romans did, with the new day starting at midnight? If so, the meeting would have taken place on Sunday night. Or did he use the Jewish way of counting, where the new day started at sundown? In this case, they would have been meeting on Saturday night. Luke in both his Gospel and the book of Acts referred to time in the Hebraic way of counting (Luke 22:7, 23:54, 24:1; Acts 2:15, 10:3), but either way, it was clearly an evening meeting, so deducing that there was regular Sunday morning fellowship and worship at this time in the Church's history is pure conjecture.

The fact that it was an evening service makes it highly unlikely that it was a formal worship service. Paul was leaving the next day, so they were gathering to see him off. He begins his oratory and literally talks Eutychus to death, as he spoke until after midnight. He stops speaking, raises him from the dead (how's that for a sermon illustration?), and continues to share with them until daybreak. Doesn't sound much like a worship service to me. Why would they have started a service after sundown anyway? The only kind of Christian service we have any history of that meets at that time is a Christmas Mass, (although modern traditions have done that on New Year's Eve as well). It's common for Jews to meet at the end of the Shabbat to see it off and welcome the new week. It's called Havdalah (separation) and starts at sundown on Saturday night. It's not so much a worship service as an informal fellowship gathering with a few traditional prayers and practices. Again, we have no indication that this is what it was, but it's a more likely explanation than a Sunday service. The fact that they broke bread after midnight and didn't disperse until after dawn would also suggest this was a highly unusual gathering as opposed to a regular one. All-night services are not the norm, even for the most verbose of rabbis and pastors.

The term "breaking bread," which Acts 20:11 says Paul did after raising Eutychus, bears attention. It says that Paul is the one who broke bread and that he spoke with the brethren until dawn. The focus is all on what Paul was doing, not what the congregation did corporately. If it was a public worship service, Luke would have told us *they* broke bread, as he does in Acts 2:46. While the term "breaking bread" later became associated with the Lord's Supper and was widely assumed to have occurred during a Sunday service, it had not done so yet at this time and was used to describe the common fellowship meal in the New Covenant writings, among other things.[96]

The Lord's Day

The verse most used to prove the switch from the Shabbat to Sunday worship is Revelation 1:10. As John was beginning to get his revelation from Yeshua about what was to come, he said:

"I was in the spirit on the Lord's Day."

The term "the Lord's Day" is almost universally accepted as Sunday. Again, it's tied in with Yeshua rising from the dead on the first day of the week, but John apparently cements this new practice with his wording in Revelation. Not only did the Messiah's resurrection occur on the first day, but John affirms this switch to a new and better day with his encounter with Yeshua on the Isle of Patmos. A closer look will help determine if that's what the apostle was really saying.

The first thing to note is that this is the only time in scripture this phrase is used. Right there we should be extremely hesitant about establishing a new practice that abrogates a direct command from the Lord to keep the Sabbath Day holy. As we have just documented, the honouring of the Sabbath is mentioned several times in the Tanakh and would seem to be very important to God, so much so that the penalty for violating it is death. To use one passage in a prophetic vision to set it aside for a new tradition is risky business, to say the least. Again, where does the authority to do this come from? The term "the Lord's Day" is never mentioned in the Gospels or the epistles, but Yeshua does declare Himself to be Lord of the Sabbath a couple of times. To say that by being Lord of the Sabbath means His intent was to change it also lacks any precedent in scripture. He says in Malachi 3:6, *"For I, the Lord, do not change."* By the way, one does not keep something holy by exchanging it for something else. Furthermore, if the term "Lord's Day" was already in regular use at the time, why would John use older, Hebraic terms in his Gospel and the book of Revelation? All of John's references to time are styled as the Jews would have referred to them, such as "the first day of the week" (John 20:1), "the Passover" (nine times in the Gospel), "a Sabbath" (John 5:9, 9:14), or "high Sabbath" (John 19:31). To suddenly switch to a brand-new term that had never been used before and develop a whole theology around it that contradicts a practice that originated at Creation and is commanded by God for us to keep forever is utterly unprecedented in scripture and, quite frankly, heretical. Does this seem like strong wording to you? How do we describe what has happened then? From a spiritual perspective, how successful do you think Satan has been in weakening the Church over the centuries by taking it out of God's cycle and pattern? While God has certainly allowed this to happen and does work through and bless Sunday keepers, once we start abrogating one part of scripture, the rest is fair game too, which is again why we have the mess we do today. There are few things left in the Bible that aren't open to question anymore, even in the Church, much less society, to which we are supposed to be salt and light.

"There is no evidence of any kind that 'the first day of the week' was ever called 'the Lord's Day' before the Apocalypse was written. That it should be so called afterwards is easily understood, and there can be little doubt that the practice arose from the misinterpretation of these words in [Revelation 1:10]. It is incredible that the earliest use of a term can have a meaning which only subsequent usage makes intelligible.

"On the contrary, it ceased to be called by its Scripture name ('the First day of the week'), not because of any advance of Biblical truth or reverence, but because of declension from it. The Greek 'Fathers' of the Church were converts from Paganism: and it is not yet sufficiently recognized how much of Pagan rites and ceremonies and expressions they introduced into the Church; and how far Christian ritual was elaborated from and based upon Pagan ritual by the Church of Rome. Especially is this seen in the case of baptism.

"It was these Fathers who, on their conversion, brought the title 'Sunday' into the Church from the Pagan terminology which they had been accustomed to use in connection with their Sun-worship.

"Justin Martyr (114–165 CE) in his second Apology (i.e., his second defense of Christianity), says, in chap. 67. on 'The weekly worship of the Christians,'—'On the day called SUN-DAY all who live in the country gather together to one place … SUN-DAY is the day on which we all hold our common assembly, because it is the first day on which God, having wrought a change in the darkness and matter, made the world; and Jesus Christ our Savior on the same day rose from the dead. For He was crucified on the day before that of SATURN [i.e., Saturn's day]; and on the day after that of Saturn, which is the day of the SUN, having appeared to his apostles and disciples, He taught them these things, which we have submitted to you also for your consideration.'"[97]

If we're going to take one of the most foundational concepts within scripture and change it, we should probably have more than pagan references and assumptions about what God was doing, especially with no direct command as our basis for doing so. There were some early on who used the term "Lord's Day" to refer to the Lord's Supper, which was the annual Passover celebration. That would actually have more merit. It's possible it started out that way but could have morphed into weekly celebration as time went on.

In order to properly understand what the Day of the Lord actually refers to, once again we need to look at the all-important context of the passage. Revelation 1 starts off by saying Yeshua was telling His followers *"the things that must soon take place."* It's commonly referred to as apocalyptic literature. "Apocalypse" comes from the Greek word for "revelation," which means "an unveiling or unfolding of things not previously known and which could not be known apart from the unveiling."[98] Developing a new theology in isolation because of one phrase is one thing, but when you add the imagery and symbolism of the first chapter of Revelation, we can see very quickly that what Yeshua was trying to convey to John was about the *time* we are in, which is His judgement on the Earth and His imminent return. It has nothing to do with the day John got the vision. When we think about it, what relevance would that even have? The Day of the Lord is said to have begun on the cross and will culminate in His Second Coming. The image of Yeshua that John sees is the glorified Lord as He will appear at His return. It is reminiscent of Daniel's vision:

"And the Ancient of Days took His seat; His garment was white as snow, and the hair of His head like pure wool. His throne was ablaze with flames, its wheels were a burning fire" (Dn 7:9).

Once again, we see a picture of God meant to frighten those who would think to oppose Him. Hebrews 10:31 warns us: *"It is a terrifying thing to fall into the hands of the living God."* You don't want to be working against Him when He returns. The constant message we get throughout scripture is that there will be a day of recompense for the wicked, and the book of Revelation gives us more detail about that time than any other book.

To further illustrate how the Lord's Day refers to the Day of the Lord and not the first day of the week, Yeshua tells John in Revelation 1:19 to write past, present, and future events. Yeshua wants John to write a panoramic view of history consistent with Revelation's purpose. Yeshua's return is a central theme of the New Covenant. Everything we go through—the suffering, the trials, the struggles, the persecution—all pale in comparison to the blessings of His return and our dwelling with Him. Our great hope and all of our sacrifices are about how He will return and deliver us from these things and judge the wicked. Joel mentions it five times alone.

"Woe for the day! For the day of the Lord is near, and it will come as destruction from the Almighty" (Jl 1:15).

"Blow a trumpet in Zion, and sound an alarm on My holy mountain! Let all the inhabitants of the land tremble, for the day of the Lord is coming; Indeed, it is near" (Jl 2:1).

"The Lord utters His voice before His army; His camp is indeed very great, for mighty is one who carries out His word. The day of the Lord is indeed great and very awesome, and who can endure it?" (Jl 2:11).

"The sun will be turned into darkness, And the moon into blood, Before the great and awesome day of the Lord comes" (Jl 2:31).

"Multitudes, multitudes in the valley of decision! For the day of the Lord is near in the valley of decision" (Jl 3:14).

All of these verses and the many more throughout the scriptures paint a terrifying picture of His return. Why do you think when John turns around and sees the Lord he *"... fell at His feet like a dead man"* (Rv 1:17)? It was a terrifying image. The Day of the Lord, the day when a holy and indignant God comes to bring judgement upon a wicked and sinful world, is a terrifying prospect, even for the righteous. Dozens of verses refer to it, but one mention of a day of the week when He rose from the dead and we now suddenly tie it in with the expression the Lord's Day in to change God's day of rest from creation? There are even many different expressions to refer to the day of His return, such as "the day of judgement" (Mt 10:15, 12:36; 2 Pt 2:9), "the day" (Mt 25:13; Rom 13:12), "the great day of God"

(Rv 6:14), "the great and notable day" (Acts 2:20), and so on.[99] Is it such a stretch to think that this could simply be another variation? John refers to Yeshua's return at least thirty times in Revelation in various ways. Why single out that one verse as referring to something different that alters God's calendar?

Looking at the expression grammatically will also help us to properly interpret it. Greek and Hebrew are very different languages in structure, so explaining the same thing is often expressed differently.

"Objection has been taken to the interpretation of 'the Lord's Day' here, because we have (in [1:10]) the adjective 'Lord's' instead of the noun (in regimen), 'of the Lord,' as in the Hebrew. But what else could it be called in Hebrew? Such objectors do not seem to be aware of the fact that there is no adjective for 'Lord's' in Hebrew; and therefore the only way of expressing 'the Lord's Day' is by using the two nouns, 'the day of the Lord'—which means equally 'the Lord's Day' (Jehovah's day). It is useless, therefore, to make any objection on this ground; for if a Hebrew wanted to say 'the Lord's Day,' he must say 'the day of the Lord.'

"In the Greek there are two ways of expressing this (as in modern languages); either by saying literally, as in Hebrew, 'the day of the Lord' (using the two nouns); or by using the adjective 'Lord's' instead. It comes to exactly the same thing as to signification; the difference lies only in the emphasis.

"The natural way of qualifying a noun is by using an adjective, as here—(kyriakee) Lord's; and, when this is done, the emphasis takes its natural course, and is placed on the noun thus qualified ('day'). But when the emphasis is required to be placed on the word 'Lord;' then, instead of the adjective, the noun would be used in the genitive case, 'of the Lord.' In the former case (as in [Revelation 1:10]), it would be 'the Lord's DAY.' In the latter case it would be 'THE LORD'S day.' The same day is meant in each case, but with a different emphasis.'"[100]

As we pointed out in chapter 1, Dr. Michael Lake tells us we have to consider language if we're to properly interpret scripture. Since most of us are not experts in biblical Hebrew or Greek, it requires extra work on our part, but when it comes to changing God's Word, it's an understatement to say we need to have all of our bases covered before we proceed.

Another point rarely discussed is that the scope of what John saw makes it almost impossible for him to have received everything in one day. Isaiah prophesied over the reign of four kings. Ezekiel, Jeremiah, and Daniel also prophesied for decades. Are we to think that John received such details about the last days leading up to Yeshua's promised return and the calamity that will befall humanity all at once? John says in Revelation 4:1–2 that he was in the Spirit again. This is clearly a different instance from 1:10, and he again gets an image of the glorified Son of Man. Since he got multiple visions over an indeterminate period of time (weeks, months, or even years), we have to ask again about the significance of a particular day of the week. Furthermore, it has no bearing on what he saw in the original vision, or on the rest of what he was shown. It's also never mentioned again. If the day of revelation were so important, there would be some details surrounding it, and it certainly would have been mentioned again somewhere else in scripture. This is known as a red herring, a literary device to distract people from the main point. The term was popularized in an 1807 novel by William Cobbett about distracting hounds from chasing a rabbit.[101] Is it possible that the evil one has used this red herring to throw God's people off track from walking in obedience and receiving the blessings that keeping the Shabbat promised? Ask the majority of Christians today whether they truly feel rested or even feel God's rest. Is it a stretch to say this might have something to do with it?

Further evidence that the phrase is about the Lord's return is the trumpet imagery John uses to describe Yeshua's voice. The sound of a trumpet is often a reference to judgement. Let's go back to Joel 2.

"Blow a trumpet in Zion, and sound an alarm on My holy mountain! Let all the inhabitants of the land tremble, for the day of the Lord is coming; Indeed, it is near" (Jl 2:1).

Further on in the same chapter, again Joel speaks of the blowing of a trumpet as a call to fasting for the deliverance of His people Israel:

"Blow a trumpet in Zion, consecrate a fast, proclaim a solemn assembly, gather the people, sanctify the congregation, assemble the elders, gather the

children and the nursing infants. Have the groom come out of his room and the bride out of her bridal chamber. Let the priests, the Lord's ministers, weep between the porch and the altar, and let them say, 'Spare Your people, Lord, and do not make Your inheritance a disgrace, with the nations jeering at them. Why should those among the peoples say, 'Where is their God?'' (Jl 2:15–17).

The trumpet sound, although used for many things throughout scripture, eschatologically is used to illustrate Yeshua's return. The entire book of Revelation is about preparing the Body for the Tribulation period and His coming. The trumpet is the warning sound to those who don't belong to Yeshua, but it's our great hope. During John's second time in the Spirit in Revelation 4:1, he hears the voice as a trumpet sound again to demonstrate judgement. There are also flashes of lightning and peals of thunder around the throne, a similar image to what we see when Israel arrived at Mt. Sinai to receive the Law. Both of these times when John is in the Spirit we see how the trumpet blast is tied in with the Day of the Lord.

The Didache

The Didache (The Teaching), also known as The Teaching of the Twelve Apostles, is an ancient document that detailed early Church ethics, practices, and order. It contains sixteen chapters and is broken down into four different sections: moral instructions, ritual practices, instructions for leaders, and end times information.[102] Chapter 14 is only three lines and says:

"1. On the Lord's Day of the Lord come together, break bread and hold Eucharist, after confessing your transgressions that your offering may be pure;
2. But let none who has a quarrel with his fellow join in your meeting until they be reconciled, that your sacrifice be not defiled.
3. For this is that which was spoken by the Lord, 'In every place and time offer me a pure sacrifice, for I am a great king,' saith the Lord, 'and my name is wonderful among the heathen.'"[103]

Estimated to have been written between 60 and 150 CE, it's one of the earliest documents we have on how the primitive believing community functioned. Once again, we have a document that some believe irrefutably shows that the Christian community corporately worshipped on Sunday, even in the earliest days.

The key phrase here in the first verse of the chapter is the "Lord's Day of the Lord." It's a rather awkward phrase when translated to English, and we are much better served if we go back to the Greek. According to Bob Thiel, Ph D:

"The Greek expression in verse 14.1 in the Didache, is:

"Κατὰ κυριακὴν δε κυριου.

"The Greek word κυριακὴν above is transliterated as kuriaki/kyriake.

"Basically kuriaki means the Lord's way. I believe I have translated verse 14.1 in the Didache, properly below (with two options):

"According to the Lord's way, even the Lord's, or

"According to the Lordly {way}, even the Lord's.

"However, it has normally been incorrectly translated by many Protestant scholars. Here are two examples:

"'On the Lord's day of the Lord,' by Kirsopp Lake.

"'But every Lord's day,' by Hall and Napier.

"There are at least two reasons that the above by Lake, as well as Hall & Napier, can be shown to be mistranslated. The first is that the translators should have realized that the Greek term for 'day' (ἡμέρᾳ) is missing in verse 14.1 and is not required by the context. The second is how each of them began the translation of this particular verse. The beginning in both translations is in error and is inconsistent with the translators [sic] other translations in this letter.

"The Greek word translated in verse 14.1 as 'On the' by Kirsopp Lake and 'But every' by Hall and Napier (Κατὰ) truly does mean 'According to' as I have translated it. Κατὰ should not be translated as 'On the' or 'But every.'"[104]

The article gets a bit technical (it's all Greek to me), but the point he's trying to make is that whether unknowingly or intentionally, an ancient manuscript is translated inaccurately. Thiel sums up his article with this:

"Since the Protestant translating scholars of the Didache did not observe an annual Christian Passover and tended to be Sunday observers, this may explain why they did not translate it literally. Instead they used terms that have, sadly, misled multitudes.

"Irrespective of why, the reality is that the Didache did not do away with the seventh-day Sabbath and replace it with Sunday."[105]

If the move from Shabbat to the first day of the week is truly a plan from the kingdom of darkness to deceive the Body of Messiah into stepping outside of God's will, we can see from this example that the conspiracy runs deep.

Any Day

In addition to the three verses Christians use to say the New Covenant proves Sunday is now the correct day, many others will point to verses that suggest whatever day we want is a Sabbath for all belong to the Lord.

The first one is Romans 14:1–6

"Now accept the one who is weak in faith, but not to have quarrels over opinions. One person has faith that he may eat all things, but the one who is weak eats only vegetables. The one who eats is not to regard with contempt the one who does not eat, and the one who does not eat is not to judge the one who eats, for God has accepted him. Who are you to judge the servant of another? To his own master he stands or falls; and he will stand, for the Lord is able to make him stand. One person values one day over another, another values every day the same. Each person must be fully convinced in his own mind. The one who observes the day, observes it for the Lord."

According to many Christians I have spoken to about this matter, this seals the deal. Each person can observe whatever day he wants unto the Lord as long as he's convinced in his own mind. The command "thou shalt" now has the addendum "if I want to" added to it because of the cross. Again, the assumption is that the authority to choose what day to approach God has been transferred to each person. Shabbat or Sunday or Tuesday are all fine with God. Except the passage isn't dealing with the Shabbat. Nowhere do we find it mentioned. So what is Paul addressing?

Verse 1 tells the Roman believers not to argue over opinions or disputable things. The Greek word is διαλογισμῶν (*dialogismōn*—from Strong's #1261) refers to a reasoning,[106] something one has decided in his own mind. Once again, we have to reiterate that the commandments of God are not up for debate, nor do we have any authority to make of them what we will. Paul references eating of meat or vegetables and fasting, none of which have anything to do with the Shabbat. Fasting is not done on Shabbat. The Talmud actually forbids it, as the Shabbat is supposed to be an *oneg*, or a delight. The Apostolic Constitution, a collection of writings similar to the Didache, written between 250–350 CE, actually forbade fasting on Sunday.[107] If Paul is mentioning fasting and the abstaining from meat, he is not addressing the corporate day of worship—either Saturday or Sunday, where a fellowship meal was eaten—but personal days of dedication to God. The Pharisee boasted in the Temple that he fasted twice a week (Lk 18:12). Zechariah 7:4 speaks of fasting in the fifth and seventh months, which wasn't biblically mandated but personally consecrated to God. One day is not better than another. Paul says if you fast, do it unto the Lord, and if you don't, do that unto the Lord. We don't have a choice when YHVH says to do something in His Word. The Roman believers were using their personal days of devotion to one up each other. They believed they were spiritually superior for what they decided in their hearts to dedicate to God. Paul is saying that whatever you offer to the Lord in the way of sacrifice, or whatever you partake of in rejoicing, don't feel you're any better than anyone else who doesn't do the same thing you do. It has nothing to do with any of the days God says we're to observe. Our opinion on those doesn't matter. Remember, Paul affirmed the law many times in Romans, so it's contradictory to say that whatever day one chooses is fine.

The next verse is Colossians 2:16:

"Therefore, no one is to act as your judge in regard to food and drink, or in respect to a festival or a new moon, or a Sabbath day—things which are only a shadow of what is to come; but the substance belongs to Messiah."

This is interpreted as meaning that we aren't to judge anyone for whatever day they decide to keep. If you keep Sunday as your day of worship, I'm not to judge you. Same goes for if you keep Christmas. It's not my place to judge. However, as we discussed in chapter 2, the context of this passage begins in verse 8, where we're told not be taken captive through by empty philosophy and the traditions of men. Further on in this passage, he speaks of things like the worship of angels in false humility, which men were using to puff themselves up, even though it went against scripture. They appear to be wise, but Paul calls those things made-up religion. This verse has nothing to do with God's commandments. Why would Paul warn people not to let anyone judge them for not doing the things they had never done to begin with? These were primarily Gentile converts. Who was going to judge them for not keeping Shabbat or a New Moon celebration? It appears that after having come out of paganism, they were being condemned for *doing* those things by their former pagan brethren. When they wouldn't come out and celebrate the emperor's birthday or some pagan deity's special day that involved ritual sex, they were ridiculed. After my wife got saved and she started going home from the clubs early on Saturday night because she had to go to church the next day, she was ridiculed by her friends, who didn't like her new-found faith. That was a good incentive to stop going altogether. Paul is encouraging the Colossian believers to remain strong and not bow to peer pressure when they're attacked for keeping God's commandments. Yet the Church today uses this verse to prevent anyone from saying anything about a brother or sister being disobedient. In Paul's exhortation to the Corinthians, he says:

"But actually, I wrote to you not to associate with any so-called brother if he is a sexually immoral person, or a greedy person, or an idolater, or is verbally abusive, or habitually drunk, or a swindler—not even to eat with such a person. For what business of mine is it to judge outsiders? <u>Do you</u>

not judge those who are within the church? But those who are outside, God judges. Remove the evil person from among yourselves" (1Cor 5:11–13, emphasis mine).

It turns out we are supposed to judge one another for not keeping God's commandments. Those who quote Matthew 7:1, where Yeshua warns us not to judge or we will be judged, once again miss the context of the Messiah's words. He's speaking about being a hypocrite. We don't get after someone about the same thing we're doing ourselves. David found that out the hard way when he pronounced judgement on the rich man who took the poor man's lamb, and then Nathan told him that *"You yourself are the man"* (2 Sm 12:7). Paul is speaking about keeping each other accountable, not condemning, which is what Matthew 7:1 addresses.

These two passages, as well as the previous three we looked at, demonstrate how believers have taken scripture completely out of context to justify disobedience to God's commandment to keep the seventh day holy, and it's to their own detriment. Old or New Covenant, God clearly lays out blessings for obedience and discipline and curses for disobedience. Christians have been missing out on peace and favour because of it.

Despite the Church repeating over and over that the Lord's Day is the first day of the week, there is no biblical imperative to do so and no evidence to confirm that historically the early Assembly did this. But there is plenty that suggest that the term refers to His return. The idea that Christians worship on Sunday because Yeshua rose from the dead is so ingrained in our theology that to even question it might seem heretical to some. However, as we have seen, the first day of the week never had any significance in scripture for anything except the creation account and the day Yeshua exited the tomb. But was the first day of the week really what mattered about His resurrection, or was there something else about that particular day that we can tie back into scripture? Why was the first day of the week mentioned in the resurrection account?

An Appointed Time

The first, or eighth, day of each week is not tied to anything specific in scripture. In reality, there's no such thing as an eighth day because the week still only has seven, so the whole concept is allegorical. Yet there must be a reason why the first day was referenced in the Gospel accounts. Everything mentioned in the Bible has some point of relevancy and often points us to something else. In Jewish exegesis (biblical interpretation), there is a type or level of interpretation called *remez*, which means a hint or something deeper. Often in scripture this is used, and Yeshua Himself employs it on many occasions. It's practised when we start with a few words of a verse that trigger our memories to what the rest of the passage says. If I say "For God so loved the world," most people with a rudimentary knowledge of the Bible will quote the rest of John 3:16, probably the most famous verse in all of the Word of God. By stating the first day of the week, the Gospel writers are indicating that it's important; therefore, we have to go back into God's Word to understand why. Jewish believers had no concept of the first day of every week being significant, but seeing as how Yeshua died on Passover, there is a first day of the week that is important.

In Leviticus 23, the appointed times, or feasts of the Lord, are listed. If you want to know on which days God does want to be worshipped and how, this is the chapter to go to. There is the weekly Shabbat and then seven annual festivals. Most occur on a particular date, such as the Passover being on the fourteenth day of the first month. However, there's a little-known celebration God commands that most of Christianity and even Judaism is completely ignorant of. It's called the Feast of First Fruits. When does it happen?

"Then the Lord spoke to Moses, saying, 'Speak to the sons of Israel and say to them, "When you enter the land which I am going to give to you and you gather its harvest, then you shall bring in the sheaf of the first fruits of your harvest to the priest. He shall wave the sheaf before the Lord for you to be accepted; <u>on the day after the Sabbath</u> the priest shall wave it. He shall wave the sheaf before the Lord for you to be accepted; on the day after the Sabbath the priest shall wave it."'' (Lev 23:9–11, emphasis mine).

The day after the Sabbath is mentioned as one of the *moedim Adonai* (appointed times of the Lord), but it's not a weekly observance but rather an annual one, as it happens right after Passover at the time of the barley harvest, which was the first harvest of the year. Those who said the Day of the Lord referred to Easter Sunday and the commemoration of the resurrection were on the right track, but since Easter is a pagan holiday, there's no connection with scripture. Looking at the Feast of First Fruits, though, we see several elements that foretell the resurrection of Yeshua.

In fact, every one of God's appointed times is given to show us His plan of salvation. We'll get into greater detail in the next chapter, but with First Fruits, the key is that the first crop that comes out of the ground has a ribbon tied around it so that when the harvest comes, the priest would wave it before the Lord. That might seem odd, and odder still when God explains, *"He shall wave the sheaf before the Lord for you to be accepted"* (Lev 9:11). Why is it important the first plant that pokes its head out of the ground be waved before God so that the people might be accepted?

"But the fact is, Messiah has been raised from the dead, the first fruits of those who are asleep. For since by a man death came, by a man also came the resurrection of the dead. For as in Adam all die, so also in Messiah all will be made alive. But each in his own order: Messiah the first fruits, after that those who are Messiah's at His coming" (1 Cor 15:20–23).

"Now I urge you, brothers and sisters: you know the household of Stephana's, that they are the first fruits of Achaia, and that they have devoted themselves to ministry to the saints" (1 Cor 16:15).

"In the exercise of His will He gave us birth by the word of truth, so that we would be a kind of first fruits among His creatures" (Jas 1:18).

"These are the ones who have not defiled themselves with women, for they are celibate. These are the ones who follow the Lamb wherever He goes. These have been purchased from mankind as first fruits to God and to the Lamb" (Rev 14:4).

"He is also the head of the body, the church; and He is the beginning, the firstborn from the dead, so that He Himself will come to have first place in everything" (Col 1:18).

"For the Lord Himself will descend from heaven with a shout, with the voice of the archangel and with the trumpet of God, and the dead in Messiah will rise first" (1 Thes 4:16).

"and from Yeshua The Messiah, the faithful witness, the firstborn of the dead" (Rev 1:5).

Apparently this idea of being the first to come back from the dead on His own power was a big deal to God. The first plant to come out of the ground represents Yeshua. Remember how He spoke in John 12:24 about the grain of wheat falling to the ground and needing to die to bear a harvest? That was what First Fruits was all about. He was the wave offering before the Lord so that we might be accepted before God. I don't find many references to egg-laying chocolate rabbits here in these passages, though. Do we see now why He rose on the first day of the week? It was because God's prophetic calendar was being fulfilled on an *annual* festival. The first day of every week means nothing, although we're certainly free to remember His death, burial, and resurrection as often as we like. On the other hand, the first day of the week after the Shabbat after the Passover means everything because God tells us so in His Word. Without understanding the feast days and our Hebraic heritage, we miss this entirely and proceed to create a new custom that is of our vain imagination and counters God's eternal plan for us.

The debate over the Sabbath day is often the most contentious of all theological issues, and I believe the reason for this is that it takes us out of God's spiritual pattern and design where peace and blessing reside into the kingdom of darkness and its cycles and patterns. Once one command can be changed by our own will, so can any other one we choose. Yeshua told the disciples that heaven and earth would have an easier time of passing away than the most minute part of the law, but the Torah looks like Swiss cheese today because we've taken so much out of it.

Christians are fond of saying that none of the other Ten Commandments have changed, but the one about the Shabbat has because we've got a better day. I have to ask again, on what basis do we make that claim, other than using these passages, which are clearly misinterpreted or misused? Besides, what benefit is there in Yeshua changing the day anyway? All of our reasoning is nothing but sophistry, and Paul tells us God's foolishness puts our wisdom to shame. Seven represents competition, perfection, and redemption. The first day represents nothing. There's no continuity with anything in the Hebrew scriptures. I believe that instead of showing God how clever we are by trying to improve upon His plan, it probably makes more sense to continue with what He's given us as a model, lived out Himself while He walked the earth, and which He's told us will last for eternity.

Chapter 7—God's Appointed Times

"The feasts teach a correct, balanced, and in-depth view of the gospel, the sanctuary, righteousness by faith, and the three angels' messages. Each feast teaches a different aspect of each these subjects. The feasts also teach many more details about the prophecies in Daniel and Revelation."

Richard and Melody Drake

"The festivals of the L-rd found in Leviticus (Vayikra) 23 were given to us by G-d so His people could understand the coining of the Messiah (Mashiach) and the role that the Messiah (Mashiach) would play in redeeming and restoring both man and the earth back to G-d following the fall of man in the Garden of Eden (Gan Eden). Although most non-Jewish Bible believers have heard of the feasts, the deep meaning and the importance of these feasts are almost universally not understood."

Eddie Chumney

Time is our most valuable resource and the thing above all in our lives that we can't control one bit. Steve Jobs once said, "It's really clear that the most precious resource we all have is time." Albert Einstein cheekily remarked, "The only reason for time is so that everything doesn't happen at once." More ominously, George Orwell said, "Who controls the past, controls the future: who controls the present controls the past."[108] Numerous songs have been written about time, like the Rolling Stones, who said time was on their side (which is debateable), or Steve Miller, who told us that time keeps on slipping into the future (a candidate for the "obviously" award). Time seems to be a fascination for a lot of us. We stress over it, would love to be able to stop it or go back in it, and spend billions every year trying to learn how to manage it better. Society is obsessed by it, as nearly every electronic device we have today has a clock included, and almost everything we do is ordered by it—from work to meals to dates. Without time, we could not function.

It's fascinating that time has not always existed, at least as we know it today. God created it when He made the heavens and the earth. Before that, time operated differently (I have no idea how). Another interesting thing is that space and time are actually interrelated, which Albert Einstein demonstrated through his theory of relativity:

"We must accept that time is not completely separate from and independent of space, but is combined with it to form an object called space-time"[109]

Studies show that everything in space and time is connected to the speed of light. Einstein proved that nothing can go faster than light. He also showed that neither space nor time are constants but are malleable. Sir Isaac Newton, in his *Philosophiae Naturalis Principia Mathematica*, stated he believed that time was absolute,[110] but Einstein's theory proved that both time and space are, well, relative. Light, which is simply energy waves (everything physical in the universe at the quantum level is composed of waves of energy), can actually bend when sufficient force is applied to it, such as gravity. The closer an object gets to moving to the speed of light, the slower it moves through time. The greater an object's mass, the more it bends or warps time and slows down movement around it. Time moves slower for an object the closer it is to the earth's core and moves quicker the farther it moves away from the earth's gravitational pull. All of my stats courses in university were obviously very close to the centre of the earth. Is your mind bending yet? Mine does when I start thinking about this, which is why I teach the Bible and not physics.

Why do I mention any of this? It's to show that the concept of time is more complicated than it appears, and that God is the creator of everything, including time. Therefore, when He gives certain instructions regarding it, we should pay attention. You're asking if we really needed the science lesson to prove that.

Time is very important to God. Galatians 4:4 explains that in the fullness of time, God sent the Messiah. God gives us time to turn back to Him and repent, affirming Him as being long-suffering (Rev 2:21). He appoints times for specific things to happen, such as returning to Abraham and Sarah to give them Isaac, the son of promise. In fact, Ecclesiastes 3:1 tells us *"There is an appointed time for everything. And there is a time for every matter under heaven—"* Just as society cannot function without a system of time keeping, our spiritual lives must also be governed by a schedule that God Himself sets up. The sacrifices in the Temple were offered at specific times of the day, and the official times of prayer coincided with them, which are known in the New Covenant as the hours of prayer. Ever hear the expression "timing is everything"? There's more truth to it than we might think.

The term "appointed time(s)" occurs forty times in the NASB. This tells us that when we approach God, it is not random, nor is it up to us when we prefer to show up. Just as we established with the Shabbat, God wants us to rest with Him on the seventh day; there are other days that He has appointed for us to come before Him.

"The Lord spoke again to Moses, saying, 'Speak to the sons of Israel and say to them, "The Lord's appointed times which you shall proclaim as holy convocations—My appointed times are these: For six days work may be done, but on the seventh day there is a Sabbath of complete rest, a holy convocation. You shall not do any work; it is a Sabbath to the Lord in all your dwellings. These are the appointed times of the Lord, holy convocations which you shall proclaim at the times appointed for them."'" (Lev 23:1–4).

Four times in this passage, God says the festivals He's introducing are His appointed times. Rarely in the scriptures do we find God repeating the same thing four times in the same thought. These festivals mean a lot to Him. He says they belong to Him, yet the world and the Church generally refer to these times as Jewish holidays. He gave them to the Jewish people to introduce to the rest of the world so everyone would know about them and celebrate them. Yet most of His children are completely ignorant of them or only casually familiar with what they are and why we have them.

The feasts have many purposes, but the three primary ones are:

1. A memorial of something amazing and wonderful that God did
2. Revelation of God's plan of salvation
3. A show of His character through types and shadows.

Everything the feasts represent and accomplish can be slotted into these three categories. If we study them in depth, we'll see that all of them are fulfilled in the Messiah. Contrast these with the pagan holidays that Christianity worships on and we have to make up how they point to Yeshua—for example, saying that the candy canes we eat at Christmas represent Yeshua because the j shape stands for Jesus (there's no j in Hebrew), the stripes represent the ones He bore for our sins, and the red represents His blood shed for us. People actually believe this stuff or at least try to convince themselves that it's true. Cue the head smacking.

The *moedim* are agricultural festivals. In today's urban society, some of the impact of the imagery is lost because we're not dependent on the ground we live on for our very sustenance. One of my neighbours from several years back told us one time "my meat grows on trees." I had a meat distributorship at the time, and she wasn't a big fan of talking about blood or discussing how an animal is actually prepared. It was easier just to imagine that food comes prepackaged from wherever in the world we can get it. But in ancient civilizations, everyone was dependent on what they grew or raised locally. God's feast days reflect that and also help us to understand that we are the actual harvest and that all the symbolism of the festival is about Yeshua and what He did for us. So Israel's life-cycle and calendar were based on the cycles of the crops. Rabbi Samuel Raphael wrote:

"The catechism of the Jew consists of his calendar. On the pinions of time which bear us through life, God has inscribed the eternal words of His soul-inspiring doctrine, making days and weeks, months and years the heralds to proclaim His truths. Nothing would seem more fleeing than these elements of time, but to them God entrusted the care of His holy things, thereby rendering them more imperishable and more accessible than any mouth of priest, any monuments, temple, or altar could have done. Priests die, monuments decay, temples and altars fall to pieces, but time remains forever, and every newborn day emerges fresh and vigorous from its bosom."[111]

All of Israel's life-cycle revolved around these times. Their lives were structured on when the crops would grow, when the harvest was to be done, and when to show up to celebrate. In fact, no matter where the Israelites lived, Moses commanded them to appear before the Lord, first at the Tabernacle but eventually at the Temple in Jerusalem three times a year.

"Three times a year all your males are to appear before the Lord God, the God of Israel" (Ex 34:23).

For some, travelling to Jerusalem would have been a long trip that required much planning. It would have taken several weeks, which means it would have had to be coordinated with the family and neighbours, as people travelled in groups. Everything in life had to revolve around those trips, including making sure the harvesting was finished. It would be safe to say Israel's very identity was woven into feasts. If that's so, what happens when we remove a key pillar of our identity? We lose it. Do we really understand what Yeshua spoke about when He lamented that the harvest was plentiful but there were (are) so few labourers available, so we need to pray for more labourers? Remember, we are the harvest. Waiting for the Easter Bunny or hanging a stocking on the chimney with care doesn't really tell us that.

When we begin our study of the feasts, we start with the fact that they are written in the book of Leviticus. This book gives instructions on how the Levites were supposed to live, and it's all about holiness. The entire book can be summed up in the verse that says:

"For I am the Lord who brought you up from the land of Egypt, to be your God; so you shall be holy, because I am holy" (Lev 11:45).

Although Leviticus contains many commandments that applied exclusively to those who served in the Temple, it is a blueprint for all of us.

"Another name for the book of Leviticus is the 'Torah of the Priests,' as much of it concerns the Tabernacle/Temple sacrifices and the priestly service. As Israel is a 'Kingdom of Priests,' this means all the people, not only the Levitical Priests, can learn about serving God."[112]

God's set-apart times to come worship Him are part of His definition of what it means to be holy. They aren't just times to gather. They distinguish us from the rest of society. Even today, the world over knows that come Passover time, Jewish people will be gathering to commemorate their deliverance from Egypt, regardless of whether they even believe the events actually happened or not. When I asked my atheist uncle years ago why he cared about these things, since he didn't believe they were true, he answered, "Because that's what our people have always done." Identity. Doesn't matter if it's true. It's what defines us. Do you think most Hindus really believe the god Ganesha actually has a snout and looks like an elephant? Doesn't matter. Identity. Identity is of greatest importance to us. When our identity is rooted in the things of God, we have assurance our identity is true.

The very first of God's *moedim* is the Shabbat. In previous passages, the Shabbat has been connected to both creation and Israel's deliverance from Egypt. Now God is emphasizing that it's part of the cycle of life. In Greco-Roman thought, time was linear. We have a straight line going from point a to point b. In Hebraic thinking, time moves in cycles and patterns. The late Brad Scott once said:

"The 'Elohiym of scriptural thought is cyclical not linear. He brings to His creation cycles, cycles of righteousness and instruction. You can see this clearly in His creation. The celestial glories go through their cycles. The moon passes through its phases every month. As a matter of fact, this is the background for understanding the New Covenant. The moon is renewed every month. The word for moon is chodesh (חדש) which is the cognate of the word for new which is chadash (חדש). The idea is something renewed. 'Elohiym placed the seasons in their cycles. The woman has her monthly cycles. The sun, moon, and stars are cyclical and are placed in the heavens for signs (le'otot (אות) or times) and for seasons (mo'ediym (מועד) or appointed festivals). The guideline for mankind's times and feasts are cyclical just as His Sabbaths and feasts are cyclical. In these Sabbaths and feasts, 'Elohiym is constantly and cyclically reminding man of who He is and who man is. This is a big part of what it means to be unchanging. 'Elohiym is not linear and He is not flippant."[113]

Everything that happens on Earth does so in a cycle. We have seasons that repeat every year and we have seasons of life. In their seminal book *The Fourth Turning*, William Strauss and Neil Howe (1997) demonstrated by tracing American history back to the pre-settlement year 1584 that there are four seasons in society that cycle about every one hundred years or so and correspond with the calendar seasons. The winter season is one of great upheaval, war, and chaos, called Crisis. The spring season follows and is when society renews and rebuilds. During summer, prosperity and consumerism set in, and in the fall society begins to decline again, leading to another winter. What's fascinating about their theory is that with each season, a generational "archetype," or defining set of attributes and values, always coincided with it. After war and chaos, when society was rebuilding, hard work and self-sacrifice always characterized that generation. Individualism wasn't as prevalent as the collective good. When the season of content and leisure arrives after a couple of decades of rebuilding, society turns to individualism, and selflessness is looked upon as antiquated and unnecessary, since the times are now good.

What the book demonstrated with hundreds of examples is that the cycles of society are long-term and multi-generational as well as shorter-term. That's why God also gave us the Sabbatical year (seven years) and the Year of Jubilee (every fifty years). The appointed times of God reinforce the cyclical nature of our lives and how time really works. Although we understand that time also moves forward in a linear fashion, and we don't subscribe to such theories as the Circle of Life as represented by reincarnation prevalent in New Age (occultic) and eastern religions, we acknowledge that things will repeat. Picture a pinwheel spinning along a line, circling as it moves forward. Robert Heidler defines a cycle as "something that goes around and moves you to a destination."[114]

After the weekly Shabbat, God introduces the cycle of annual festivals. Care to guess how many of them there are? Of course, you knew there were seven! They are:

1. Passover

2. Unleavened Bread
3. First Fruits
4. Shavuot or The Feast of Weeks
5. Feast of Trumpets or Festival of Blowing
6. Yom Kippur or The Day of Atonement
7. Sukkot or Tabernacles

The first four are called the Spring Feasts and the last three the Fall Feasts. They have both an historical as well as prophetic component to them, so we remember what God has already done but also look forward to what He's going to do. We also understand the character of God better by studying them. While we will briefly go over the three elements with each festival, my intention isn't to delve into the deep theological wonders of the appointed times of the Lord. There are many terrific resources out there solely dedicated to that topic. The intent of this tome is to demonstrate that they are important, that God wants all of His children to keep them, and the Body of Messiah is missing out on blessings by not doing so.

Passover

The first *moed* (appointed time) is the Passover. While most people think it lasts eight days, Passover and Unleavened Bread are two distinct holy days. The commemoration of an act of God is well remembered in the Exodus story, one of the most famous events in history. After four hundred years of slavery, God raised up a deliverer to bring the people out of bondage into freedom. Moses confronts Pharaoh, who was king of the most powerful nation on earth at the time, to let the Israelites go. When Pharaoh keeps refusing, Moses brings the ten plagues on the Egyptians. The last plague was the slaying of the first born, God's judgement on Pharaoh for killing the male children of Israel by having them thrown into the Nile River eighty years before.

What is fascinating about this story is that Israel was completely protected from the first nine plagues while they were hidden away in the land of Goshen. They didn't have to do anything to safeguard themselves. The tenth one, however, was different. God instructed the Israelites to stay in their houses that night and smear the blood of a lamb on the door frame so the Angel of Death would "pass over" them. If they didn't, they would die too, which means this last plague wasn't just a judgement against the Egyptians but against all mankind and sin. Israel obeyed, and after four centuries of slavery, they were delivered in one night. They came down to Egypt as a few dozen members of one family and left as a nation of several million.

Prophetically, this incredible event points to how all of mankind is delivered from slavery; 1,500 years later, John the Baptist declared Yeshua to be the "*Lamb of God who takes away the sin of the world*" (John 1:29). Every Jew would have known what the reference was, and there would have been several cases of whiplash as people looked to see who was fulfilling the long-awaited prophecy of the Redeemer of Israel finally arriving. Egypt represents the kingdom of darkness and the bondage of sin. Pharaoh represents Satan, who will not let humanity go. When Yeshua was crucified, He hung there for three hours as God poured His wrath on the innocent and perfect lamb, our substitution. As the spear was thrust into His side and His blood poured out on the ground, God's righteous requirement of blood atonement for the remission of sin and the defeat of death was completed. Just as Israel trusted God's Word and applied the blood on their doorposts in Egypt so they would not die in the final plague, all who trust in Yeshua's death and are "covered" by His blood and will not see spiritual death but spend eternity with God. Those who reject the Messiah's atoning sacrifice will be as the Egyptians who ignored Moses' warning and will experience death or separation from God forever, tormented in a lake of fire. And just as there was wailing in Egypt for those who did not cover their doors with blood and stay inside, "*in that place there will be weeping and gnashing of teeth*" (Mt 13:42).

To further demonstrate how Yeshua fulfills this feast and is the Lamb of God, the Lord gives an odd command as He institutes the Passover:

"*Speak to all the congregation of Israel, saying, 'On the tenth of this month they are, each one, to take a lamb for themselves, according to the fathers' households, a lamb for each household. Now if the household is too small for a lamb, then he and his neighbor nearest to his house are to take one according to the number of persons in them; in proportion to what each one should eat, you are to divide the lamb. Your lamb shall be an unblemished male a year old; you may take it from the sheep or from the goats. You shall keep it until the fourteenth day of the same month, then the whole assembly of the congregation of Israel is to slaughter it at twilight"* (Ex 12:2–6).

Israel was to take the lamb they were about to sacrifice and keep it within the house for five days, from the tenth to the fourteenth. It was in essence to be a pet, which was unusual because Jews didn't normally have animals inside the house, for cleanliness purposes. It's one of the reasons why whenever disease outbreaks have happened, such as the Black Death, or the bubonic plague epidemic in the mid-1300s, Jews were not as adversely affected. It's also why you can be sure that when Yeshua was born whether it was in a barn where they usually housed the animals or if it was in a sukkah, since He was born during the Feast of Tabernacles and they just brought in the manger and cleaned it out for him to lie in, there were no animals present like in every Nativity scene you see at Christmas time.

Part of the reason why the lamb was to be kept in the house was that it was to be observed and inspected to make sure it was perfect or unblemished. After five days they killed it and put its blood on the door-posts to protect them from their own death. When Yeshua came riding into Jerusalem on the back of a donkey and the crowds were shouting "Hosanna to the Son of David," which was a Messianic title, He came in on the first day of the week (John 12:12). It was the tenth of Nisan, which would make Thursday the fourteenth, which was the day He died, right on the day of Passover and when the lamb was supposed to be slaughtered and its blood poured out. Yeshua was brought into Jerusalem (the home), inspected for five days, declared unblemished by God, and killed with His blood poured out so that the Angel of Death might pass over all who trust in His sacrifice. The symbolism is fantastic, but if all we're doing is taking a communion wafer and little glass of grape juice once a month because of rote tradition, we understand none of this.

Passover reveals several things about God's character. It shows His fierce wrath against sin and His absolute holiness. Many are living this life hoping to get a free pass on the day of judgement, believing that God will just overlook all the ways they've transgressed His Torah and let them into heaven anyway. Passover, and the rest of the sacrificial system that God instituted in Israel, proved that someone has to die and blood needs to be spilled for sin.

"For the life of the flesh is in the blood, and I have given it to you on the altar to make atonement for your souls; for it is the blood by reason of the life that makes atonement" (Lev 17:11).

This to me is the key verse in all of Torah. God gives the Law, over six hundred commandments to follow, which no one in all of history, save Yeshua, has been able to keep perfectly. So God makes a provision that by the shedding of blood, we won't be judged for our violation of His perfect standard of righteousness. That shows His mercy and grace and unbreakable love for humanity, that He would come in the flesh Himself and live the life we couldn't and die the death we should have so we could have the forgiveness and the freedom we don't deserve. When believers don't celebrate Passover, they miss out on this.

Passover is commemorated through a Seder (order), which is a ceremonial meal. The entire service revolves around the four glasses of wine or grape juice that are drunk throughout the evening, symbolizing the four promises God made to Israel in Exodus 6:6–7.

"Say, therefore, to the sons of Israel, 'I am the Lord, and I will bring you out from under the labors of the Egyptians, and I will rescue you from their bondage. I will also redeem you with an outstretched arm, and with great judgments. Then I will take you as My people, and I will be your God; and you shall know that I am the Lord your God, who brought you out from under the labors of the Egyptians.'"

1. The Cup of Sanctification—"I will bring you out from under the labours of the Egyptians."
2. The Cup of Judgement—"I will rescue from their bondage."
3. The Cup of Redemption—"I will also redeem you with an outstretched arm."
4. The Cup of Joy or Praise—"I will take you as My people, and I will be your God."

Four promises, and each one is represented by a glass of wine.

The entire service follows a book called a Haggadah (the telling) and gives the traditions to follow, the meanings behind them, and the prayers to be said or sung throughout the evening. There is a Seder plate with various elements on it, including the bitter herbs and the unleavened bread that scripture commands (Ex 12:8) and other extra-biblical ones too. There's no one right way to conduct a Seder, no rigid formula. Every one has a different flavour. The point isn't all the details in how we do it but to celebrate the Passover and honour God.

Of course, Passover is celebrated through the institution of the Lord's Table or Communion. The third cup, the Cup of Redemption, clearly points toward Yeshua redeeming us with an outstretched arm(s). At the Last Supper in John 13, He took the bread and the wine, which Jews had been partaking of ever since Abraham met with Melchizedek, and proclaimed that they now represented His body and blood. This was the third cup, and He was instituting the New Covenant (Lk 22:20), promised from Jeremiah 31:31 to have the Law written on our hearts. The Lord was fulfilling a six-hundred-year-old prophecy and letting everyone know He was the Promised One. When we take those elements, we again commemorate His great sacrifice in which He died so that we could be delivered from sin. It's serious business, and that's why Paul warned the Corinthians that anyone who treats the Lord's Supper lightly and doesn't reflect on their sin to repent of it brings judgement on themselves.

"Therefore whoever eats the bread or drinks the cup of the Lord in an unworthy way, shall be guilty of the body and the blood of the Lord. But a person must examine himself, and in so doing he is to eat of the bread and drink of the cup. For the one who eats and drinks, eats and drinks judgment to himself if he does not properly recognize the body. For this reason many among you are weak and sick, and a number are asleep" (1 Cor 11:27–30).

Passover is the first of God's set-apart times that He gave us to come worship Him. Through it, He reminds us of the consequences of rebellion against Him, which is death. Paul affirms this in Romans 6:23 when he says, *"The wages of sin is death."* It doesn't get any clearer than that. We all sin, we're all guilty, and we all are going to die at some point. That's the bad news. The good news, though, is that just as Abraham prophesied *"God will provide for Himself the lamb*" (Gen 22:8), Yeshua came as that sacrificial lamb and took our place, shedding His blood and defeating the consequences of sin. When God sees the blood of the Lamb, He passes over us. The symbolism is so incredibly rich, and God wants us to understand all of this, which is why He commanded us to celebrate it every year. To those who say that the feast days were done away with: How could something be done away with that is still in effect today? What benefit is there in not gathering together to remember God's faithfulness in Egypt and also at Calvary? Sure, the Church today takes the Lord's Table, but how many understand the significance and origins of what they're doing? Very few, I would estimate, and I've done Passover presentations at over one hundred churches over the years. Most people who see the Passover presented are amazed at the connection, but if Christianity was to start keeping God's appointed times, more would understand what they are doing and God's heart on the issue.

Unleavened Bread

The day after Passover, which again falls on the fourteenth day of the first month of the year (Ex 12:3) is the Feast of Unleavened Bread. As with Passover, Unleavened Bread is instituted as they are leaving Egypt.

"Now this day shall be a memorial to you, and you shall celebrate it as a feast to the Lord; throughout your generations you are to celebrate it as a permanent ordinance. For seven days you shall eat unleavened bread, but on the first day you shall remove dough with yeast from your houses; for whoever eats anything with yeast from the first day until the seventh day, that person shall be cut off from Israel. And on the first day you shall have a holy assembly, and another holy assembly on the seventh day; no work at all shall be done on them, except for what must be eaten by every person—that alone may be prepared by you. You shall also keep the Feast of Unleavened Bread, for on this very day I brought your multitudes out of the land of Egypt; therefore you shall keep this day throughout your generations as a permanent ordinance. In the first month, on the fourteenth day of the month at evening, you shall eat unleavened bread, until the twenty-first day of the month at evening. For seven days there shall be no dough with yeast found

in your houses; for whoever eats anything with yeast, that person shall be cut off from the congregation of Israel, whether he is a stranger or a native of the land. You shall not eat anything with yeast; in all your dwellings you shall eat unleavened bread" (Ex 12:14–20).

Passover is one day and Unleavened Bread is seven. They're intertwined with each other, and even the Gospels sometimes interchange them. Yet they represent two different aspects of our salvation experience. Passover is about our justification. If we trust in the blood, we are passed over, or saved. That's an instantaneous experience. Paul says confess and believe.

Unleavened Bread is about the new life that we live. The old life dies and is buried. We're to get rid of the leaven. Jewish people will scour their houses from top to bottom to get rid of every last breadcrumb. It's a tradition called *Bedikat Chametz* (the search for chametz) that Chabad.org refers to as a "search and destroy mission."[115] I even heard of one family in central Asia that would take two months and used to wash their mattresses to prepare. It's most likely where the tradition of spring cleaning came from. As Jews were in the Diaspora (dispersion), they would thoroughly go through their houses in preparation for Passover and likely influenced their neighbours to do likewise.

Two words are used for leaven in Hebrew, both of them in Exodus 12:15. The first one is חָמֵץ (*chametz*—Strong's #2557).[116] It refers to bread that is leavened or raised with a leavening agent. The second word is שְׂאֹר (*seor*—Strong's #7603)[117] which means leavened but most often refers to the leavening agent itself, which is usually yeast but can also be unpasteurized beer, buttermilk, ginger beer, kefir, or sourdough starter (a piece left over from an old lump). Old dough was allowed to ferment until it became sourdough or yeast. A piece was then added to flour and water to help it rise as the leaven spread through the entire pastry. Unleavened bread is entirely new. It doesn't rely on the corruption of something old to make it. Leavened bread symbolizes our old lives, while unleavened symbolizes new.

Yeast spores are everywhere. They're in the air that we breath. That's why in Jewish tradition, dough that is to be used to make unleavened bread, or matzah, isn't allowed to sit for more than eighteen minutes or it will be considered *chametz*, or leavened. Matzah is flat and not very tasty (although today you can get a variety of flavours, but not when I was growing up). It's also known in scripture as the bread of affliction (Deut 16:3). God commanded Israel to remove the leaven from their houses for seven days (completion) to represent the getting rid of the old life and entering into the new one. So what's the big deal about yeast, you might ask. Yeast is a single-celled organism that converts carbohydrates (energy, life) to carbon dioxide (death) and alcohol (intoxication). It literally corrupts the dough. The production of carbon dioxide gas inflates the dough and puffs it up, so leaven represents the puffing up of a person, or the sin of pride. Although observant Jews today ban anything that rises, including baking soda and even rice or corn, it was the yeast the Lord wanted out because it affected everything around it. Baking soda, although it does help things rise, only raises what touches it directly. It doesn't spread.

As God was leading Israel out of bondage (the old life of unbelief) into a new life of freedom, they had to make a clear distinction between the old life and the new. They had to clean out their houses of the leavening agent that produces pride and move into the new life with a clean break. A complete cycle of one week signifies a complete severing from the old life of sin and bondage and being sanctified or separated into the new life of purity and humility, which is completely contrary to the world system and its values.

The New Covenant actually speaks of five different types of pride. The leaven of the Pharisees is hypocrisy and legal bondage (Lk 12:1). They added to the Word of God (Mk 7:6–8). The Pharisees would come to a place to teach and hand out bread to gain an audience. Yeshua also did that (He just made the bread on the spot) but taught with purity.

The leaven of the Sadducees represented religious corruption. The Sadducees were the priestly class who ran the Temple, which during Yeshua's day had become terribly corrupt. The high priesthood was actually bought and sold and no longer dependent on lineage from Aaron's descendants. Although they weren't as liberal in their understanding of the Torah as the Pharisees, who added thousands of rules in their interpretation, the Sadducees weren't opposed to mixing a little paganism in to keep the Romans happy. They were all about power and money and held the common people in contempt. Many of today's politicians probably read the Sadducean handbook on how to run things.

Herod's leaven was political corruption. Herod the Great was an Idumean, or a descendant of Esau. His father, Antipater, was a convert to Judaism, but it was about as authentic as Constantine's conversion to Christianity. The Herod clan were murderous thugs and ruled with an iron fist. When Herod the Great found out about Yeshua's birth, his first instinct was to have him killed, for he would have no rival to the throne. The pride of the Corinthians was licentiousness and disorder. Most of Paul's writings to them dealt with their turmoil and lack of morality. The Galatians had the opposite problem and had issues with legalism that, as we discussed in chapter 1, leads to a works-based salvation.

Each leaven refers to a type of pride. James 4:6 explains that *"He gives a greater grace. Therefore it says, 'God is opposed to the proud, but gives grace to the humble.'"* Lucifer's five "I wills" in Isaiah 14:13–14 were the origins of pride and have brought both man and angel down ever since. Pride puffs up and glorifies self, while humility gives God the glory.

Moses tells us specifically why we are to celebrate Unleavened Bread:

"For seven days you shall eat unleavened bread, and on the seventh day there shall be a feast to the Lord. Unleavened bread shall be eaten throughout the seven days; and nothing with yeast shall be seen among you, nor shall any dough with yeast be seen among you in all your borders. And you shall tell your son on that day, saying, 'It is because of what the Lord did for me when I came out of Egypt.' And it shall serve as a sign to you on your hand, and as a reminder on your forehead, that the law of the Lord may be in your mouth; for with a powerful hand the Lord brought you out of Egypt. Therefore, you shall keep this ordinance at its appointed time from year to year" (Ex 13:6–10).

It reminds us of what God did for us. He delivered us from bondage into freedom, and then as a sign on our hand and forehead (whatever we think or do) that the *Torah* shall be in our mouth (what we say). If we don't believe we need to keep the commandments of God, Unleavened Bread really serves no purpose anymore. The whole point was that God took us out of bondage, brought us into freedom, and then gave us the instructions on how a free people live.

Is there any specific instruction within the New Covenant to celebrate Unleavened Bread?

"Your boasting is not good. Do you not know that a little leaven leavens the whole lump of dough? Clean out the old leaven so that you may be a new lump, just as you are in fact unleavened. For Messiah our Passover also has been sacrificed. Therefore let's celebrate the feast, not with old leaven, nor with the leaven of malice and wickedness, but with the unleavened bread of sincerity and truth" (1 Cor 5:6–8).

The Apostle to the Gentiles tells them that boasting (pride) is no good and that a little bit of it will spread to the entire community. He then commands them to clean out the old leaven and celebrate the feast in the right way. I've heard many say that this was only a spiritual exercise and we don't have to do it physically. That would be like me saying I only have to come to work spiritually while I sleep in, or your children saying they will do their homework spiritually as they play video games. You're not fooling anyone. The principle is that when we keep the command physically, the Ruach Ha Kodesh (Holy Spirit) goes to work on us spiritually. When we clean out our physical houses of physical leaven, God cleans out His house, which is our bodies, His temple, of spiritual leaven, which is pride and wickedness. Once believers start keeping this feast according to the commandment, God shows us where the leaven in our souls is and how we can clean it out. We have to take the step in faith to do what He commands first and then receive the spiritual benefit after. If we just spiritualize it, it doesn't have the same effect. Our faith is very practical.

Unleavened Bread represents a new way of living. Passover is about our redemption, while Unleavened Bread is about our transition to a holy life, pleasing to God. As the old life is buried, it prepares us for God's instruction on how to live the new.

First Fruits

As we discussed in our last chapter, First Fruits (*Bikkurim*) is about the resurrection. On the third day, the tomb was empty, as Messiah had fulfilled the typology of being the first out of the ground. It's interesting that after He was resurrected and Mary Magdalene was at the tomb, He says to her, "*Stop clinging to Me, for I have not yet ascended to the Father*" (Jn 20:17). It's not clear if this was literal and she was hugging Him, or metaphorical and she was still dependent on Him being with her physically (probably both). But the reference to Him not yet ascending to the Father is an allusion to the wave offering of First Fruits. He had been pulled out of the ground but not waved before the Father for the people to be accepted. In John's Gospel, after speaking about the grain falling to the ground and dying, He foretells His own death and becoming the wave offering when He says,

"*And I, if I am lifted up from the earth, will draw all people to Myself.' Now He was saying this to indicate what kind of death He was going to die.*"

The term "wave offering" comes from the Hebrew root word נוּף (*nuph*— Strong's 5130), which means to move to and fro[118] but usually infers up and down too.

"What was the symbolism of waving the offering to God? Waving was also done with the peace offerings where God, the priests and the offerers all got to share in the eating of the animal sacrifice.

Traditionally, the ceremony of 'waving' seems to have meant that parts of the sacrifice were swung or elevated towards the altar, signifying that they were given to God, and then swung back again, indicating that they were given back by God to the priests for them to eat."[119]

This is one of many reasons why He had to die by crucifixion instead of the Jewish method of capital punishment, which was stoning to death. Many speak of Him being lifted up as being exalted, but it was a reference to dying on a Roman cross. Crucifixion victims were lifted up, and when they had died, they were taken down.

A dispute has been going on for a couple of thousand years on what day First Fruits was supposed to be celebrated. This stretches back to even before Yeshua's time and continues to this day. The confusion actually stems from the clarification of when Yeshua was crucified. The Church holds Friday because it says He died the day before the Sabbath, but in our analysis of Leviticus 23, we see there are other Sabbaths besides the weekly one, called High Sabbaths. There are seven of them, and both the first and last days of Unleavened Bread are shabbats. So when Leviticus 23:11 says the day after the Sabbath the priest shall wave it, we're now left with the question "Which Sabbath?" Is it the weekly Shabbat or the first day of Unleavened Bread, a High Shabbat? And you thought studying the Bible was as easy as just picking it up and reading it.

The Sadducees, who were more literal in their interpretation of the Torah, held to the weekly Shabbat, which meant Yom Ha Bikkurim is always on the first day of the week. However, the Pharisees said it was after the first day of Unleavened Bread, which means that it always fell on the sixteenth of Nisan (the first month in the Hebrew calendar), regardless of the day of the week. Many trees have given their lives in trying to solve this dilemma. Josephus, the famed Jewish historian, held to the Pharisaic view, and almost all orthodox rabbis of today (the successors to the Pharisees) celebrate it on Nisan 16. Karite Jews of today, who like the Sadducees are literalists in their interpretation of the Torah and reject the Talmud, also keep it on the first day of the week. Although the answer isn't obvious, it also isn't too difficult to figure out.

The key lies in the command in verse fifteen to count off seven more Sabbaths to bring us to the next Holy Day, which is Shavuot, or the Feast of Weeks (shavua means week):

"You shall also count for yourselves from the day after the Sabbath, from the day when you brought in the sheaf of the wave offering; there shall be seven complete Sabbaths. You shall count fifty days to the day after the seventh Sabbath; then you shall present a new grain offering to the Lord" (Lev 23:15–16).

For continuity, if the day after the Sabbath is the first day of Unleavened Bread, a High Sabbath, then the seven Sabbaths that we count must also be High Sabbaths. Since there are only seven in the entire year, that would take us to the last one, which is the ending of Sukkot (Tabernacles) in the fall. Furthermore, they're not consecutive. If, however, the Sabbath is a weekly one, then we have seven weekly Sabbaths and the next day is the fiftieth day, which also corresponds to the Jubilee year. We can't be mixing and matching Sabbaths when they're in the same sentence. The sentence is clearly talking about the same type of Sabbath. They're either both one or the other.

Another indicator is that after the fifty days, when Shavuot falls, it says it happens the day after the seventh Sabbath. If First Fruits was always on the sixteenth day of Nisan, the first month, Shavuot, would always fall on the sixth of Sivan, the third month. If you look at all the holy days that fall on a specific date, scripture says what that date is, but First Fruits and Shavuot are both dependent on a specific day of the week.

This all gets quite technical, but without becoming obsessed about these things, which some have a tendency to do, it does show that rightly dividing the word of truth and showing up on the right day is important.

The Counting of the Omer

The Counting of the Omer is a tradition that on each day between First Fruits and Shavuot, the day is counted and remembered. As we saw in Leviticus 23:15, once the sheaf has been brought in from First Fruits, we are to count down to the Feast of Weeks. The Omer can be both a sheaf or a stalk of grain, but it's also a measurement of volume, which is about how much a bundle of sheaves would be. One Omer is fifteen dry cups, or 3.5 litres. The Counting of the Omer is the waiting with anticipation for Shavuot. First Fruits is the barley harvest, but Shavuot is the wheat harvest and the most important one calorie-wise for the year. Barley is more often used for animal feed, while the fall harvest is mainly about fruits. They may taste good, but since they're mostly sugar, they won't get you through the winter very comfortably. The abundant harvest of wheat was key to a society's well-being, so the counting raises the anticipation and excitement level at what God was going to provide.

Jewish tradition has the Counting of the Omer as a time of mourning, for the Talmud says that Rabbi Akiva lost 24,000 of his students in a plague during this time. It says they died for not showing respect for each other.

The belief was that it was their failure to bring about the Messianic age. Observant Jews will not have weddings or other festivities during these days to commemorate the tragedy except for on the thirty-third day where the plague was supposed to have stopped.

Since the destruction of the Temple, instead of bringing an actual Omer, a blessing is pronounced on each day. Rabbinic tradition dictates that if a day of reciting the blessing is missed, one can continue to count but not say the blessing, as it breaks the chain.

For believers, the Counting of the Omer is a discipline that helps us to prepare for the next *moed*, the Feast of Shavuot.

Shavuot (The Feast of Weeks)

The early spring feasts are done, and fifty days have passed, which brings us to Shavuot. The Counting of the Omer is now complete, and we have arrived at the second major harvest in Israel. This is the fourth of the seven m*oedim* Adonai (feasts of the Lord) and the second appearance feast where all males had to go up to Jerusalem and present themselves before the Lord.

Shavuot is a special and unique holiday. It's in the centre between the three early spring and the three fall feasts. It's the most critical of the three harvests, as bread was the key staple for the ancient Middle East, so this was a joyous harvest. And when there's a harvest, God ordains a festival to celebrate it to give Him glory for His provision.

Among the sin and peace offerings, an unusual wave offering was given. The priests were commanded to offer two loaves *baked with leaven* (Lev 23:17). This is the only time of year the priests were to offer anything leavened, as even the weekly showbread was to be unleavened. The whole focus of the barley harvest and the Passover season was getting rid of the leaven to illustrate the purity of the new life, yet to end the perfect seven sevens of weeks off, the people were to offer something full of leaven. And there are two loaves waved.

"Contrary to the common rule of the Sanctuary, these loaves were leavened, which, as the *Mishnah* informs us (Men. V. 1) was the case in all thanks-offerings. The common explanation—that the wave-loaves were leavened because they represented the ordinary food for the people—only partially accounts for this. No doubt these wave-loaves expressed the Old Testament acknowledgment of the truth which our Lord embodied in the prayer, 'Give us this day our daily bread.' But this is not all. Let it be remembered that these two loaves, with the two lambs that formed part of the same wave-offering, were the only public peace- and thank-offerings of Israel; that they were accompanied by burnt- and sin-offerings; and that unlike ordinary peace-offerings, they were considered unlikely as 'most holy.' Hence they were leavened, because Israel's public thank-offerings, even the most holy, are leavened by imperfectness and sin, and they need a sin-offering. This idea of a public thank-offering was further borne out by all the services of the day. First, the two lambs were 'waved' while yet alive; that is, before being made ready for use. Then, after their sacrifice, the breast and shoulder, or principal parts of the each, were laid beside the two loaves, and 'waved' (generally towards the east) forwards and back-wards, and up and down. After burning the fat, the flesh belonged, not to the offerers, but to the priests. As in the case of the most holy sacrifices, the sacrificial meal was to take place within the Temple itself, nor was part of it to be kept beyond midnight."[120]

The two loaves are suggested to represent the Old and New Covenants, but most likely they represent both Jew and Gentile, with whom God wants to sup. Both are filled with sin, which is why a sin offering had to be made before the peace offerings. Unless sin is dealt with, we can have no peace with God. So many of the Old Covenant scriptures point toward the Gentiles coming into the fold, and even Moses declares God's intent in the Torah:

"Now it is not with you alone that I am making this covenant and this oath, but both with those who stand here with us today in the presence of the Lord our God, and with those who are not with us here today (for you know how we lived in the land of Egypt, and how we passed through the midst of the nations through which you passed" (Dt 29:14–15).

The covenant that God made with Israel was to include all the Gentiles who were going to come later, once Yeshua finished His work of redemption for mankind on the cross. Amos 9:13 speaks of the *"Gentiles who are called by name."* Yeshua declares in John 10:16

"And I have other sheep that are not of this fold; I must bring them also, and they will listen to My voice; and they will become one flock, with one shepherd."

That's why Paul says in Galatians 3:28 that in Messiah, nobody has any distinction, no matter race, gender, or social status. All of humanity is sinful and all are saved by grace (Eph 2:8–9). The two loaves represent the equality of everyone, who are sinful and still accepted by God because of His mercy. They show us God's provision for all mankind. In Leviticus 23:22, YHVH Elohim says:

"When you reap the harvest of your land, moreover, you shall not reap to the very edges of your field nor gather the gleaning of your harvest; you are to leave them for the needy <u>and the stranger</u>. I am the Lord your God" (emphasis mine).

This is why the book of Ruth is so important to us. Ruth, a Moabitess (from Moab, the incestuous descendent of Lot who was a sworn enemy of Israel and banned from the Temple for ten generations in Deuteronomy 23:3) was a sojourner, an alien in Israel. Because of God's commandment in Leviticus 23:22, she was able to scrabble together enough food for her and her mother-in-law to eat, and God redeemed her through Boaz. Not only was she provided for, but she ended up becoming part of the Messianic line by giving birth to King David's grandfather, Obed (Ruth 4:21). God cares about all humanity!

Although it's not stated specifically, because of the theme of Shavuot and the time stated in the Bible, it's generally accepted that the commandments were given by God to Moses at this time.

"In the third month after the sons of Israel had gone out of the land of Egypt, on that very day they came into the wilderness of Sinai" (Ex 19:1).

The arrival at Sinai happened in the third month. In our North American understanding, that would be around ninety days because we think of full months. However, the way the Bible counts, a partial month is still counted.

Therefore, since Israel left Egypt on the fourteenth of the first month, that's fourteen days. The second month (Iyar) was twenty-nine days, which means they arrived sometime after the forty-third day, in the third month. They had to consecrate themselves, and on the third day God gave the Ten Commandments. Since God uses His *moedim* to commemorate a monumental event, the giving of the commandments on a harvest festival lines up perfectly with how God operates. The fifty days from First Fruits to Shavuot also point to the fifty years of the year of Jubilee, a year of release and redemption. What better way to demonstrate Israel's redeemed status than to be given the commandments on how a free people live? Remember, the Torah wasn't given to Israel in bondage. They had to be set free first so they *could* keep the commandments. A people enslaved in Egypt or to sin cannot keep God's holy instructions. Yet the Church today thinks those very instructions and guidelines are what we need to be freed from. That is twisted logic.

The covenant is confirmed with the people when Moses sprinkles them with blood.

"Then Moses came and reported to the people all the words of the Lord and all the ordinances; and all the people answered with one voice and said, 'All the words which the Lord has spoken we will do!' And Moses wrote down all the words of the Lord. Then he got up early in the morning, and built an altar at the foot of the mountain with twelve memorial stones for the twelve tribes of Israel. And he sent young men of the sons of Israel, and they offered burnt offerings and sacrificed bulls as peace offerings to the Lord. Moses took half of the blood and put it in basins, and the other half of the blood he sprinkled on the altar. Then he took the Book of the Covenant and read it as the people listened; and they said, "All that the Lord has spoken we will do, and we will be obedient!" So Moses took the blood and sprinkled it on the people, and said, 'Behold the blood of the covenant, which the Lord has made with you in accordance with all these words' (Ex 24:3–8).

Sadly, the people did not keep their word, and as soon as Moses went up the mountain to receive the tablets of stone on which the commandments were to be written, they coerced Aaron to build the golden calf so they could worship it instead. As a result, three thousand died when Moses returned. The Torah reveals sin and the death that ensues when we commit it. The prophetic fulfillment of Shavuot also confirms it was the time of the giving of the Torah. As the disciples were in the upper room and waiting on Yeshua's promise for the giving of the Ruach Ha Kodesh (Holy Spirit), they met daily, devoting themselves to prayer. Yeshua walked amongst them for forty days and ascended to heaven, which was still during the Omer count. Then, on the day of Pentecost (from the Greek *Pentēkostē*) meaning "fiftieth"),[121] we're told the Spirit came rushing upon them with a noise like a great windstorm, which was reminiscent of the scene at Mt. Sinai when God gave the Ten Commandments. And there was great thunder, the blast of the shofar, and smoke and fire. It was quite the spectacle that no one would ever forget.

When the Ruach had come upon them and they started sharing the gospel in different languages, it was a confirmation of the new or renewed Covenant from Jeremiah 31:31.

"Both the Hebrew chadash (Jer. 31:31) and the Greek kainos (Heb. 8:8) words for 'new' may be more properly translated "renewed" as opposed to "new" or "brand-new" in certain contexts.

"Chadash may mean new in quality, not new in time (1 Sam. 11:14; 2 Chron. 15:8; 24:4, 12; Job 10:7; Psa. 103:5; 104:30; Isa. 61:4; Lam. 5:21). It may also mean to 'renew' or 'repair.' For instance, in Psalm 51:10 David says, 'Create in me a clean heart, O God; and renew a right spirit within me.' David uses the same word as in Jeremiah 31:31 (chadash). David was not asking for something brand-new, but was asking for a renewal of what he had previously. In 2 Chronicles 24:4, 12 we see the use of the terms repair and restore (root, chadash) with the already existent house of the Lord. So, in all these verses, there is a renewal, a repairing, a restoring of that which was already in existence. The same is true for Jeremiah 31.

"In the New Testament, of the eight times that 'new' is applied to the New Covenant, seven of them use the term kainos, meaning 'renewed,' or 'new in quality,' not necessarily time (Matt. 26:28; Mark 14:24; Luke 22:20; 1 Cor. 11:25; 2 Cor. 3:6; Heb. 8:13; 9:15) as opposed to neos (meaning new in time—Heb. 12:24). The use of term kainos means there was a pre-existing covenant to which Jesus gave a qualitative difference."[122] Yes, kainos and chadash can both refer to brand new and are used interchangeably in scripture, however,

"Although Greek scholar David Stern in his Complete Jewish Bible still uses the term new testament and new covenant instead of renewed covenant, he does discuss the word kainos in his Jewish New Testament Commentary in his comments on Hebrews 8:8 (p. 690). There he gives the reasons why he translates kainos as new, but also explains why it can also mean "renewed" in that "the New Covenant renews the Old Covenant" (his exact words). He then goes on to prove his point how the New Covenant is a renewed version of the Old Covenant"[123]

This renewing of the covenant that God made through Moses at Mt. Sinai was different in that it was now written on our hearts. As long as the command-ments were on tablets of stone, they couldn't penetrate and change our hearts. It was constant frustration and only led to condemnation. Once God gave us a heart of flesh to replace that heart of stone when we accepted Yeshua as Lord and Saviour, He could now inscribe those commandments of righteousness on our hearts for us to do them. When the Torah was given, three thousand died. Paul refers to the Torah as a covenant that kills (2 Cor 3:6), but this renewed covenant gives life. On the day of Shavuot, when the Holy Spirit came and they preached the Gospel, three thousand came to faith.

The main distinctive about Shavuot is the two loaves of bread offered. Yeshua calls Himself the Bread of Life:

"*I am the living bread that came down out of heaven; if anyone eats from this bread, he will live forever; and the bread which I will give for the life of the world also is My flesh*" (John 6:51).

Eating of His flesh means partaking of the Word, for He was the Word that became flesh, and then believing what that Word says. He was the manna that fell from heaven every day to nourish the Israelites in the desert. He said to the disciples at the well in Samaria when they encouraged Him to eat that "*I have food to eat that you do not know about*" (John 4:32). He also reminded the devil that "*man shall not live on bread alone but on every word that comes out of the mouth of God*" (Mt 4:4).

On Shavuot, it's customary for Jews to eat dairy. Although there are many reasons given for this, one mentioned in the scriptures is that the Torah is like milk.

"The Torah is the spiritual nourishment of the Jews, just like a mother gives milk to nourish a newborn baby. It (Torah) is necessary to grow and thrive!"[124]

Peter calls the scriptures "*the pure milk of the word*" (1 Pt 2:2), and Isaiah exhorts us:

"*Why do you spend money for what is not bread, and your wages for what does not satisfy? Listen carefully to Me, and eat what is good, and delight yourself in abundance. Incline your ear and come to Me. Listen, that you may live; and I will make an everlasting covenant with you, according to the faithful mercies shown to David*" (Is 55:2–3).

Shavuot is about the wheat harvest. Physically, the Father gives us bread because He loves us, wants to provide for us, and even wants to dine with us—a sign of intimacy. The Table of Showbread in the Temple told us that. Our great hope is the Marriage Supper of the Lamb. Spiritually, that bread is His Word that nourishes our souls. The Law was given on Shavuot at Mt. Sinai. The Holy Spirit took those commandments and wrote them on our hearts when we came to faith. If we say we don't have to keep them, we're in conflict with our own nature. If as believers we don't celebrate and remember these things, we are robbing ourselves of our understanding of the heart of God, and we end up thinking we don't have to keep that which God majestically brought about for our great benefit.

The Feast of Trumpets

The spring feasts have finished and the long summer of tending to the fields is done by the time we reach the seventh month, the month of Tishrei. Just like the early spring feasts, the three fall festivals occur quite close together and conclude the growing season to begin the agricultural rest of the winter months. In Judaism, they are called the High Holy Days, as even non-observant Jews will pay some attention to them.

Yom Teruah (The Day of Blowing), or the Feast of Trumpets, is the fifth of God's *moedim*. It's distinct from the others in that we aren't told why we're celebrating it. We're only told to have a Shabbat (rest), a memorial of blowing the shofar, hold a holy convocation (gathering to worship together), and offer a sacrifice. On the surface, it doesn't seem like much, but the beauty of God's Word is like an iceberg: there's so much more below what we can see.

Yom Teruah is also known as Rosh Hashanah (head of the year). Although the biblical new year actually starts two weeks before Passover (Ex 12:1), Jews turn the calendar in the seventh month. For those new to Torah and the keeping of the commandments, this causes a lot of consternation with some. However, there are actually four different new years in the Jewish calendar (yes, my people are complicated). We have

1.   Nisan 1 (first month—March/April): Months on the calendar and the counting of the reign of kings
2.   Elul 1 (sixth month—August/September): New year for tithing animals
3.   Shevat 15 (eleventh month—January/February): New year for trees
4.   Tishrei 1 (September/October): Sabbatical and Jubilee years

The reason the new year is celebrated at the beginning of the seventh month certainly has some influence from Babylon, where Israel spent seventy years in exile.

"We don't know what the religious life of the Jews was like during the Babylonian exile. But we do know that by the time the Jews returned to Israel, and at the beginning of the Second Temple period (516 BCE), Jewish religious practices had profoundly changed compared with the pre-exile era.

"For one, the names of the months that we use to this very day are the Babylonian names. Tishrei for example is a Babylonian month whose name derives from the Akkadian word tishritu—'beginning.'

"In addition, the Babylonians took their New Year's Day celebrations very seriously. They called the holiday Akitu (from the Sumerian word for barley) and Resh Shattim, the Akkadian equivalent of the Hebrew Rosh

Hashanah. This was celebrated twice a year, at the beginning of Tishrei and the beginning of Nisan, and lasted for 12 days."[125]

Before the exile, the months were called different names. What Israel had been practicing in Babylon came back with them, which included celebrating the new year at the beginning of fall. But there are other reasons as well.

"But our God is a God of multiple new beginnings, new seasons, and fresh starts! Instead of celebrating once a year, God asks that the beginning of every month, each new moon, is celebrated—that's twelve new beginnings instead of one! This is called 'Rosh Chodesh,' or 'head of the month.' It's interesting that the word for month, 'chodesh,' is from the root word for new: 'chadash.'"[126]

The fact that Yom Teruah is a rosh chodesh (head or beginning of a new month) provides a clue to what God wants us to remember.

"The sons of Aaron, moreover, the priests, shall blow the trumpets; and this shall be a permanent statute for you throughout your generations. And when you go to war in your land against the enemy who attacks you, then you shall sound an alarm with the trumpets, so that you will be thought of by the Lord your God, and be saved from your enemies. Also on the day of your joy and at your appointed feasts, and on the first days of your months, you shall blow the trumpets over your burnt offerings, and over the sacrifices of your peace offerings; and they shall be as a reminder of you before your God. I am the Lord your God" (Nm 10:8–10).

Israel was commanded to make the two silver trumpets, which were to be blown at the appointed feasts (Lev 23) and on the first day of the month over the sacrifices. Israel's calendar is based on the lunar cycle but is also adjusted to match up with the solar one to ensure the seasons don't get completely out of alignment (a lunar year is 360 days, whereas the solar year is 365.25 days). A new month starts when the new moon appears. In fact, the new months and feast days were announced at the sighting of the new moon.

"The Jewish calendar, or the fixed Hebrew calendar, months are determined by the New Moon conjunction. This calendar, credited as being finalized by the Nasi of the Sanhedrin, Hillel II (330–365 CE), though foundationally based on God's calendar, is lunisolar, meaning it keeps in sync with the natural cycles of both the Sun and the Moon."[127]

The Feast of Trumpets occurs on the beginning of a new month, and scripture doesn't explain why we are to celebrate that either, just that we are to commemorate it and blow the shofar as a memorial. But to what?

The shofar or trumpet is used for many purposes throughout scripture. They include:

1. To summon Moses to the top of the mountain to receive the Commandments—Exodus 19:19–20
2. A call to war—Joshua 6:16
3. A call to worship and the announcement of the appointed times, including the New Moon—Psalm 81:3–4, 89:15
4. Repentance—*"Wake up sleepers from your slumber, look at your ways and repent and remember your Creator"*—(Moses Maimondes from the Mishneh Torah), (Ezek 33:2–4)
5. Musical accompaniment—Psalm 98:6
6. To declare the arrival of the Messiah—Zechariah 9:14
7. Regathering of Israel—Isaiah 27:13
8. Judgement—Revelation 8:2

The memorial of blowing can be a reminder of all of these things. The life of a believer is one of readiness for war, praising God at all times, constantly repenting, and being ready to come to worship Him. Those who don't do these things must expect the judgement that will eventually come to all who reject Him.

Each Rosh Chodesh is announced with a shofar blast to wake people up. It's a reminder of who made the universe. Psalm 19:1 says, *"the heavens tell of the glory of God; and their expanse declares the work of His hands,"* while Paul warns us that *"For since the creation of the world His invisible attributes, that is, His eternal power and divine nature, have been clearly perceived, being understood by what has been made, so that they are without excuse"* (Rom 1:20). Creation itself testifies to God's handiwork and that it was He who created everything, but because humanity has a short memory and is prone to rebellion, the blast of a horn is there to help remind us.

Even the very word *teruah* (תְּרוּעָה—Strong's #8643) means a shout, a blast of war, alarm, or joy.[128] The very day of this memorial is a call to war against the kingdom of darkness and the pervasive enemy of sin. It's how Jericho was taken down. Israel marched around the city blowing the shofar. Then they took down the walls with both the shofar blast and a shout. Even though the shofar is a call for us to awake and assemble, it's also a signal to God we're ready for Him to go ahead of us in battle. It represents His voice as a warning to the enemy. In battle, the shofar was blown when Israel was on the offensive, whereas the silver trumpets were to be sounded as an alarm when they were being attacked (Nm 10:9). Psalm 98:4 tells us, "*With trumpets and the sound of the horn shout joyfully before the King, the Lord.*" In this instance, both were used. When King Asa instituted reforms and Judah renewed covenant with God, we are told:

"*Moreover, they made an oath to the Lord with a <u>loud voice, with shouting, trumpets, and with horns</u>. All Judah rejoiced concerning the oath, for they had sworn with all their heart and had sought Him earnestly, and He let them find Him. So the Lord gave them rest on every side*" (2 Chr 15:14–15, emphasis mine).

Although the seventh month isn't when the new year starts, it's when the Jubilee Year begins. This is the super sabbatical that happens every fifty years and is a time of release and redemption. It's to be announced by the blowing of the shofar on Yom Kippur (The Day of Atonement), which occurs in the seventh month. The Talmud also tells us that some rabbis believe that the world, or perhaps man, was created on the first day of Tishrei:

"It's no coincidence that Rosh haShannah of Tishrei is commemorated with the blowing of the shofar. According to Jewish tradition, the Creation of man took place on this day, when God breathed (or blew) His breath into man. We listen to the sound of the shofar on this day, perhaps as a memorial to that first breath from God—the giving of a divine soul, a little piece of God."[129]

We have no way of knowing this for sure, and it really doesn't matter, but the commemoration of the new moon at Rosh Chodesh seems to be for the purpose of reminding us that God created the heavens and the earth. If we're going to celebrate the act of creation, Yom Teruah is as good a day as any to do so.

Jewish tradition says that the binding of Isaac, when Abraham almost sacrificed him, also occurred on this day. When God stopped him, He provided the substitute, and even though Abraham told Isaac that God would provide a lamb (Gn 22:8—a prophecy about the coming Messiah), God instead provides a ram, one of the animals we get a shofar from.

Prophetically, the Yom Teruah points toward the ἁρπαγησόμεθα (*harpagēsometha*, from harpazó—Strong's # 726), which means caught up or snatched away,[130] which we commonly refer to as the Rapture.

"For the Lord Himself will descend from heaven with a shout, with the voice of the archangel and with the trumpet of God, and the dead in Messiah will rise first. Then we who are alive, who remain, will be caught up together with them in the clouds to meet the Lord in the air, and so we will always be with the Lord" (1 Thes 4:16–17).

"Behold, I am telling you a mystery; we will not all sleep, but we will all be changed, in a moment, in the twinkling of an eye, at the last trumpet; for the trumpet will sound, and the dead will be raised imperishable, and we will be changed" (1 Cor 15:51–51).

At some point before He returns to Earth to set up His Millennial Kingdom, those who are still alive will be caught up with Him in the clouds and be taken to heaven. It's the great hope of all believers to be delivered from this wicked world, and no matter when you think the *harpazó* occurs (pre-tribulation, mid-trib, pre-wrath, or post-trib), at some point we go to be with Yeshua and remain with Him forever, as we return with Him when He comes back.

On Yom Teruah, the shofar is blown many times. In the modern synagogue, it's customary for it to be blown 100 or 101 times. I'm not sure who's responsible for counting, but if it's the one blowing the shofar, which is most often the chazzan (cantor) at the synagogue, he's liable to lose count (as well as consciousness) by blowing that much, as I've often experienced.

There are four different notes that are sounded on Yom Teruah.

1. Tekiah (a long blast)—Tradition says it is for the crowing of the king
2. Shevarim (comes from the Hebrew word "to break," three medium blasts)—Sounds like sobbing or crying, which symbolizes the mourning Jewish heart over his sin
3. Teruah (nine stacato notes)—Alarm or the wakeup call for us to get back to God but also a warning of impending judgment
4. Tekiah Gedolah (great tekiah)—Associated with Messianic redemption

These are repeated throughout the day. The message is loud and clear: repent, mourn over our sin, come back to God before judgement comes, and be ready for the battle against wickedness. Once the victory has been obtained, blow the trumpet or shofar in praise of our King.

The Days of Awe

Yom Teruah begins what is known in Judaism as the ten Days of Awe. It's the time between Yom Teruah and Yom Kippur, the Day of Atonement. Jews the world over endeavour to get serious about preparing for the holiest day of the biblical calendar by reflecting on their lives. Yom Kippur is the day that God designated for Israel's sins to be *covered* (kippur) for another year. As many of us know, the act of repentance is sometimes something that we need to prepare ourselves for, since admitting we're actually wrong is counterintuitive to our carnal nature. Our tendency is to defend and justify our actions, so reflection on our behaviour leads to a softening of our hearts toward God's righteous standard where we can fully acknowledge how far short we have come. Therefore, ten days of contemplation on where we are at is a very helpful exercise in righting our hearts before our Creator.

The Hebrew root word for repentence is שׁוּב (*shub*—Strong's #7725).[131]

"The word Teshuvah is usually translated as repentance. In fact, there is a well known [sic] prayer recited on the High Holy Days that Teshuvah, Tefillah, and Tzedakah, translated as 'Repentance,' 'Prayer,' and 'Charity' can avert the evil decree.

"This translation is not entirely accurate. Teshuvah is better translated as 'return' and signifies a return to the original state.

"Classically, Teshuvah is comprised of three ingredients: regret of misdeed, decision to change, and verbal expression of one's sins. Technically, whenever one sins, one is mandated to do Teshuvah. However, the Ten Days of Teshuvah between Rosh Hashanah and Yom Kippur are specifically designated for Teshuvah, when the gates of prayer and repentance are more open than at any other time during the cyclical Jewish year."[132]

While God's doors to repentance and returning to Him are open 24/7/365 because of Yeshua's finished work during the spring feasts, what the rabbi is trying to say is that repentance goes beyond just confessing our sins. It means changing our minds and then our behaviour. In order for *teshuvah* to be legitimate, there must be evidence that our confession is more than just lip service. Jacob (or James, changed to appease King James) says in his epistle, "*But prove yourselves doers of the word, and not just hearers who deceive themselves*" (Jas 1:22). True repentance is evidenced by Yeshua's command to the woman caught in adultery: "*Go. From now on do not sin any longer*" (Jn 8:11).

A tradition that many follow during these days is called *tashlich*. It comes from the Hebrew word for "to cast off." Jews will go to a body of water, like a stream, river, or a lake, and throw either bread crumbs or even stones. The tradition, which started in the thirteenth century, symbolizes the casting away of our sins. Micah 7:18–19 says:

"*Who is a God like You, who pardons iniquity and passes over the rebellious act of the remnant of His possession? He does not retain His anger forever, Because He delights in unchanging love. He will again have compassion on us; He will tread our iniquities under foot. Yes, You will cast all their sins into the depths of the sea.*"

"*Cast your bread on the surface of the waters, for you will find it after many days*" (Eccl 11:1).

"*As far as the east is from the west, so far has He removed our wrongdoings from us. Just as a father has compassion on his children, so the Lord has compassion on those who fear Him. For He Himself knows our form; He is mindful that we are nothing but dust"* (Ps 103:12–14).

What a magnificent thing to know that God takes the sins we're letting go of and separates us from them by an infinite distance. That is a wonderful definition of mercy!

Yom Teruah reminds us that God created the universe. It's a special *rosh chodesh* when the new moon appears and it's a call to assemble, to worship, and to repent. It's also a warning of judgement plus a call to arms in spiritual war. When we hear the blast of the shofar, God is trying to get our attention.

Prophetically, it points to the ultimate call to assemble, when He will gather the remnant in the Rapture as we go to be with Him for eternity. All of this understanding makes the sound of the shofar so much more exciting.

Yom Kippur

"Then the Lord spoke to Moses, saying, 'On exactly the tenth day of this seventh month is the Day of Atonement; it shall be a holy convocation for you, and you shall humble yourselves and present an offering by fire to the Lord. You shall not do any work on this very day, for it is a Day of Atonement, to make atonement on your behalf before the Lord your God. If there is any person who does not humble himself on this very day, he shall be cut off from his people. As for any person who does any work on this very day, that person I will eliminate from among his people. You shall not do any work. It is to be a permanent statute throughout your generations in all your dwelling places. It is to be a Sabbath of complete rest for you, and you shall humble yourselves; on the ninth of the month at evening, from evening until evening, you shall keep your Sabbath'" (Lev 23:26–32).

Ten days after Yom Teruah and with the completion of the Days of Awe, we arrive at the most solemn day on the biblical calendar. It's the only day God commands all of Israel to fast (*you shall humble yourselves*). Jews all over the world fast on this day, many of whom aren't even observant. Orthodox Jews will wear sneakers to synagogue so as not to wear leather shoes because they won't even wear clothing made from an animal we eat.

The rabbis say it is the one day of the year that determines whether our names are written in the Book of Life for one more year.

Yom Kippur, or the Day of Atonement, is when Israel would gather with trepidation. With the protocols clearly laid out in Leviticus 16, right after the deaths of Nadab and Abihu, the path to clear forgiveness of sins was now set.

The cohen gadol (high priest) was the only one allowed into the Holy of Holies on this one day of the year. Instead of the normal bright colours of gold and blue, his garment would be completely white, and he would continually wash himself throughout the day as he performed his duties.

"The simple white of his array, in distinction to the 'golden garments' which he otherwise wore pointed to the fact that on that day the high-priest appeared, not 'as the bridegroom of Jehovah,' but as bearing in his official capacity the emblem of that perfect purity which was sought by the expiations of that day. Thus, in the prophesies of Zechariah the removal of Joshua's 'filthy garments' and the clothing him with 'change of raiment,' symbolically denoted—'I have caused thine iniquity to pass from thee' (Zech. 3:3, 4). Similarly those who stand nearest to God are always described as arrayed 'in white' (see Ezek. 9:2, etc; Dan. 10:5; 12:6). And because these were emphatically 'the holy garments,' therefore the high priest had to 'wash his flesh in water, and so put them on' (Lev. 16:4), that is, he was not merely to wash his hands and feet, as before ordinary minis-trations, but to bathe his whole body."[133]

The clothing was a big deal for the priest. Coming before the Lord to minister to Him on behalf of the people, which was the priest's main job, was serious business. I shake my head in disbelief in today's Western church, where I've seen pastors even get up before the congregation in sandals and shorts! A big part of our problem in Christianity today is that we've lost the awe and reverence of a holy God and are far too familiar in our approach to Him. The cohen gadol had to wear specific garments before coming before Him. When God gave the commandments on how to design the priestly garments, He specified the robes needed to be made, with little bells in the hem:

"You shall make on its hem pomegranates of violet, purple, and scarlet material all around on its hem, and bells of gold between them all around: a golden bell and a pomegranate, a golden bell and a pomegranate, all around on the hem of the robe. It shall be on Aaron when he ministers; and its sound shall be heard when he enters and leaves the Holy Place before the Lord, so that he will not die" (Ex 28:33–35).

Why make a robe with bells in it? We don't often think of the solemn duties of the high priest being performed all the while tinkling like some little girl's dress-up costume. But the bells let us know something—the priest was still alive!

"Each time the listeners heard the music of the golden bells, their hearts were gladdened by three wonderful truths: (1) they had a living high priest; (2) the high priest was successful in making intercession for them; and (3) their sacrifices had been accepted."[134]

Nobody but the priests could enter the inner court of the Tabernacle/Temple, and nobody but the high priest could enter the Holy of Holies, and only on Yom Kippur. If a priest came before the Lord in an unworthy manner, he could be struck dead. That was the lesson of Nadab and Abihu. One does not just sashay into the throne room before a holy and just God, full of iniquity and rebellion in his heart, and live. In fact, the people used to tie a rope around the cohen gadol's leg before he went into the Holy of Holies, and if they didn't hear the bells for a while, they knew he had probably been judged and had died. But since nobody else was allowed in to get him, they needed a way of getting the body out. Can you imagine if every pastor had to be concerned for his life before he stood up in the pulpit to address the congregation? We would have a much different looking Body today.

As the holiest of days began, the High Priest would first make an offering for him and his family (Lev 16:6), as one whose sin that was not dealt with could not minister on behalf of others. He then would take the two identical goats selected and draw lots for them. One would become the sin offering for the tabernacle, including the Holy of Holies (v. 16), because even the place of God's presence on Earth had been defiled because of sin. And then the most unusual of occurrences: the second goat would have the sins of Israel confessed over it, a scarlet thread tied around one of its horns, and instead of killing it, the priest would run it off into the desert. This second goat was known as the Azazel, or scapegoat, a word or name whose origins are not entirely clear.

"The word 'scapegoat' was coined by William Tyndale from (e)scape + goat, a literal rendering of the Hebrew word עזאזל –'Azazel'– in Leviticus 16:8, 10, 26. Azazel comes from עז (ez, 'goat') and אוזל (ozél, 'escapes'). In modern English, the word scapegoat has evolved its own misleading definition, but we should read this word more properly as escapegoat: The scapegoat is the goat that escapes!"[135]

In addition,

"The word Azazel appears nowhere else in Scripture, and three major theories emerged as to its meaning. According to the Sages and Rashi it means 'a steep, rocky or hard place,' in other words a description of its destination. According to Ibn Ezra (cryptically) and Nachmanides (explicitly), Azazel was the name of a spirit or demon, one of the fallen angels referred to in Genesis 6:2, similar to the goat-spirit called Pan in Greek mythology, Faunus in Latin."[136]

As we saw in chapter 3, the Book of Enoch tells us that Azazel taught men the art of weapon-making and warfare. In fact, he is the personification of Satan, so the confessing of the sins of Israel onto the goat and then chasing it off into the wilderness is symbolic of sending our sins back to where they came from and then removing them from outside the camp.

The scapegoat was driven into the wilderness, and in order to prevent it from coming back into the camp with all of last year's sins, Alfred Edersheim tells us that a series of ten booths were set up and manned so that the goat was escorted until it reached the edge of a cliff. The thread would be split in half, with part still tied to the goat and the other half tied to a rock by the cliff, and the goat was then shoved off to his death. Thus, the translation "rocky place," describing the place where it ended its life. Tradition tells us the red thread around the rock would then turn white, which the monitor would communicate back to each booth until word reached the Tabernacle/Temple with great rejoicing that Israel's sins had been atoned for one more year.

This use of the two goats was both unique and quite strange. At no other time of year was this done. And why was the Azazel not killed but released into the wilderness? Its blood was not shed. To answer this, we have to understand how the offerings worked. Rabbi Lord Sacks tell us:

"Why was this ritual different from all other sin or guilt offerings? Why two goats rather than one?

"The simplest answer is that the High Priest's service on Yom Kippur was intended to achieve something other and more than ordinary sacrifices occasioned by sin. The Torah specifies two objectives, not one: 'On this day atonement will be made for you, to cleanse you. Then, before the Lord, you will be clean from all your sins' (Leviticus 16:30). Normally all that was aimed at was atonement, kapparah. On Yom Kippur something else was aimed at: cleansing, purification, tahara. Atonement is for acts. Purification is for persons. Sins leave stains on the character of those who commit them, and these need to be cleansed before we can undergo catharsis and begin anew."[137]

The scapegoat was not slain and its blood not sprinkled on the altar to help us to realize that what the priest was doing was *covering* Israel's sins, not washing them completely away. That's because as Hebrews 10:4 reminds us, *"For it is impossible for the blood of bulls and goats to take away sins."* Animal sacrifices didn't provide טָהֵר (*taher*—Strong's #2891).[138] They only provided a temporary covering (*kippur*), which is why they had to be done over and over again. Only Yeshua's blood is able to cleanse us of sin. Most Christians say that Yeshua died to forgive us of our sins, which would essentially be a type of *kippur*, or covering over. He didn't just die to have our sins forgiven: He died to wipe away the effect of sin, which is death (Rom 6:23). His blood literally washes us clean of the stain of sin.

"What does atonement mean?" Leon Morris writes. "The atonement is the crucial doctrine of the faith. Unless we are right here it matters little, or so it seems to me, what we are like elsewhere." Erickson and others agree. The atonement is the critical point of the Christian faith. But if you ask most believers what "atonement" means, they are hard-pressed to provide a clear answer. And if they suggest something about forgiving sins or the mercy seat or covering our guilt with the blood, they will have enormous difficulties when it comes to a verse like this one in Leviticus.

"Read the verse again. Here 'atonement' isn't about forgiveness. It is about cleaning up pollution in the Tabernacle. The verb is kipper. Here it is in the Piel tense. In fact, in all the verses related to sacrifice, this verb is never in the Qal tense. It is always Piel. Why does this matter? Because in the Qal, the verb means 'to wipe something on to a surface' but in the Piel it means 'to wipe something off of a surface.' In other words, we often think of atonement as though God is wiping the blood of the Lamb over our sins so that He no longer sees them. This idea is common in the expression that the blood of Yeshua covers our transgressions. But when this verb is used in the context of sacrifice, it never means 'covering over.' It means 'cleaning away.' Atonement removes pollution."[139]

"Though your sins are as scarlet, they shall become as white as snow; though they are red like crimson, they shall be like wool" (Is 1:18).

That's why the priest's garments were linen and completely white. They pointed toward the fact that when Yeshua died and we trusted in His blood, we were finally *tahered*, not just *kippered* in the usual sense. It's more emphatic. How do we know?

"Every priest stands daily ministering and offering time after time the same sacrifices, which can never take away sins; but He, having offered one sacrifice for sins for all time, sat down at the right hand of God" (Heb 10:11–12).

Conspicuously absent from the Holy of Holies was anything to sit down on. The cohen gadol's work was never done. Yet Yeshua sat down beside the Father when He arrived in heaven. Of interest as well, Hebrews also tells us that with His blood He cleansed the heavenly temple (Heb 9:23). The fallen angels appearing before God's throne have also brought their defilement there, and it too had to be cleansed (Job 1:6).

The whole day's rituals demonstrate for us the utter incapability of the Torah in saving us.

"For, on the one hand, there is the nullification of a former commandment because of its weakness and uselessness (for the Law made nothing perfect)" (Heb 7:19).

It only condemns us. The Bible itself calls the Torah useless in helping our dire condition, but it's absolutely necessary in helping us find the solution. The New Covenant with Yeshua's death and resurrection, and the writing of the Law on our hearts, saves us. If we dispense with the Torah, we're wandering aimlessly without knowing where we are spiritually or where we're going.

Yeshua is the fulfillment of this festival in so many ways. He represented both goats in that while on the cross, the Father confessed all of humanity's sins on Him so He could be our scapegoat. How many times have we heard that when Yeshua cried *"My God, My God, why have you forsaken Me?"* (Mt 27:46) the Father turned His face away from Him and could not look at Him because He had become sin? Second Corinthians 5:19 says:

"Now all these things are from God, who reconciled us to Himself through Messiah and gave us the ministry of reconciliation, namely, that God was in Messiah reconciling the world to Himself, not counting their wrongdoings against them, and He has committed to us the word of reconciliation."

How could He be looking away when He was in Him? How could sin be so powerful that it even separated the Godhead, that it overcame God's love for His Son? It couldn't. What was Yeshua doing then? He was teaching, even from the cross. In chapter 6 we discussed the teaching method called *remez*, which gave part of the scripture to reference the point the one speaking wanted to make. It assumes the listener knew the scriptures well enough to make the connection. Yeshua was quoting David in Psalm 22, which starts off with that line. In verse 24, David tells us:

"For He has not despised nor scorned the suffering of the afflicted; nor has He hidden His face from him; but when he cried to Him for help, He heard."

That's not just a minor issue. This theology of God separating from His Son changes His *very nature*. That's what happens when we don't use proper interpretive methods to try and understand scripture. We must look through the eyes of the author and the audience and understand the issue before trying to figure out what the passage means.

So the Father unloads His wrath for all of the sins ever committed throughout history on Yeshua in a three-hour period He was on the cross. And people think the physical aspect of crucifixion was what terrified the Messiah. But unlike the Azazel, His blood actually was poured out. At the same time, He also represents the other goat, the one for the Lord who died to cleanse the sanctuary.

The Azazel had a scarlet thread tied to him. Yeshua had a scarlet robe put on Him. The scapegoat was released. Barabbas (meaning son of the father), who was a murderer, was released. Yeshua's blood expiated or washed away all sin from all of history. The Talmud even mentions that forty years before the destruction of the Second Temple in 70 AD, the thread stopped turning white. Coincidence?

Prophetically, Yom Kippur points to Israel's national atonement. The prophet Zechariah says:

"And I will pour out on the house of David and on the inhabitants of Jerusalem the Spirit of grace and of pleading, so that they will look at Me whom they pierced; and they will mourn for Him, like one mourning for an only son, and they will weep bitterly over Him like the bitter weeping over a firstborn" (Zec 12:10).

After the Rapture (Yom Teruah) and the remaining Church is removed, God turns His full attention to Israel, and the time of Jacob's Troubles (The Great Tribulation) begins. At the end of the seven-year tribulation period, when the Antichrist is about to wipe out Jerusalem, Yeshua returns to deliver them, and as Paul says in Romans 11:26, *"all Israel will be saved."* When the remnant of Israel looks up and sees Yeshua returning to save them, they will realize the mistake they made in rejecting Him, and Israel will finally have recognized her Messiah.

Although Yom Kippur is a day when we still mourn our sins and unfaithfulness to God's covenant, it is also a day of rejoicing for believers, for Paul assures us that *"Therefore there is now no condemnation at all for those who are in Messiah Yeshua"* (Rom 8:1). Because of His shed blood, we can now be sure that if we truly *shub,* our clothes are white, the colour of righteousness.

"We might ask, 'Why don't Christians celebrate such a wonderful day?' The answer seems to be connected not simply with a turn away from Jewish practices. The answer seems to also involve the idea that forgiveness was accomplished once and for all time on the cross (so there is no longer a need for some annual reminder of God's goodness) and the idea that grace is uniquely a 'New Testament' concept. This combination of anti-Judaism, cross-forgiveness and Lutheran grace keeps us from relishing a day when we are caught up in the festive emotion of God's love for His people. It's rather sad, don't you think?"[140]

The Feast of Tabernacles

Five days after Yom Kippur, the last of the *moedim Adonai* is celebrated. Sukkot or Tabernacles is the final of the seven feasts, the third appearance feast, and it's probably the most joyous of all the festivals. It's when we celebrate the harvest that was prayed for at Passover. It's such a happy festival that it's sometimes called *Z'man Simchateinu* (the Time of Our Rejoicing). Now the final harvest is done, so the people can look forward to a rest during the winter months. Sukkot is the crowning time in the cycle of the year and the culmination of the year's work in the field. The harvest that was prayed for in the spring has come in, and now prayers are made for the winter rains to provide for the next year's harvest. Continual dependence on God and great joy at his abundant provision! The Talmud gives a vivid description of the mood in Israel during Sukkot:

"As the pilgrims journeyed, they sang the songs of Zion, the psalms. On one side of the road, a family would sing from Psalm 121: 'I lift up my eyes to the hills.' Across the road, the response would come: 'Where does my help come from?' And all together: 'My help comes from the Lord, the make of heaven and earth.'

"Others would sing: 'I rejoiced with those who said to me, "Let us go to the house of the Lord." Our feet are standing in your gates, O Jerusalem, Jerusalem is built like a city that is closely compacted together. That is where the tribes go up, the tribes of the Lord, to praise the name of the Lord according to the statute given to Israel (Psalm 122:1–4).

"It was Sukkot, the Feast of Tabernacles. The tribes of Israel, their hearts overflowing with praise to the Lord, were going up to Jerusalem to render unto Him honor and praise and glory."[141]

Sukkot gets its name from the tabernacles or booths that Israel was instructed to build and live in for seven days:

"So you shall celebrate it as a feast to the Lord for seven days in the year. It shall be a permanent statute throughout your generations; you shall celebrate it in the seventh month. You shall live in booths for seven days; all the native-born in Israel shall live in booths, so that your generations may know that I had the sons of Israel live in booths when I brought them out from the land of Egypt. I am the Lord your God" (Lev 23:41–43).

In addition to Sukkot being a harvest festival and bringing an offering to the Lord, Israel was to live in sukkot, or booths, for seven days. It was a reminder that when they were settled in the land of promise in their permanent houses that God dwelt with them in the desert and took care of their needs, even though much of that time they were in rebellion. How much comfort does that provide for us, that even when we are outside of God's will in our behaviour, He still looks after our needs and provides for us? Whether we are established or in transition, the cloud of glory remains with us at all times. When Jews build a sukkah today, usually in their back yards or on their balconies if in an apartment, the roof must be able to let the sun and starlight in to show that we are subject to the elements and dependent on God's protection and shelter as opposed to our own resources. It is customary to invite *ushpizin* (guests), who might even be strangers, into the sukkah and dine with them to show hospitality.

The temporary nature of the sukkah was also to point to the temporary nature of our own lives and bodies:

"For we know that if our earthly tent which is our house is torn down, we have a building from God, a house not made by hands, eternal in the heavens. For indeed, in this tent we groan, longing to be clothed with our

dwelling from heaven, since in fact after putting it on, we will not be found naked. For indeed, we who are in this tent groan, being burdened, because we do not want to be unclothed but to be clothed, so that what is mortal will be swallowed up by life. Now He who prepared us for this very purpose is God, who gave us the Spirit as a pledge" (2 Cor 5:1–5).

Paul calls our bodies our "earthly tents." We're borrowing these bodies for a few decades and discarding them for a permanent home for our souls, which will be our resurrected bodies. Sukkot reminds us of that.

At Sukkot, what are called "The Four Species" are bundled together and waved before the Lord. This comes from the command:

"On exactly the fifteenth day of the seventh month, when you have gathered in the crops of the land, you shall celebrate the feast of the Lord for seven days, with a rest on the first day and a rest on the eighth day. Now on the first day you shall take for yourselves the foliage of beautiful trees, palm branches and branches of trees with thick branches and willows of the brook, and you shall rejoice before the Lord your God for seven days" (Lev 23:39–40).

An etrog (citrus fruit like a lemon) and the lulav, which consists of a willow branch, date palm branch, and myrtle branch bundled together, are all gathered. Each has different practical uses for medicine or other practices and different symbolic meanings, depending on which rabbi you ask (two Jews, three opinions) but they represent the various foliage of the land. The three branches are native trees to Israel, but the etrog is not. It appears to originate from Persia, where many Jews were in exile after the Babylonian Empire fell, and made its way eventually to Israel as an exotic fruit.[142] The lulav and etrog are waved in all directions, including up and down, again signifying God's omnipresence and how He is Lord of everything, including the harvest.

Hoshana Rabbah (The Great Salvation)

On the seventh day of Sukkot, a special service occurs that has its origins in both biblical and Talmudic traditions. It's called the Hoshana Rabbah, or The Great Hosannah (The Great Salvation). It comes from Psalm 118:25, which says *"Please, O Lord, do save us; Please, O Lord, do send prosperity!"* The Hebrew phrase for save us is הוֹשִׁיעָה נָּא (*hoshia na*), but it became an expression of great joy for God's deliverance.

Hoshana Rabbah was the culmination of a great buildup throughout Sukkot. Every day, a procession was made around the altar with the lulav and etrog, but on Hoshana Rabbah, the procession went around seven times. The priest would beat the lulav on the ground five times to symbolize the casting away of our sins. Rabbinic Judaism and kabbalistic thought believes that our names have to be renewed in the Book of Life every year and that time of judgement occurs on Yom Teruah, is sealed on Yom Kippur, and is delivered on Sukkot, so the greeting at Sukkot is *pitka tava* (a good note), that we might receive a favourable judgement for the year. Thankfully, because of Yeshua's resurrection and the conquering of death, we know that our names do not need to be renewed every year.

Huge bowls of oil would be lit, the priest's old robes being used as wicks to light them. All of Jerusalem could see them. These huge bowls were lit in reference to passages in scripture such as:

"No longer will you have the sun for light by day, nor will the moon give you light for brightness; but you will have the Lord as an everlasting light, and your God as your glory" (Is 60:19).

or

"On that day there will be no light; the luminaries will die out. For it will be a unique day which is known to the Lord, neither day nor night, but it will come about that at the time of evening there will be light" (Zec 14:6–7).

The rabbis remembered that God Himself is light. Revelation 21:23 says that in the new heavens and new earth, there won't be any sun because the Lord Himself will be our light. That was why when Yeshua said He was the light of the world in John 8:12 it was such an audacious statement.

The climax of Hoshana Rabbah is what is called the Water Libation Ceremony (*Nissuch Ha-Mayim*). The priest on duty would draw water from the Pool of Siloam and pour it out at the base of the altar while the people sang songs. This ritual invoked the promise in Isaiah 12:2–3, which said, *"Behold, God is my salvation, I will trust and not be afraid; for the Lord*

God is my strength and song, and He has become my salvation. Therefore you will joyously draw water from the springs of salvation."

"This was the most joyous of the temple ceremonies. The Mishnah says that 'he who has not seen the rejoicing at the place of water-drawing has never seen rejoicing in his life' (Sukkot 5:1). The ceremony was accompanied by a torch-light procession, dancers, singing and chanting by the Levitical choir of the fifteen pilgrim psalms, the songs of ascents (Psalms 120–134), to the accompaniment of musical instruments."[143]

There was great Messianic expectation at this time. Then, something profound happened.

"Now on the last day, the great day of the feast, Yeshua stood and cried out, saying, 'If anyone is thirsty, let him come to Me and drink. The one who believes in Me, as the scripture said, "From his innermost being will flow rivers of living water"'" (Jn 8:37–38).

Right after the Water Libation Ceremony and the golden bowls had been extinguished, Yeshua stood up and announced that He was the fulfillment of this prophecy and was the long-awaited Messiah. The shock that must have gone through the Temple grounds must have been ground-shaking. Even scripture says it got everyone talking about who He was. The Lord certainly had a flair for the dramatic. Many say Yeshua never claimed to be God or the Messiah. What utter foolishness! As C.S. Lewis said these claims that He makes about Himself throughout the Gospels would be the ravings of a madman if they weren't true. Nobody gets to walk around saying they're the Bread of Life or the Door or the Light of the World. Those are all titles of divinity. Yeshua had to be God in the flesh.

After the Rapture and Israel's purifying fire through the Great Tribulation, leading up to her national salvation, the only major event left on the prophetic calendar is Yeshua's return and the establishment of His one-thousand-year reign on Earth. The main themes of Sukkot are God's provision through the harvest and His actual dwelling amongst the Israelites. The Bible speaks about three different times of God's dwelling with us. The first is in the desert as the Angel of the Lord (Ex 23:20), where He was the pillar of cloud and fire.

The second was when He actually came to Earth as a human being. Many believe that Yeshua was actually born during Sukkot. Not only does tracing the timeline through John the Baptist's birth and Mary's pregnancy six months later suggest that, but the name (or title) of the child born of a virgin in the Isaiah 7:14 prophecy would be Emmanuel, which means "God is with us," the same reason the Lord gave for Israel dwelling in sukkot. Yeshua performed all the signs the prophecies from the Tanakh (Hebrew scriptures) said He would, to prove His Messiahship and that the Messiah would be God.

"For a Child will be born to us, a Son will be given to us; and the government will rest on His shoulders; and His name will be called Wonderful Counselor, Mighty God, Eternal Father, Prince of Peace. There will be no end to the increase of His government or of peace on the throne of David and over his kingdom, to establish it and to uphold it with justice and righteousness from then on and forevermore" (Is 9:6–7).

This was the hardest thing the Jews had to wrap their heads around. A man couldn't become God, which is correct, despite what Adam and Eve were told in the garden. Anyone who claimed that committed blasphemy, which many pagan kings did. But God could become a man, and He did and lived amongst us. Isaiah prophesied correctly, though, that we wouldn't recognize Him when He came, which John validates:

"This was the true Light that, coming into the world, enlightens every person. He was in the world, and the world came into being through Him, and yet the world did not know Him. He came to His own, and His own people did not accept Him" (Jn 1:9–11).

What a tragedy that the very people Yeshua came to save rejected and eventually demanded His death. But God knew this, which is why we the plan isn't finished.

The Jewish people have always struggled with the contradictory prophecies about the Messiah. Many of them talk about His victorious reign over the entire world and how He will bring peace. Yet others speak of His suffering and even death. The rabbis resolved this by coming up with two different Messiahs. One was Moschiach ben Yosef (Messiah, son of

Joseph), the suffering servant, and the other was Moshiach ben David (Messiah, son of David), the conquering king. Little did they understand it wasn't two Messiahs but two comings of the same one. The first time Yeshua came, it was as the Lamb of God who takes away the sin of the world. He said:

"If anyone hears My teachings and does not keep them, I do not judge him; for I did not come to judge the world, but to save the world" (Jn 12:47).

As He said, He did not come to judge but to save. That was the first time. The second time He comes, though, it will be a different story.

Prophetically, the third time God dwells amongst us is when He returns. This time it's not as the Lamb of God but as the Lion of Judah. It's as *"King of Kings and Lord of Lords"* (Rev 19:16). The judgement that was not delivered when He came two thousand years ago will now be doled out without restraint. He will rescue Israel, judge the wicked, and destroy His enemies. The prophecies about when He comes back are truly terrifying for those who reject Him, but they are the great hope for the believer.

Sukkot also figures prominently in Yeshua's Millennial reign. The prophet Zechariah says:

"Then it will come about that any who are left of all the nations that came against Jerusalem will go up from year to year to worship the King, the Lord of armies, and to celebrate the Feast of Booths. And it will be that whichever of the families of the earth does not go up to Jerusalem to worship the King, the Lord of armies, there will be no rain on them. And if the family of Egypt does not go up or enter, then no rain will fall on them; it will be the plague with which the Lord strikes the nations that do not go up to celebrate the Feast of Booths. This will be the punishment of Egypt, and the punishment of all the nations that do not go up to celebrate the Feast of Booths" (Zec 14:16–19).

Whoever survives the final battle and enters into the Millennial Kingdom will be required to go up to Jerusalem to worship Messiah at Sukkot every year. These are the Gentile nations. And the ones who don't? They don't get rain. And what does rain bring? Harvest. It's intriguing that Zechariah singles out Egypt for a warning against not being obedient, since Egypt has figured so prominently in Israel's history for both good and bad but is also called by God as His people (Is 19:25). Incidentally, for those who insist on celebrating Yeshua's birthday, this might very well be the time if He truly was born on this festival.

When He returns, every nation will worship Him. Sukkot is for everyone, no matter what their racial heritage, for in Messiah, there are no distinctions. We are all equal before Him, and we see that fulfilled when He returns. In Numbers 29, the sacrifices for Sukkot constitute seventy bulls over the eight days. The rabbis believe that the seventy bulls represented the seventy nations mentioned in Genesis. In other words, Israel, as a priestly nation, was offering up sacrifices for the entire world. The Talmud even suggests that if the Romans had known the function of the Temple, they would have protected it instead of destroying it.[144] Yeshua is the fulfillment of this practice, where He becomes the High Priest for all nations as the world tabernacles with Him.

Sukkot is the final holiday on the yearly calendar cycle. It caps off the harvest season and reminds us of Israel's nomadic wanderings before God planted them in the promised land. That points to our wanderings as aliens and sojourners here on Earth (1 Pt 2:11) in our temporary bodies until we're brought to our eternal home in our eternal bodies. Sukkot also foreshadows Yeshua's return to destroy the counterfeit Messiah and his armies and set up His eternal reign with man.

As we have seen, God is very precise about time. It's important to Him that we keep His appointments when He says to. Even in Leviticus 23, as the feast days are being decreed, God makes sure we understand that there's no flexibility in a) that we keep them and b) when we keep them.

"These are the appointed times of the Lord which you shall proclaim as holy convocations, to present offerings by fire to the Lord—burnt offerings and grain offerings, sacrifices and drink offerings, each day's matter on its own day" (Lev 23:37, emphasis mine).

The *moedim Adonai* (feasts of the Lord) are special appointments to meet with God so we can remember His faithfulness, understand His plan of salvation, and know more about His character. Each one helps us to appreciate how much the Lord loves and cares for us. You simply can't do that when we try to Christianize pagan holidays. Furthermore, when we keep His festivals, we please Him. Don't we all have appointed time? Aren't our special days made better when our loved ones remember them and celebrate with us, or made worse when we're ignored on them? How do we think God feels when we don't show up? What happens when husbands forget their wedding anniversaries? A shiver just went down the spine of every married man reading this book or within earshot of someone else reading it. How much more so God, who on His appointed times wants to remind us of what He's done for us and His plan of salvation for humanity. When we keep these special days, blessings come our way. We experience God's rest through His shabbats as we flow in His frequency. By not coming and fellowshipping with Him, we disappoint Him. In order to survive and even prosper in the end days before His return, keeping His *moedim* is going to be essential for the Remnant.

Chapter 8—Food

"Louisiana consistently ranks as one of the unhealthiest states in
the union. National decadence with the consumption of biblically
"unclean" protein sources may provide more grounds for poor
health than environmental causes."

Dr. Joe C. Guthrie Jr.

"He was a bold man that first ate an oyster."

Jonathan Swift

If you want to get people's emotions going, start talking about their favourite dishes. Entire nations, like Italy, are known for their cuisine. Eating food isn't only a necessity of life but also a very intimate experience. A man wanting to impress a woman and take her out often goes to a nice restaurant (at least that's what I did). Numerous studies have shown that families that eat together tend to be closer and have healthier relationships with each other. In the previous chapter, we discussed how in the Tabernacle, the Table of Showbread was set up to demonstrate that God wanted to dine with us.

Food is pleasurable. Thinking about our favourite dishes elicits a physical response. Pavlov showed that with his famous experiment with the dogs. A quick search in Google for recipes produced almost 2.3 billion results. Apparently, food takes up a lot of space on the internet. Research is constantly being conducted into the use of different spices to make the dish just so. Food is an experience. The late comedian John Pinette made an entire career of making jokes about food. He hilariously spoke of nothing else for almost thirty years.

God designed our bodies to consume food for fuel. He said when He created man:

"Then God said, 'Behold, I have given you every plant yielding seed that is on the surface of all the earth, and every tree which has fruit yielding seed; it shall be food for you; and to every animal of the earth and to every bird of the sky and to everything that moves on the earth which has life, I have given every green plant for food'; and it was so" (Gn 1:29–30).

The principle we need to understand through this verse is that God designed our bodies and those of the animals with every intricate detail in mind, and He determined what they should use as food. In the Garden of Eden, it was plants. We were all vegetarians. After the fall, though, things changed, and the Lord is the one who changed them.

The first time we see meat being mentioned was after the flood. As Noah comes out of the ark, God tells him:

"Every moving thing that is alive shall be food for you; I have given every-thing to you, as I gave the green plant" (Gn 9:3).

It seems that the Earth had changed since the canopy of water blocking the sun's radiation was now removed, and life was different. People went from living close to 1,000 years to being capped at 120. It also appears that their digestive systems would now be able to handle meat. However, what isn't explicitly stated in the Bible is whether people were able to digest meat after the fall but before the flood. It's curious that God would have people sacrifice animals as an offering before the flood but not eat them. That would be wasteful and contradictory to God's nature, but again, nothing is said, so we can't come to any concrete conclusions.

What God deemed acceptable to eat gets clarified in Leviticus 11. The entire chapter details what God considers clean and unclean animals. On the surface, Genesis 9:3 seems to say that if Noah could catch it, he could eat it. Nothing was forbidden. The restrictions didn't come until centuries later. Except that's not quite accurate, because when Noah was gathering the animals to come onto the ark, God tells him:

"You shall take with you <u>seven pairs of every clean animal</u>, a male and his female; and two of the animals that are not clean, a male and his female; also of the birds of the sky, seven pairs, male and female, to keep their offspring alive on the face of all the earth" (Gn 7:2–3, emphasis mine).

Even during Noah's time, God had already distinguished between clean and unclean animals. Noah was told to take seven pairs of clean ones, because the moment he got off the ark, he offered a sacrifice of each of the clean animals. If it was only two of a kind, like all the Sunday school classes say, every clean animal in Leviticus 11 would have become extinct after the second one of the pair died.

Religious Jews today eat food that is called kosher. Although most of what constitutes kosher today are man-made rules (as is the vast majority of rabbinic Judaism), the idea originally came from two issues in the Bible: what was eaten and how it was slaughtered.

"Kashrut is the body of Jewish law dealing with what foods we can and cannot eat and how those foods must be prepared and eaten. 'Kashrut' comes from the Hebrew root Kaf-Shin-Reish, meaning fit, proper or correct. It is the same root as the more commonly known word 'kosher,' which describes food that meets these standards."[145]

Kashrut is the commands or ordinances about what we eat, and something that is kosher is the actual food. Biblically, it only dealt with meat. Today, Orthodox Jews won't eat anything that's not certified as kosher, including things such as salt or pastries. It's a big business but very little has a biblical basis. In fact, the Bible never calls food kosher. It refers to טָהֵר (*taher*—clean) and טָמֵא (*tameh*—unclean).

What exactly constitutes a clean animal, and why does God insist on it, with two chapters dedicated to the subject within Torah? (Deuteronomy 14 repeats the commandments.) There are different categories of animals, depending on where they dwell. For land animals, the command is:

"Whatever has a divided hoof, showing split hoofs, and chews the cud, among the animals, that you may eat" (Lev 11:3).

In order to be considered *taher* (clean), the animal must have a split hoof and also chew the cud. The split hoof part is fairly straightforward, but what does it mean to chew the cud? Hope Eagan in her terrific book *Holy Cow!: Does God Care about What We Eat?* says:

"Remember that one of the characteristics of animals designated as clean in Leviticus 11 is that they must 'chew the cud,' which is a complex digestion process. Known as 'ruminants,' these animals essentially regurgitate their food for another pass at chewing. Yum. Once I can get beyond this aspect of God's design, I am fascinated. God gave ruminants a unique, multi-stomach digestive system that removes toxins from their food, before it is absorbed into their flesh. Dr. Colbert compares the ruminant's stomach to a washing machine that has four wash and rinse cycles. Like a washing machine running through its cycles, the ruminant's four stomach changers must each digest the food before it is properly metabolized. The food is expelled upward for re-chewing after it has entered the second pouch, but before it reaches the third. By the time their Genesis 1:29 food has reached their flesh, it is nearly free from anything that might be harmful to humans."[146]

The reason God insisted that animals considered *taher* must chew the cud is that they are designed to purify their food before they become food for us.

The second thing to consider is what animals considered *taher* eat. Ruminants eat, as Eagan says in the above quotation, a Genesis 1:29 diet. It consists of plants that bear seeds and trees that grow fruit. In other words, they're vegetarians. None of the clean animals eat meat because their systems can't handle it. Eagan says herbivores' digestive systems are several times longer than their bodies, which allows for the multiple stomachs and times through the system to eliminate toxins before the food is absorbed into their flesh.

Contrast this with meat eaters. Eagan goes on to say:

"On the other hand, omnivores do not chew the cud and are designed quite differently. Pigs, for example, have a simpler, shorter digestive system that does not detoxify their food before it reaches their flesh. Considering pigs as a food source is troublesome. Why? Because on their own, pigs will eat everything, including mice, dead animals and feces."[147]

Not only will pigs eat all of the above, including their own dead (making them cannibals), but they'll eat humans too. Robert Pickton, Canada's most notorious serial killer, was a pig farmer, and many of the prostitutes he murdered in Vancouver in the 1990s and early 2000s ended up being fed to his pigs. Then off to market they would go. I realize that's a revolting image, but why should it be necessary to have to illustrate something so extreme in order to understand why God prohibited the eating of certain animals? Why can't we just accept what the word says to begin with? This is a fundamental problem with people: they either need to understand everything before they'll obey or they think that God wasn't serious when He gave the command. Or, as in the case of the Shabbat, they think they can even improve upon what He has established.

Eagan further mentions that the city of Philadelphia has used pigs for over one hundred years to eat garbage and sewage. You are what you eat.

"Scientific studies support the apparent wisdom of the biblical food laws. A Johns Hopkins University study illustrates how pigs and other unclean mammals, bird, fish and insect have significantly higher toxicity levels than clean ones, like cows. Another study, in which medical students were fed organic pork that was trichinosis-free, revealed serious changes in the subjects' blood chemistry after the pork was eaten. The longer-term study could not be completed, since the subjects stopped eating pork after the initial testing." [148]

Pork was also common used in paganism. It was standard practice for those who worshipped Dionysus to sacrifice a swine. The ancient Greek historian Herodotus said:

"The only deities to whom the Egyptians consider it proper to sacrifice pigs are Dionysus and the Moon. To both of these they offer pigs at the same time, at the same full moon, and afterwards eat the flesh ...

"Everyone, on the eve of the festival of Dionysus, sacrifices a hog before the door of his house ... "[149]

When Yeshua met the Demoniac of the Gerasenes and cast the demons out of him, they requested they be allowed to enter into the swine because it was familiar to them. Not a herd of cows or flock of sheep, but a bunch of pigs. Swine flesh is filthy and a comfortable place for an evil spirit. Do we really want to be consuming what unclean (*tameh*) spirits deem a preferable home?

The creatures in the water that were acceptable had to have both fins and scales. Any fish that has both are perfectly acceptable. Anything else isn't and that's because of what they eat and how their bodies are designed. Shellfish are considered unclean, primarily because they're bottom feeders and clean the water of filth. Remember the Disney cartoon *Finding Nemo*? When Nemo was captured and put into the dentist's fish tank, Jacques the shrimp's job was to clean the tank. Shellfish are the vacuum cleaners of the oceans, and when we eat them, we're putting toxins into our systems. Lobster must be boiled alive in order to be safe to eat, a heinous practice:

"Lobster and other shellfish have harmful bacteria present on their flesh called vibrio bacteria, which thrive once the shellfish dies and begins to decay—and it doesn't take days for the vibrio bacteria to become a problem, they multiply rapidly with the first few hours. Even the high heat used to cook these crustaceans won't destroy these harmful bacteria, and preparing them alive is the best way to avoid this nasty foodborne illness. Abdominal cramping, nausea, vomiting, and fever would be just a few side effects if you were to eat a lobster covered with these little critters."[150]

If we have to go through all of that to eat something and not get sick, it's probably best to just avoid it. Shellfish is the biggest killer of any food type and also causes allergies to develop, as well as increasing cholesterol levels. Once again, we see the veracity in God's instructions for us. Other fish that don't meet the standard are catfish, because they don't have scales and are bottom feeders, and sharks, because like pigs, they eat anything they can catch and don't filter it before it gets absorbed into their flesh.

When it comes to birds, there are no defined characteristics as to which ones are *taher* (clean), only which ones are not permissible. If you study the list, you'll find that they're all scavengers and meat eaters. Science again bears out the wisdom of God. Yet Christians will fight vigorously for the right to ignore God's protection of us.

All insects except the order of orthopetera, which include grasshoppers, locusts, crickets, and katydids, are forbidden to eat. All of these have hind jumping legs. Any other insect is considered unclean and to be avoided altogether.

"Clean-eating, kosher conscious persons should avoid eating all food and drinks with carmine, cochineal, or natural red 4 in its list of ingredients, as this red dye is an extract from the cochineal—a small, flat, oval-shaped, parasitic, scale unclean insect. Cochineal extract is used to dye food, drinks, and cosmetics (lipstick). Cochineal extract consumption has been linked as a cause of allergen cases ranging from mild hives and itchy skin to severe life-threatening anaphylaxis reactions."[151]

For those who claim that when God said every animal it meant every animal without any restrictions, what do they believe about plants? Can we really eat every plant? Are there not plants and fruit that we avoid eating because they're toxic to us? Many varieties of mushrooms are to be avoided because eating them will make you sick, or in the case of the Destroying Angel or the Death Cap Amanita (they're even named to terrify us), will kill you.[152] The manchineel fruit, sea buckthorn, or winter berries can make you very sick,[153] so when the Bible says all, it doesn't necessarily mean *all*.

Scripture

There are a number of scripture verses that people use to demonstrate how God has abrogated His own Torah, which is absurd. Again, Malachi 3:6 says He does not change, and the physiology of these animals hasn't either since Leviticus 11 was given, so how is it that something that was no good for us before is now ok?

The most common of these verses is Acts 10, Peter's famous vision:

"On the next day, as they were on their way and approaching the city, Peter went up on the housetop about the sixth hour to pray. But he became hungry and wanted to eat; but while they were making preparations, he fell into a trance; and he saw the sky opened up, and an object like a great sheet

coming down, lowered by four corners to the ground, and on it were all kinds of four-footed animals and crawling creatures of the earth and birds of the sky. A voice came to him, 'Get up, Peter, kill and eat!' But Peter said, 'By no means, Lord, for I have never eaten anything unholy and unclean.' Again a voice came to him a second time, 'What God has cleansed, no longer consider unholy.' This happened three times, and immediately the object was taken up into the sky" (Act 10:9–16).

There you have it. God made shrimp kosher. If a pig eats a human a few days before being sent off to the slaughterhouse, Adonai said it was ok. Even though it contradicts many other scriptures, throw a live lobster into the boiling water for me.

To start with, Peter argues with God. He actually tells Him no. Large swaths of Christendom would look at that as heretical, believing Peter should have been primed for a lightning bolt. Except that God doesn't punish Peter, because He knows his heart. Why was Peter arguing? He was defending God's reputation. It was the Lord who said not to eat these things, and now He was telling Peter to violate the same command. We see Moses doing the same thing several times in the Torah. God was so upset with Israel that He was ready to wipe them all out, but Moses told God He couldn't because of His promises and that He would look like a failure to the rest of the nations for not being able to deliver Israel. Ezekiel does the exact same thing when God tells him to cook his food over human dung. He complains because it would cause him to become defiled, so God allows him to use cow dung instead. He wouldn't allow God to violate His own rules about holiness without an argument. We see Job doing this as well.

"'Though He slay me, I will hope in Him' (13:15a) is a beautiful expression of faith, widely quoted and familiar to many Christians. However, the rendering is based on marginal notes in the Hebrew rather than on the accepted Hebrew text. The word 'Though' should read 'Behold' and the words 'in Him' should be replaced by the word 'not,' so that the verse reads 'Behold, He will slay me; I do not have hope.' Not only is that a more accurate rendering of the Hebrew, but it also correlates better with the preceding verse. Job fully anticipated that his self-defense would result in his being killed by God. But he was more concerned for maintaining justice than for maintaining his life: 'Nevertheless I will argue my ways before Him.'"[154]

Job was willing to die for the defence of God's reputation. So when Peter is disputing with God about this strange command, it's because he knows it doesn't line up with God's perfect and holy character.

The second thing we need to address is the fact that Peter himself didn't understand the vision. After God told him not to call *tameh* what He had made *taher*, the very next verse (17) says "*Now while Peter was greatly per-plexed in mind as to what the vision which he had seen might mean.*" If it was so clear that God was removing the restrictions on what animals could be eaten, why was Peter perplexed? It's because God wasn't referring to animals He had cleansed. The passage continues by saying:

"*Behold, the men who had been sent by Cornelius had asked directions to Simon's house, and they appeared at the gate; and calling out, they were asking whether Simon, who was also called Peter, was staying there. While Peter was reflecting on the vision, the Spirit said to him, 'Behold, three men are looking for you. But get up, go downstairs and accompany them without misgivings, for I have sent them Myself'*" (Acts 10:17b–20).

The Lord wasn't talking about animals at all. He was talking about people. Peter received the vision three times, and three men show up, whom God tells Peter to follow without reservations. Peter then tells Cornelius when he arrives at his house that:

"*You yourselves know that it is forbidden for a Jewish man to associate with or visit a foreigner; and yet God has shown me that I am not to call any person unholy or unclean*" (Act 10:28).

Peter himself in recorded scripture tells us what the vision meant. There's no reason to guess or speculate. There's no need to develop a new theol-ogy. If you recall back in chapter 3 when we discussed Christmas, the only thing God sanctifies is people. He doesn't make what started out *tameh* to be *taher*. Pork is no less toxic for us now then 3,500 years ago when the Torah was given. We also need to remember that Yeshua died not so we can now sin, which is a violation of the commandments, but so that the effect of sin, which is death, is now neutralized. Not one jot or tittle of the Torah has been done away with, so unclean animals remain that way and will always be so.

So why did God use the image of the sheet to give this message to Peter? Peter says that it's unlawful for a Jew to associate with or visit a Gentile. Technically that wasn't true. There's nothing about a Gentile per se that would automatically defile someone according to the commands of Torah. The Talmud (the Oral Law), which puts a fence around the commandments by adding extra prohibitions to ensure we never violate the commands themselves, does say "The dwelling places of Gentiles are unclean (m.Ohlot 18:7).[155] But that isn't scripture. However, if there was a stuffed pig with an apple in its mouth on the table, or a household idol that the pig had been offered to staring at you when you walked in the door, now you would be defiled. Leviticus 11:8 says not to eat the animal or even touch their carcasses. What made it unlawful for a Jew to go to a foreigner's house was primarily his pagan idols and what he ate. That's why at the Council of Jerusalem, three of the four initial commands given to the Gentiles had to do with food. God was letting Peter know that his ingrained prejudices based on oral tradition needed to be put aside because the door to the gospel going to the nations was about to be unlocked. Cornelius was a God-fearer. Although a Gentile, he kept the commandments and did everything Torah said to. He just wasn't circumcised, so he wasn't a convert. Therefore, there was nothing in his house that would have caused Peter to become ritually unclean.

Another commonly-referenced verse is in Mark 7:

"After He called the crowd to Him again, He began saying to them, 'Listen to Me, all of you, and understand: there is nothing outside the person which can defile him if it goes into him; but the things which come out of the person are what defile the person.' And when He later entered a house, away from the crowd, His disciples asked Him about the parable. and He said to them, 'Are you so lacking in understanding as well? Do you not understand that whatever goes into the person from outside cannot defile him, because it does not go into his heart, but into his stomach, and is eliminated? (Thereby He declared all foods clean.) And He was saying, 'That which comes out of the person, that is what defiles the person. For from within, out of the hearts of

people, come the evil thoughts, acts of sexual immorality, thefts, murders, acts of adultery, deeds of greed, wickedness, deceit, indecent behavior, envy, slander, pride, and foolishness. All these evil things come from within and defile the person" (Mk 7:14–23, emphasis mine).

When it says He declared all foods clean, most commentators I have read say that Yeshua Himself right there nullified the food commands. Number one, He cannot violate His own law because He said it would last until heaven and earth are destroyed. Secondly, it says He declared all *foods* clean. Unclean animals are not considered food. Food is what is suitable for consumption, so a pig, eel, or cockroach are not considered food. Calling something unclean food is an oxymoron. If it's unclean, it isn't classified as food. When He said it's not what goes into a man's mouth that makes him unclean, the assumption was that man was eating actual food. If we come into contact with or eat the carcass (or a steak) of an unclean animal, then we most certainly will become ritually impure and there will be a high probability of adverse health consequences.

Third and most importantly, we have to look at the context. The issue they were dealing with is clearly laid out at the beginning of the chapter:

"The Pharisees and some of the scribes gathered to Him after they came from Jerusalem, and saw that some of His disciples were eating their bread with unholy hands, that is, unwashed. (For the Pharisees and all the other Jews do not eat unless they carefully wash their hands, thereby holding firmly to the tradition of the elders; and when they come from the marketplace, they do not eat unless they completely cleanse themselves; and there are many other things which they have received as traditions to firmly hold, such as the washing of cups, pitchers, and copper pots.) And the Pharisees and the scribes asked Him, 'Why do Your disciples not walk in accordance with the tradition of the elders, but eat their bread with unholy hands?'" (Mk 7:1–5).

The issue was that the disciples weren't washing their hands according to the standard the Pharisees had set up for themselves. They weren't violating any commandment of Torah but the *traditions of the elders*. The conflict had nothing to do with what they were eating but how they washed up beforehand. Matthew's telling of the story helps to clarify that even further:

"These are the things that defile the person; but to eat with unwashed hands does not defile the person" (Mt 15:20).

Washing your hands before eating is generally good practice, but if you happen to be out in the field and wish to snack on something, it's not mandatory, especially with the complicated ways the religious leaders had established. To develop a theology based on such a gross misinterpretation of the Word of God is a sure-fire way to get yourself into trouble. The number of people who suffer from ill health as a direct consequence of eating what God said to avoid is proof of that.

What about 1 Timothy 4?

"But the Spirit explicitly says that in later times some will fall away from the faith, paying attention to deceitful spirits and teachings of demons, by means of the hypocrisy of liars seared in their own conscience as with a branding iron, who forbid marriage and advocate abstaining from foods which God has created to be gratefully shared in by those who believe and know the truth. For everything created by God is good, and nothing is to be rejected if it is received with gratitude; for it is sanctified by means of the word of God and prayer" (1 Tm 4:4).

I recently had a man in ministry tell me that because I say we shouldn't be eating pork, I am violating this passage and practising the doctrine of demons. Imagine saying the keeping of God's commandments is now the doctrine of demons. That's the same as the Pharisees accusing Yeshua of casting out demons by Beelzebul, the ruler of demons, in Matthew 12:24. Yet many today claim that being obedient to God's instructions is demonic.

The meaning of the passage is quite clear. Once again, we're dealing with manmade traditions. Many different sects of Christianity and other religions believe in human-designed rituals regarding what's permissible and what isn't. He might have well been prophesying about the Catholic Church, which forbids marriage for the priests and disdains meat on Fridays. Paul was emphatic about liberty in Messiah on all matters in which there is freedom. However, none of these restrictions have anything to do with the commandments of God. Paul wouldn't even think of violating any command of Torah. That isn't liberty: that is sin.

"On this verse, some have said that in fact *kashrut* must be abolished completely (that we should enforce liberty, so to speak). However, Paul is talking about pagan asceticism here, and his reasoning continues: 'for it is sanctified by means of the word of God and prayer.' Since *kashrut* was obviously a matter of 'the word of God,' it is unwise to base a sweeping rejection of food laws on this verse."[156]

Romans 14 is another go-to chapter to prove we no longer have to abide by the food commands.

"I know and am convinced in the Lord Yeshua that nothing is unclean in itself; but to the one who thinks something is unclean, to that person it is unclean. For if because of food your brother or sister is hurt, you are no longer walking in accordance with love. Do not destroy with your choice of food that person for whom Christ died. Therefore do not let what is for you a good thing be spoken of as evil; for the kingdom of God is not eating and drinking, but righteousness and peace and joy in the Holy Spirit. For the one who serves Christ in this way is acceptable to God and approved by other people. So then we pursue the things which make for peace and the building up of one another. Do not tear down the work of God for the sake of food. All things indeed are clean, but they are evil for the person who eats and causes offense. It is good not to eat meat or to drink wine, or to do anything by which your brother or sister stumbles. The faith which you have, have as your own conviction before God. Happy is the one who does not condemn himself in what he approves. But the one who doubts is condemned if he eats, because his eating is not from faith; and whatever is not from faith is sin" (Rom 14:14–23).

Paul says he is convinced that nothing is unclean, but if someone thinks it's unclean, then it is to him, but obviously not to everyone. Again, it's a complete misrepresentation of the issue at hand. Since we've already addressed Romans 14 as being about matters of one's own opinion, it cannot be speaking about God's direct commandments about animals unfit for consumption. God does not change His mind.

A clue to what Paul is speaking to occurs when he mentions eating meat or drinking wine (v. 20). There's nothing *tameh* about wine itself. So what would cause someone to stumble over wine? If it was sacrificed to idols. The common practice at the time was that the pagans would take their meat and their wine and offer it up to their gods before either consuming it or selling it at the marketplace. In fact, anytime Paul addresses the issue of eating or not eating meat, it's always in the context of idolatry. He says to the Corinthians:

"Therefore, concerning the eating of food sacrificed to idols, we know that an idol is nothing at all in the world, and that there is no God but one. For even if there are so-called gods whether in heaven or on earth, as indeed there are many gods and many lords, yet for us there is only one God, the Father, from whom are all things, and we exist for Him; and one Lord, Yeshua the Messiah, by whom are all things, and we exist through Him. However, not all people have this knowledge; but some, being accustomed to the idol until now, eat food as if it were sacrificed to an idol; and their conscience, being weak, is defiled. Now food will not bring us close to God; we are neither the worse if we do not eat, nor the better if we do eat. But take care that this freedom of yours does not somehow become a stumbling block to the weak. For if someone sees you, the one who has knowledge, dining in an idol's temple, will his conscience, if he is weak, not be strengthened to eat things sacrificed to idols? For through your knowledge the one who is weak is ruined, the brother or sister for whose sake Christ died. And so, by sinning against the brothers and sisters and wounding their conscience when it is weak, you sin against Christ. Therefore, if food causes my brother to sin, I will never eat meat again, so that I will not cause my brother to sin" (1 Cor 8:4–13).

This is why Daniel, Hannaniah, Mishael, and Azariah refused to eat of the king's delicacies (meat and wine). They had been offered up to idols. The prohibition in Torah (Ex 34:15) about not eating food sacrificed to idols was to prevent Israel from adopting the pagan practices and worshipping their gods, which God knew they were prone to do. Paul is clear here that we know there's no such thing as an idol, so we can eat the food without participating in the idolatry itself, if we are mature and grounded in our identity in Messiah. I can show up to a Christmas party without participating in and embracing the rituals of Christmas. We are to be in the world but not participating in it (the world system), just as Yeshua was in the world but not defiled by it. We can pray over it (1 Tm 4:4), and whatever god (demon) that has been invited to affect the food is now commanded to leave. I pray this over my food all the time, because who knows what spirit it has been affected by? The new or immature believer, though, may still struggle with his old ways. Paul says if that's the case, we're not supposed to abuse our liberty and risk causing him to stumble or tempt him to fall back into idolatry or be adversely offended by the practice.

So when it comes to everything being clean, it has to be according to what God defines as clean to begin with and then defiled by ritualistic practices. It has nothing to do with God suddenly declaring clean what He had classified as unclean in Torah. I reiterate, Paul and the other apostles never advocated for the breaking of any commands of Torah, not even one time.

Another thing to consider is how important the food commands were to the identity of the Jews, illustrated by the struggle Peter had with even the notion of eating something *tameh*. If the food commands were suddenly being changed, do we not think there might have been just a little resistance? The Judaizers were insisting Gentiles be circumcised to be saved, which was never commanded for them, even in Torah, and there had to be a meeting with all the apostles to clarify the issue. How much more would the abrogation of a direct commandment cause a disturbance? Yet we don't see any mention of this coming up in Acts or any of the epistles. We just assume that unlike every other issue the early Church wrestled through, when it came to food, everyone just accepted the new way without any argument or pushback. We believe that everyone was excited about not being restricted on what they could eat because shark-fin soup was something everyone always craved. I can assure you there would have been rioting in the assembly meetings had that been what was actually happening, and it would have taken years and decades to settle. It wouldn't have been universally accepted just because Peter had a vision. For there to be no mention of such an explosive issue anywhere should indicate to us that nobody was suggesting ham sandwiches were now ok.

The last chapter of Isaiah clearly deals with Yeshua's one-thousand-year-reign on earth. Isaiah speaks of Him coming in fire (judgement) and

Jerusalem being a joy, which it most certainly isn't to the world now, and all flesh worshipping before the Lord. Verse 17 of chapter 66 says:

"'Those who sanctify and purify themselves to go to the gardens, following one in the center, who eat pig's flesh, detestable things, and mice, will come to an end altogether,' declares the Lord.'"

The exact meaning of this passage is rather obscure, with reference to "the centre" possibly being about a pagan ritual, but what's abundantly clear is that God considers swine flesh a detestable thing. Same with unclean sea animals (Lev 11:12). That's strong language but it's how God sees us when consuming animals He made for purposes other than food. If in the Millennium pig is detestable and was when the Torah was given, why do we assume the Torah is put on hold now? Even if you're a dispensationalist, logically it doesn't make sense that God would forbid something, allow it, and then forbid it again. He isn't confused like we can be, changing our minds because we get new information or our feelings change.

Another question we need to ask is: Did Yeshua eat anything unclean? He couldn't have, since that would have been sin and disqualified Him from being the perfect sacrifice for us. Besides, He is the Word (Torah) that became flesh. To eat what He himself prohibited would have contradicted Himself, and He is not the author of confusion (1 Cor 14:33). Therefore, He also could not have declared it ok for others to do so.

Going back to the story of my encounter at the pizza parlour, we clearly see that enjoying your liberty in Messiah does not include violating God's commands. Certain animals were made for consumption, and the ones that were not have a different function on earth, namely cleaning it up. Most of us wouldn't even think of eating a common housefly, since they eat garbage, rotting flesh, and fecal matter. Yet swine and shellfish are no different, but Christians love to indulge in those things, and some get downright hostile if you should suggest they perhaps shouldn't, even if it's for their own good, because of their liberty. I recently contacted a church regarding using their facility to hold a Passover Seder. I was told we could not. And the reason? Because I believe in the keeping of the food commands. The chairman of the leadership team said, "Our largest concern was the position you take regarding the ceremonial laws in Leviticus and that they are still binding to believers today." First of all, I was very specific with him that I don't impose my beliefs on others, especially those who are not part of my community, and secondly, we weren't even going to be discussing the food commands. We were going to celebrate the Exodus from Egypt and the death, burial, and resurrection the Messiah. Yet the unity of the Spirit was broken because they were imposing their "freedoms" on me. The food commands, as with every other one in scripture, not only have a spiritual foundation but wisdom in the physical as well. Keeping them can only be to our benefit.

Chapter 9—Anti-Semitism

"With satanic joy in his face, the black-haired Jewish youth lurks in wait for the unsuspecting girl whom he defiles with his blood, thus stealing her from her people."

Adolf Hitler

"These men, Jews as they are, are causing our city trouble, and they are proclaiming customs that are not lawful for us to accept or to practice, since we are Romans."

Acts 16:20

We've dealt with a number of different issues in this book, and all of them have to do with our obedience to God's instructions. What has caused the Body of Messiah to stray so far from the truth? Are all of these just random issues that Satan has tripped us up on, or is there a common factor behind them all? How has the evil one been so successful in corrupting the Word of God so that our theology and practices clearly go against God's basic instructions for our lives?

According to psychologist Dr. Shad Helmstetter in his ground-breaking book *What to Say When You Talk to Yourself*, in order for us to act a certain way, we have to feel that way. In order for us to feel something, our attitude must be such that it will generate that feeling. Our attitudes are molded by our beliefs, and our beliefs are determined by our programing.[157] In other words:

- Behaviour is determined by feelings
- Feelings are determined by our attitudes

- Attitudes are determined by beliefs
- Beliefs are determined by our programming or what we are taught

It all starts with programming. A baby's mind is like a blank slate when it comes into the world. It has no opinions, and the only thing God has programmed into it at this point is instinct. Everything a person knows must be taught, either through experience or from someone else. What we're taught will dictate what we believe, and how we act will be based on those beliefs. That's why advertising is so powerful and so many billions of dollars are spent on it every year. The whole point of advertising is to convince you that your life will either be better with the product or service being promoted or you won't be happy without it. If advertisers can generate an emotional response in you about their product, there's a good chance the buying process will have begun.

Our minds are divided into three different parts, much like a computer. Many people suggest the computer was designed to be like the human mind. The conscious mind is what's going on actively: conversations, tasks, and problems to be worked out. That's like the desktop, where programs are actively running. Studies have shown that the conscious mind has about two thousand neurons firing per second of activity. The subconscious mind is like the RAM in your computer. It's all the programs that are running behind the scenes. We're not actively accessing or using them, but they're still operating. In the same second of activity, the subconscious mind has four billion neurons functioning. That's two million times the number in the conscious mind.[158] This is because the subconscious mind works in images and memories and emotions. They take far more active neurons to create.

The unconscious mind is like our hard drives—all the dormant things stored in memory. Every single experience we've had in life is stored in our unconscious mind, but most of it isn't accessible. We don't remember the vast majority of what we've experienced in life. People who have photographic memories have a better understanding of this in that they can access their unconscious minds much more easily.

The subconscious mind is where our emotions come from, so it's a major component of our soul. What's most important to know about the subconscious mind is that it has no ability to differentiate between what is real and what is not. That's the job of the conscious mind. The subconscious mind believes whatever information it receives to be true. That's why information put into it is called "programming," and if the subconscious mind is two million times as large as the conscious mind, once an emotion or belief is accepted, despite the fact that it may being irrational, it most often cannot be countered by mere logic or reason. Emotions and beliefs are far more powerful than facts since they take so many more neurons to create. Also, our brains are wired so that when a thought enters into it, it goes through the part of the brain that produces emotion before it goes to the logic centre. You will always have an emotional reaction first and then decide what to do with it. That's why the conscious mind simply can't win a battle against the subconscious mind on its own. The subconscious mind must be reprogrammed to change beliefs and attitudes.

For example, most fears are irrational. Unless you're a tightrope walker, being high up isn't dangerous, yet millions of people are afraid of heights, even if they're inside a building. It's the same with the vast majority of insects. Unless you live in Australia, where it seems everything crawling or slithering around can kill you, most tiny bugs are quite harmless, including spiders. Yet some people are petrified of them. Same thing with nyctophobia, which is fear of the dark. Dark alleys can be dangerous, but bedrooms for the most part are not (stubbed toes being the exception). In fact, Merriam-Webster classifies a phobia as "an exaggerated usually inexplicable and illogical fear of a particular object, class of objects, or situation."[159] Just because we believe something doesn't make it true. Many of our beliefs are the result of trauma or lies we've been told, or even formulated in our own heads.

Understanding all of this is important because when it comes to prejudice, we must know that it's a learned attitude based on the belief that some people are superior to others. When it comes to racial prejudice, that superiority is determined by the colour of our skin or a number of other genealogical factors. Racism has been the scourge of humanity since there have been different-looking people on the earth. Untold millions have died throughout history because of it.

In reality, there's only one race—the human race. We're all created in the image of God and all have the same DNA. All are precious in God's eyes, all are sin-fallen, and all need to be redeemed by the blood of Yeshua. While some may have more pigmentation in their skin, making it darker than others, or some people's eyes are rounder or more slanted than others, our genetic makeup is no different from any other human's. The belief that some "races" are superior to others isn't based on fact but on *programming*. Proof of this is that if you put a bunch of young children of different colours, languages, or accents, who haven't been taught racism, together in a playground, the only thing they're concerned about is what game they're going to play next. They couldn't care less about those differences. It's only when we get older and start to *learn* that some colours or nationalities or classifications of people are inferior to us that we don't like or trust them. Sadly, for many this starts at a very young age.

Anti-Semitism has been called the oldest hatred in the world. From the time of God's promise to Abraham in Genesis 12:3 that through him, all of the nations of the world would be blessed, there has been prejudice against God's people and attempts to destroy them. No other group of people has been so systematically targeted in history, and were it not for God's promise in Jeremiah 31:34 that He would never let them be destroyed, most assuredly they would have been.

Anti-Semitism, a term coined by German racial agitator Wilhelm Marr in 1873, refers to the hatred of the Jewish people.[160] The name Semite is actually derived from the descendants of Shem, Noah's eldest son, and would technically include the Arab people, whose countries ironically are some of the worst promulgators today of hatred of the Jews. But anti-Semitism has universally become applicable exclusively to Jewish people. So anti-Semitism is a relatively new phenomenon, whereas anti-Judaism is an age-old issue. It's a subtle difference but important, as anti-Semitism is based solely on genetics, whereas anti-Judaism is based on religious practices. With the latter, one could technically convert and escape the dislike (by becoming one of us), whereas with the former, one is hated no matter what he believes. However, as we saw with "Conversos" in the middle-ages, even when Jews converted to Catholicism, they were still looked at as inferior, so it isn't so obvious where one line stops and the other begins.

Opposition to the "chosen people" begins soon after the nation is established. Once the patriarchs died in Egypt and the Israelites began to grow in number, Pharaoh decided to try and eliminate them by first enslaving them and then killing all the male babies by drowning them in the Nile River. Were that operation to have been successful, the women would have been absorbed into Egyptian culture, and the Jews would have ceased to be. Although there had been battles between various nations before, this was the first instance of attempted genocide in the scriptures—the attempted destruction of a people because of who they were, not what they had done. This would be a pattern seen throughout the history of anti-Semitism. Haman also attempted to eliminate the Jewish people in Persia, seemingly for one man's refusal to pay homage to him, which might seem like a bit of an overreaction. He devised a whole plan, even setting a date for the massacre to happen. The story is recorded for our benefit in scripture to help us realize the visceral hatred the enemies of God have for the people of God.

In the inter-covenantal period between Malachi and the Gospel accounts, the famous Maccabean revolt against Antiochus Epiphanes is recorded in the apocryphal books of Maccabees. Once again, a national leader exhibits a hatred for the Jewish people and uses brute force to try and exterminate them. Antiochus IV, the Syrian king from 175 to 164 BCE, forbade the Jews under his rule to practise Torah or even circumcise their children, under the threat of death. Thousands gave their lives instead of submitting to his tyranny until the Maccabees, led by Judah Maccabee (Hammer), finally drove the Seleucid Army out of Israel. Although many foreign kings had oppressed the Israelites, Antiochus was unique in his zealousness to Hellenize the Jewish people and get them to abandon the ways of God, embrace pagan customs, and assimilate with the people around them. If that campaign had ever been successful, the Jewish people would have ceased to be a distinct nation, which would have had the same effect as killing them off.

Throughout history, this seems to be a common theme. Entire books have been written on the subject, and the number of times throughout history people tried to exterminate the Jews are too numerous to count. What is it that drives this hatred of the Jewish people? The Holocaust during WWII was unique in that never before had an entire nation structured itself for the primary purpose of destroying a distinct people group. One of the reasons Hitler lost the war was that even as the tide was turning against the Germans, resources were pulled away from the battlefront in order to ensure the concentration camps could continue their grisly task of murdering Jews. That was their number one priority. The tanks and planes or even the bullets weren't as important as the crematoriums. It's hard to wrap our heads around the sheer evil of such a concept, yet we witnessed it less than a hundred years ago.

What produces this irrational disdain for the Jews? What causes people time and again throughout history to rise up to want to destroy them? The Emperor Claudius expelled the Jews from Rome, and many monarchs did so in the subsequent 1,900 years until the rebirth of the modern state of Israel in 1948. This repeated pattern, with expulsion and confiscating of their possessions, gave credence to the term *wandering Jew*. But again, we have to ask why.

For the most part, Jews are not an aggressive people. Rarely throughout history do we see them waging campaigns to conquer foreign lands and initiate wars. Jews had a reputation when they were in the land, both ancient and modern, as being fierce warriors in defending themselves. In the third war against Rome in the Bar Kochba Revolt in 132–135 CE, Israel actually came very close to defeating the Roman Empire, but we hardly ever see them starting battles or wars of aggression. Jews have never been known as imperialistic. The image one might have of Jews today is of someone smaller in stature, bookish, and not terribly athletic. While many Muslims resorted to terrorist attacks against Jews and any other people they wish to conquer, including with suicide bombings, the worst someone Jewish might do to you is debate you to death. So why the vitriol against them?

A Blessing to Others

The Jewish people have, without exception, been an asset to every country they've lived in. They mind their own business, keep focused on being productive and successful, and only want to be left alone. And wherever they go, they bring the Torah with them, which is the universal formula for success. With their focus on education, family, and hard work, combined with the blessing of God to Abraham, where those that bless them also get blessed, society benefits when Jewish people are around. They are immensely productive, don't really bother others, and, as a rule, bring good moral values with them. According to author Thomas Cahill:

"The Jews started it all—and by 'it' I mean so many of the things we care about, the underlying values that make all of us, Jew and gentile, believer and atheist, tick. Without the Jews, we would see the world through different eyes, hear with different ears, even feel with different feelings. And not only would our sensorium, the screen through which we receive the world, be different: we would think with a different mind, interpret all our experience differently, draw different conclusions from the things that befall us. And we would set a different course for our lives.

"By 'we' I mean the usual 'we' of late-twentieth century writing: the people of the Western world, whose peculiar but vital mentality has come to infect every culture on earth, so that, in startingly precise sense, all humanity is now willy-nilly caught up in this 'we.' For better or for worse, the role of the West in humanity's history is singular. Because of this, the role of the Jews, the inventors of Western culture, is also singular: there is simply no one else remotely like them; theirs is a unique vocation. Indeed, as we shall see, the very idea of vocation, of a personal destiny, is a Jewish idea."[161]

Cahill postulates here that the Jewish people are responsible for the very way we think, which is a pretty audacious claim but one with much validity. The revelation of Yehovah Elohim to the world through His people via the scriptures did indeed transform the world from darkness to light. The coming of the Light of the World in human flesh was the culmination of that revelation. Because of the Torah, Yeshua, and the Ruach HaKodesh as our deposit until He returns, we now have the mind of God instead of the mind of Satan. Therefore, it's not such a leap to say the Jewish people are responsible for the way we think today in the West, which is founded on Judeo-Christian values.

If that is the case, and they have been such a blessing, why do so many people hate them? When the Catholic Church banned the charging of interest for every Catholic in 1179, it was the Jews who stepped into the money-lending trade and who pretty much were the financiers for most kingdoms in Europe during the Middle Ages. Although Shakespeare's *Merchant of Venice* certainly painted Shylock the Jew in a negative light as a money-lender, that role was vital in keeping society running. Yet after serving faithfully to many monarchs, time after time those same monarchs would expel the Jews from their land, and it always was to that country's detriment. Jews, while constituting a mere .2 per cent of the world's population, own twelve per cent of the Nobel Prize awards. While jealousy can be part of the problem, it doesn't explain the continuance and intensity of the hatred. It still doesn't make any sense.

When the Bubonic plague hit Europe in 1348–1349 and a third of the population of Europe died, the Jews weren't as adversely affected, mainly because of their adherence to the commandments of washing and cleanliness laid out in the Torah. They didn't let the animals into the house to live with them, so the fleas that would go from the rats to the livestock didn't bite them and transfer the disease. Instead of finding out from the Jews what they were doing to battle the epidemic more successfully, their neighbours accused them of using witchcraft, and they were persecuted as well as even killed. There are no boundaries for the stupidity of humankind. What is the source of this irrational hatred that has no valid reason? Why would people malign a source of knowledge and wisdom to lead more successful lives and attack it instead of embracing it?

As we've already discussed, prejudice, especially of the racial kind, is a learned behaviour. It isn't natural. Therefore, we must conclude that racism is a *spiritual* disease and comes from the Father of Lies himself. Hatred of anyone based on genetic differences is satanic and not godly, no matter what verses people have cherry-picked out of the Bible to justify it, as did people in the southern US to claim that the slavery of Black people was God's will. Because all sin is a battle of the mind, and the devil and his minions can suggest things to us, we must constantly battle those lies with the truth of God's Word.

Anti-Semitism is no different. Is it any surprise that the kingdom of darkness would continue to speak lies about the Jewish people? Should we be shocked that there's always been a systematic campaign to revile the nation God chose as His instrument from which to bring His Word and His Messiah? Knowing that God's promise of redemption and the defeat of Satan was going to come through the lineage of Abraham, Isaac, and Jacob, it would make perfect sense for Satan to attack it with every trick in his arsenal. Every person the devil can convince to distrust and despise the Jewish people, he is more than happy to empower. Whether it be Sanballat and Tobiah trying to thwart the rebuilding of Jerusalem, or the entire nation of the Edomites, Esau's descendants, who were always sworn enemies of the Jews and who gladly helped Nebuchadnezzar destroy Jerusalem, there have always been willing participants coming against the apple of God's eye (Zec 2:8).

At this point you might be saying that hatred of the Jewish people has always been a problem in the world, but what does that have to do with the Church and the issues we have been addressing in this book? Again, what would be the source of such opposition to being obedient to God's word? It's not just a misconstruing of the meaning of the various passages, even if you take into account the lack of understanding of the language and culture of the time and the lack of discipline for most believers to learn proper hermeneutics. There's a driving force behind the opposition to taking the Word of God at face value, and that started right after the foundation of the Body of Messiah in Acts 2. I may appear to be belabouring this point a little, and you might be saying "get to the point already," but it's important we understand what's really at the heart of the subject of this book so the problem can be rectified.

We see elements of the battle against anti-Semitism in the book of Acts and in the epistles. Paul caused a riot in Acts 16 when he cast the demon out of the slave girl who was prophesying. As a result he was accused of causing trouble because he was Jewish and had different customs that weren't lawful for Romans to practise. Well, there were many Jews around who hadn't ruined the slave girl's owner's way of making a living, but right away it was because of Paul's ethnicity that they were able to get people incited.

Haman did the same thing with King Ahasuerus. Mordechai upset him by not bowing down to him, but when Haman found out he was Jewish, he decided to put the whole race to death. Now, it might seem extreme to want to annihilate an entire people because one of them disrespected you, but if we consider that Haman was an Agagite, which might have referred to Agag, the king of the Amalekites, some pieces start coming together. Saul was instructed to exterminate them from the land, but he spared the king and others as trophies of war. Samuel put Agag to death, but some of the prisoners escaped, and there are those who believe that Haman was a descendent and therefore was looking to take revenge on something that had happened five hundred years before.

Haman used the same tactic as the slave girl's masters to convince the king to let him kill the Jews. He said:

"Then Haman said to King Ahasuerus, 'There is a certain people scattered and dispersed among the peoples in all the provinces of your kingdom; their laws are different from those of all other people and they do not comply with the king's laws, so it is not in the king's interest to let them remain. If it is pleasing to the king, let it be decreed that they be eliminated, and I will pay ten thousand talents of silver into the hands of those who carry out the king's business, to put into the king's treasuries" (Est 3:8–9).

Haman's method of getting the king's approval for his plan consisted of three basic steps. He explains to the king:

1. There is a people that is different from them in his kingdom
2. It is not in the king's best interest to keep them around
3. He offers to pay for their elimination

This is a tried-and-true way of demonizing a particular group. Ensure that people look at them as different, explain that the difference is not a good one but is detrimental to the community or nation, and suggest getting rid of them one way or another. It's been done countless times throughout history in almost every nation and works every time because the heart of humanity is bent on evil.

If we believe that different people are a threat to us, we will always regard them with suspicion, and the first opportunity that comes up, we'll blame them for whatever might be going wrong in our lives. Some women who have been abused by men look at all men askance and will blame them for their unhappy lives. The belief may not be true, but psychology and human history have shown us that truth is irrelevant to people's behaviour. It's perception of truth that matters, because what people perceive to be true will determine how they act.

The Early Assembly

Hostility to the Jewish people makes its appearance in the early days of the Church, not only amongst the people who lived around the Jews but within the Church itself. Paul spent a lot of time emphasizing that in Messiah, we're all the same. He tells the Jews to stop regarding Gentiles as inferior or second-class citizens, as in Ephesians 2 or Romans 2. However, he also has to address the mistrust of the Jews by the Gentiles. In Romans 1, he says that the gospel is to the Jew *first*. The word "first" is the Greek word πρῶτον (*proton*—Strong's #4412),[162] which is where we get our word prototype from. Israel is God's original model, and 1Corinthians 10 tells us that everything that happened to them was an example to us. That tells us that God works with the Body today the same way as He did with Israel. We've been convinced that somehow the Father deals with the Church entirely differently from how He worked with Israel in the Old Covenant, but that's hardly the case. Romans 9–11 is all about Paul's (and the Lord's) burden for Israel and reiterating that God is not done with them. Why would Paul feel the need to dedicate so much ink to defending this position unless it had to be addressed strongly? There were obviously those within the Gentile community who had less-than-favourable attitudes toward their Jewish brethren. As we discussed earlier, just because we get saved doesn't mean the old man (nature) with all of his stinking thinking volunteers to lie down on the altar. We have to crucify him, and that includes all of his prejudices. I have met several believers who once hated the Jewish people but when they got saved developed a love for them. Sadly, that's not always the case. God doesn't deliver everyone from all their bad habits immediately. Sometimes we have to struggle to develop the mind of Messiah. These pagans who came to know Yeshua in Rome didn't all suddenly shed their old programming, so Paul needed, through the inspiration of the Ruach HaKodesh (Holy Spirit), to give them new programming. The only way we can counter years and decades of the lies we've believed is to hammer them with the truth. But as is the case with most issues in our believing life, that is a process.

There are some who incredulously claim that the New Covenant itself is anti-Semitic. They refer to John's use of the "the Jews" in his Gospel, or Paul's statement to the Thessalonians, where he says:

"For you, brothers and sisters, became imitators of the churches of God in Messiah Yeshua that are in Judea, for you also endured the same sufferings at the hands of your own countrymen, even as they did from the Jews, who both killed the Lord Jesus and the prophets, and drove us out. They are not pleasing to God, but hostile to all people, hindering us from speaking to the Gentiles so that they may be saved; with the result that they always reach the limit of their sins. But wrath has come upon them fully" (1 Thes 2:14–16).

When John spoke of the Jews being opposed to Yeshua in numerous passages, he was clearly referring to the Jewish leadership that Yeshua battled against. Paul is referring to the same unbelieving leadership that had the prophets killed, such as King Jehoiakim, who killed Uriah when he spoke against him, or Manasseh, who had Isaiah sawn in half inside a log. He's also speaking of the Sanhedrin, who petitioned Pilate to have Yeshua crucified, or the Jews who would follow him around interfering with his preaching of the gospel. Neither of them was speaking of all Jews because they were Jewish, and many Jews did believe. To say that either John, Paul, or any other contributor to the New Covenant scriptures was anti-Semitic and that the Bible affirms it to justify their own prejudice against the Jewish people is utterly ludicrous.

The Church Fathers

This prevailing attitude toward Jewish people that Paul was writing against sadly did not go away. It got worse. Things really began to intensify with the first revolt against Rome. With the numerical dominance of the Gentiles, combined with the Jewish rejection of their Messiah, a toxic combination of circumstances was now in place that would be deadly for the Jewish people. Up until 70 CE, Messianic Judaism had been considered just another branch of Judaism, along with the Essenes, Pharisees,

Zealots, and Sadducees.[163] However, after the destruction of the Temple in the Roman revolt in 70, a series of events occurred in domino-like fashion. First, the unbelieving Jews, angry at the believers for not supporting them in their revolt against Rome (which Yeshua specifically warned them about in Matthew 24) rejected them from being part of the community.

"A new Regime took over, after the destruction of the Temple, and perhaps fearing for its own security and very existence, after Roman oppression and persecution, they themselves became vicious persecutors of the Nazarenes and pushed them outside the confines and bounds of Judaism!"[164]

This schism widened further during the third Roman revolt under Bar Kochba from 132–135 CE. Supported by Rabbi Akiva as the Messiah, Simon Bar Kochba led a brutal four-year war against the Romans that necessitated Hadrian to recall his top general, Julius Severus, from the British front to quell the uprising. The Christians might have even been willing to stand with the Jews against Roman tyranny except that in doing so, they would have had to acknowledge Bar Kochba as the Messiah, so they declined to fight. Bar Kochba ordered his followers to kill the Messianic believers who would not renounce their faith and follow him.[165] The cost to the Romans was tremendous, and after Bar Kochba and Rabbi Akiva were killed, Roman vengeance on the Jews was merciless. Emperor Hadrian had intended to build a new city on the ruins of Jerusalem before the rebellion, naming it Aelia Capitolina, and he was going to build a temple to Jupiter on the Temple Mount. This might have been the catalyst for the Bar Kochba rebellion, but after, he added insult to injury and renamed Judea to Philistia, after the Philistines, the ancient arch-enemy of the Jewish people. In English, we pronounce that *Palestine.*

Bar Kochba's rejection and persecution of the Messianic Jews completed the separation between them and the rabbinic community. No longer would they be seen as brothers but enemies. When believers would go into the synagogues for worship and witness to the Jews, they countered with a liturgical prayer (the Amidah), pronouncing a curse against heretics, referring to anyone who said there was any other God except YHWH. This was a direct attack on anyone who proclaimed Yeshua to be God, which believers of course could not recite. This led to the total separation of worship and community between believing and unbelieving Jews.[166]

With the unbelieving Jews now openly hostile to the believing community, and the Messianic community now predominantly Gentile, it's not hard to see where this would go. With the separation, the believing community had lost its connection to Judaism. Although Judaism itself was now tainted, as it had made the transition from a faith based on the sacrificial system to one of prayer, mitzvot (good deeds), and repentance, it was still the root. This separation would prove disastrous for the Messianic community and even worse for the Jewish community as a whole. Without being connected to the Old Covenant, the Torah, and its Jewish heritage, Christianity had been freed to go any direction its current practitioners decided to go, and the anti-Jewish element found its way in within a very short period of time. Systematically, *"the foundation of the apostles and prophets"* (Eph 2:20) was stripped away as church leader after church leader became more and more virulent in his views and attitudes toward the Jewish people and the Jewish customs and traditions that the Christian faith had been built upon.

Ignatius, the Bishop of Antioch who was martyred in 107 CE, said in his Epistle to the Magnesians:

"It is absurd to profess Christ Jesus, and to Judaize. For Christianity did not embrace Judaism, but Judaism Christianity" and "It is absurd to speak of Jesus Christ with the tongue, and to cherish in the mind a Judaism which has now come to an end." [167]

A mere seven decades after Yeshua's death and resurrection, and one of the leaders of the Church is already spouting anti-Jewish rhetoric.

Less than one hundred years later, Tertullian, another of the Church fathers from Carthage, wrote in his *An Answer to the Jews*:

"It follows accordingly, that, in so far as the abolition of carnal circumcision and of the old law is demonstrated as having been consummated at its specific times, so also the observance of the Sabbath is demonstrated to have been temporary.

"For the Jews say, that from the beginning God sanctified the seventh day, by resting on it from all His works which He made; and that thence it was, likewise, that Moses said to the People: 'REMEMBER the day of the sabbaths to sanctify it: every servile work ye shall not do therein, except what pertaineth unto life.' Whence we (Christians) understand that we still more ought to observe a sabbath from all 'servile work' always, and not only every seventh day, but through all time. And through this arises the question for us, *what* Sabbath God willed us to keep? For the Scriptures point to a sabbath of eternal and a sabbath temporal."[168]

The very name of his work tells you all about his attitude toward the Jews and what he perceived to be of the Jews, namely Torah. Why did he feel that he had to answer the Jews? I know we ask a lot of questions, but as we will see, many of the Church fathers wrote polemics against what they considered Jewish things. In reality, these attacks were against God's things. Israel was only the vehicle God used to bring His revelation to the world.

Furthermore, his conclusions are unscriptural. Which verses does he use to prove that both the physical Shabbat and circumcision were temporary and point to spiritual ones? That's gnostic philosophy, and it permeated a lot of the Gentile Church fathers' thinking and writings. We've already explored what the scriptures say about Shabbat, and it will last as long as heaven and earth do. While we fully agree physical circumcision is useless without the circumcision of the heart, it's most certainly not done away with. What we see here is that these theologians are beginning to transfer their dislike and distrust of Jewish people toward God's Word. Claiming that the Old Covenant is Jewish, they infer it is no longer relevant in the life of a believer, since the old is done away with and we now have a new and better way. This idea is completely heretical, but it became more and more widely accepted.

Marcion

One of the most influential and therefore dangerous contributors to the misleading of Christians is a man by the name of Marcion. He was the son of the Bishop of Sinope and was excommunicated by his own father for his heresies. According to Irenaeus: "… that Polycarp of Smyrna, meeting with Marcion in Rome, and being asked by him: 'Dos thou know me?' answered: 'I know the first-born of Satan.'"[169]

Marcion was a Gnostic who believed in dualism, that the spirit realm and physical realms never intersect. In his version of the Bible, he redacted the Gospel of Luke, took out the Jewish elements of Paul's letters, and got rid of the Pastoral Epistles altogether. Marcion was also the one who actually developed the idea that the Old and New Covenants were separate and went so far as to say that the gods of each were actually different.

"In his understanding, the key to all mysteries was to be found in Paul's antithesis between grace and works. He said that there are two Gods - the evil inferior God of the Old Testament, which he called the Demiurge, and the superior good God of the New Testament. The Demiurge created the physical world and was only the God of the Jews, whose law emphasised [sic] justice and punishment for sins through suffering and death. By contrast, the God of the New Testament was the Heavenly Father, a universal god of compassion and love, who regards human beings with benevolence and mercy.

"According to his distinction and antithesis between love and justice, Jesus came, not as the Jewish Messiah, but as the agent of the good God, whose mission was to destroy the work of the Demiurge. Jesus was merely a manifestation of the true God, without any actual birth of death. This is a similar teaching to the Docetists, who denied that Jesus had a physical body, but only appeared to have one. The way to attain the spirituality of Jesus was to free the body from all desires of the flesh through strict asceticism, including the rejection of marriage.

"He wrote a book called 'Anthitheses' which is now lost, in order to expose the incompatibility between the Law and the Gospel and between the Demiurge of the Old Testament and the Heavenly Father of the New Testament, bringing a complete discontinuity between Judaism and Christianity."[170]

As we can see, the concept of "Old Testament" and "New Testament" did not originate in the Bible but with Marcion, and they came with their own respective gods. Nowhere in scripture do we find the word or concept of testament. According to Merriam-Webster, a testament is a tangible proof or tribute or an expression of conviction.[171] We testify to things that we believe. Except God didn't make testaments with His people, which are simply proclamations. He made covenants, which are binding agreements between two or more parties. The Torah is called the Mosaic *covenant*, where God used Moses to convey to Israel His promises to do certain things if Israel would hold up their end of the agreement. However, most covenants that God made were unconditional. We didn't have to do anything but receive them. Abraham's promise of becoming a great nation necessitated no action on his part. David's promise to always have one of his descendants on the throne was made by God without any requirements of David. When God makes a covenant, He commits to doing what He says He is going to do. In the New Covenant from Jeremiah 31:31, God said He would write the Torah on our hearts. The only obedience it requires from us is that we believe God. Second Timothy 2:4 says "*If we are faithless, He remains faithful, for He cannot deny Himself.*"

By reducing the covenants of God to mere testaments, Marcion has done irreparable harm to how the Church has viewed the scriptures throughout the centuries. Much of that was based on his view that the Hebrew scriptures were given by the "finite, imperfect, angry Jehovah of the Jews."[172] If the God of the Jews was so distasteful, what does that make the Jews? Although Marcion was branded a heretic by many of the Church fathers, he gained quite a following, and as we can see, his theology has remained incredibly influential over 1,900 years later.

The tone has now been set amongst Christians that Christianity needed to be separated from its "Jewish" roots. God's plan of revelation and salvation by using Israel was no longer sufficient and needed to be discarded for something better. However, separating Christianity from Judaism would be a lot more difficult if Christians didn't view Jews themselves with suspicion, so the Church fathers made sure they attacked both.

Interestingly enough, according to James Carroll in his work *Constantine's Sword*, while the Church fathers worked hard to demonize the Jewish people and Judaism, the rabbis who were forming rabbinic Judaism after the destruction of the Temple felt no need to do likewise.

"In contrast to the equivalent foundational texts of Christians, which included as canonical the anti-Jewish polemic, the Mishnah, in the words of the Christian scholar Clemens Thoma, 'does not contain a single passage clearly denouncing Jesus or Christianity. At a time when the Church fathers loudly and aggressively preached and wrote against the Jews, such refraining from polemics is proof of considerable inner strength.' It is also an indication that rabbinic Judaism had no need to define itself against what could be dismissed as a minority breakaway sect. In this it was unlike nascent Christianity, which of necessity – here is the legacy of Marcion – defined itself against a Jewish negative. Nevertheless, the gulf between the sibling rivals grew, even if its insurmountability was more openly insisted upon by Christians than by Jews. The Mishnah became an emblem of a new rabbinic identity with which few Christians had any acquaintance. As such, it calcified the Jewish side of the growing break, while the newly canonical Christian writings did as much for those who followed Jesus. In other words, while Christians were devising structures that would separate them from the community once designated 'Israel,' rabbis were inventing forms of religion in which Christians could not participate, even if they wanted to. The books both symbolized the break and reified it."[173]

Justin Martyr

Justin (the) Martyr was a Christian philosopher during the second century, who was martyred for his faith in 165 CE. He was extremely influential in establishing Christian doctrine. In his work *Dialogue with Trypho*, a debate with a Jewish man (although there are some within the Jewish community who feel Trypho was just a made-up figure so Justyn Martyr could expound upon his views),[174] several of his arguments are decidedly anti-Jewish in nature. In chapter 11, in speaking about the Torah, he says:

"But we do not trust through Moses or through the law; for then we would do the same as yourselves. But now—(for I have read that there shall be a final law, and a covenant, the chiefest of all, which it is now incumbent on all men to observe, as many as are seeking after the inheritance of God. For the law promulgated on Horeb is now old, and belongs to yourselves alone; but this is for all universally. Now, law placed against law has abrogated that which is before it, and a covenant which comes after in like manner has put an end to the previous one; and an eternal and final law—namely, Christ—has been given to us, and the covenant is trustworthy, after which there shall be no law, no commandment, no ordinance."[175]

In chapter 12, when discussing how God feels about their observances, he states:

"The new law requires you to keep perpetual sabbath, and you, because you are idle for one day, suppose you are pious, not discerning why this has been commanded you: and if you eat unleavened bread, you say the will of God has been fulfilled. The Lord our God does not take pleasure in such observances:"[176]

God does indeed say in Psalm 40 that He was not pleased with their offerings, but only because they did so with the wrong heart. Justin makes the assumption that God didn't want them at all, which would be ludicrous since He was the one who required them in the first place.

In chapter 16, he goes after circumcision:

"For the circumcision according to the flesh, which is from Abraham, was given for a sign; that you may be separated from other nations, and from us; and that you alone may suffer that which you now justly suffer; and that your land may be desolate, and your cities burned with fire; and that strangers may eat your fruit in your presence, and not one of you may go up to Jerusalem.' For you are not recognised among the rest of men by any other mark than your fleshly circumcision. For none of you, I suppose, will venture to say that God neither did nor does foresee the events, which are future, nor foreordained his deserts for each one. Accordingly, these things have happened to you in fairness and justice, for you have slain the Just One, and His prophets before Him; and now you reject those who hope in Him, and in Him who sent Him—God the Almighty and Maker of all things—cursing in your synagogues those that believe in Christ."[177]

Justin makes two horrendous claims here. First, he says circumcision is a physical mark to distinguish Israel from the rest of the nations and from them (Christians) for judgement. He essentially equates circumcision with the mark of Cain. God is the one who gave the covenant of circumcision to Abraham as a sign of His promise to make a great nation out of his descendants. How could he then say that it was for judgement?

Secondly, the calumny he states here and in many other places is that the Jews killed Yeshua. He expands on this claim in chapter 17, where he says that they killed Yeshua, and not only did they not repent for doing so but they sent out men from Jerusalem to oppose the gospel. The charge of deicide (the killing of God) was one that became a mantra from supposed Christians throughout the ages and has led to untold horrors being committed against the Jewish people. The term "Christ killers" has been thrown at Jewish people before attacking them countless times throughout history.

In chapter 18, he further accuses:

"For we too would observe the fleshly circumcision, and the Sabbaths, and in short all the feasts, if we did not know for what reason they were enjoined you—namely, on account of your transgressions and the hardness of your hearts. For if we patiently endure all things contrived against us by wicked men and demons, so that even amid cruelties unutterable, death and torments, we pray for mercy to those who inflict such things upon us, and do not wish to give the least retort to any one, even as the new Lawgiver commanded us: how is it, Trypho, that we would not observe those rites which do not harm us—I speak of fleshly circumcision, and Sabbaths, and feasts?"[178]

He claims here that circumcision, the Shabbat, and all of the *moedim* in Leviticus 23 were because of the hardness of their hearts, not because of God's righteousness, and that they were supposed to be a blessing to Israel and all the world. In chapter 23, he even calls the feasts and circumcision ridiculous and absurd!

In chapter 30, he equates Judaism with a virus:

"For such institutions seemed to be unreasonable and unworthy of God to many men, who had not received grace to know that your nation were called to conversion and repentance of spirit, while they were in a sinful condition and labouring under spiritual disease."[179]

Justyn Martyr was one of the earliest Church fathers and extremely influential. Since he was so against the Shabbat, he also obviously advocated for Sunday worship, using many of the same arguments that we covered in chapter 6. As the Jewish and Christian communities continued to grow further and further apart, Justyn's attitude toward the Jews and the Torah helped pave the way for some very dark times for the Jewish people at the hands of the Church, the very institution they birthed.

Irenaeus, a disciple of Polycarp, who was a disciple of the Apostle John, wrote in *Against Heresies*:

"They indeed, had they been cognizant of our future existence, and that we should use these proofs from the Scriptures, would themselves never have hesitated to burn their own Scriptures, which do declare that all other nations partake of [eternal] life, and show that they who boast themselves as being the house of Jacob and the people of Israel, are disinherited from the grace of God."[180]

In his view, the Jews would have burned their own scriptures had they known Christians would have used them to witness against them. This is a preposterous accusation, but a mere one hundred years after Yeshua established His Assembly, its leaders were now throwing all kinds of wild and unfounded accusations against His people in order to create animosity against them.

More seriously, though, this is one of the first times someone had accused the Jews of being cut off from the grace of God. It wouldn't be the last. Now, not only are they guilty of killing the Lord, but they are no longer redeemable and, therefore, are to be vilified and treated without mercy.

Origen of Alexandria, famous for having himself castrated to control his lusts, continues this charge by saying:

"… the blood of Jesus falls not only on the Jews of that time, but on all generations of Jews up to the end of the world."[181]

Furthermore, he states:

" … on account of their unbelief, and the other insults which they heaped upon Jesus, the Jews will not only suffer more than others in that judgment which is believed to impend over the world, but have even already endured such sufferings ... these calamities they have suffered, because they were a most wicked nation, which although guilty of many other sins, yet has been punished so severely for none, as for those that were committed against Jesus."[182]

The Epistle of Barnabas (quite obviously not written by the apostle in scripture), tells us that although the Jews had been given the covenant at Sinai, they lost it, and Christians would be "'adding to your sins' and saying, 'The covenant is both theirs and ours.'"[183] He is actually postulating that by keeping the commands of Torah, Christians are now *adding* to their sins.

Cyprian of Carthage, when discussing the Lord's Prayer, claims:

"In repudiation of these, we Christians, when we pray, say Our Father; because He has begun to be ours, and has ceased to be the Father of the Jews, who have forsaken Him. Nor can a sinful people be a son ... "[184]

In other words, because of Jewish rejection of Yeshua, God has now rejected them as His people. This despite the scriptures saying in both Old and New Covenants that God would never disown His people. He may discipline them, sometimes quite severely, and obviously anyone who dies without believing is eternally condemned, but not nationally. Paul says to the Roman assembly:

"I say then, God has not rejected His people, has He? Far from it! For I too am an Israelite, a descendant of Abraham, of the tribe of Benjamin. God has not rejected His people whom He foreknew" (Rom 11:1–2).

Jeremiah 31:3 says He loved them with an *everlasting* love. To claim that the Jews are forever condemned because of their rejection of Messiah is outright heretical and an abomination against God. Many of these Church fathers arrived in heaven after they died and were most likely horrified at how wrong they were about this issue.

<u>Constantine</u>

For almost three hundred years, Christianity had been at odds with the Roman Empire. Steeped in paganism, Rome fluctuated between Christianity being a curious nuisance, to it being an enemy of the state or a scapegoat for other atrocities. Christianity had suffered severe persecution under various emperors, most notably Diocletian, who even had many churches destroyed. They were crucified, fed to the lions for the sport of the masses, and generally looked upon with disdain. Most came from the slave and lower economic classes.

Interestingly enough, the persecution increased as Christianity moved further away from Judaism. Under the Roman Empire, Judaism was considered an ancient religion and, therefore, offered special protection. Once Christianity distanced itself from Judaism and endeavoured to become different, Rome looked at it as one of many upstart faiths, and it was persecuted accordingly.[185] Jews weren't conscripted, but Christians were, and conscripts were expected to offer sacrifices to the right gods. When Christians wouldn't, they were punished or executed.

Under Diocletian, the Empire was split into two parts, with each having an Augustus, who in turn had a second-in-command, or a Caesar, under him. A man named Constantinus, a general, was one of those. When Diocletian retired, a skirmish ensued for control of the Empire. When Constantinus died while on the British Isles, his son Constantine took over and led his army back to Rome and challenge his rival for the unified throne. Although Constantine's army was tired and worn out, a vision came to the young general the night before the battle at Milvian Bridge, on the Tiber River. It was a cross in the sky with the words *In Hoc Signo Vinces*—In This Sign, Conquer. The troops rallied, and Constantine won, becoming both the emperor of an again-unified empire as well as a Christian. This would have a profound effect on Christianity, Western civilization, and the Jewish people. Carroll so eloquently states:

"When the power of the empire became joined to the ideology of the Church, the empire was immediately recast and reenergized, and the Church became an entity so different from what had preceded it as to be almost unrecognizable. It goes without saying that the conversion of

Constantine, for Church and empire both, led to consequences better and worse—although not for the Jews, for whom, from this, nothing good would come."[186]

It's not a stretch to postulate that Constantine's conversion is one of the most profound and important events in post-flood human history, maybe even more than any other next to Yeshua's resurrection itself. Christianity, and as a consequence, Western civilization, would be forever and radically transformed. Many of the things we take for granted, such as the calendar, days of worship, and even the structure of our worship services, came about as a result of this incredibly ambitious man.

The greatest problem with Constantine's "conversion" is that while the vision may or may not have been authentic, he spent more time reforming Christianity by fusing his pagan ways to his newfound faith as opposed to being radically transformed by it. After coming to faith, he had his son, wife, brother-in-law, and nephew all murdered. All of the reforms he made were to bring paganism into Christianity as opposed to driving it out of Roman society. Constantine's greatest claim to fame was that he transformed the Church into an institution, and belonging no longer became an issue of true faith. You just needed a membership card through baptism. A transformation of the heart wasn't necessary anymore.

Another aspect of Constantine's influence that drastically affected theology was the emphasis on the cross. The Gospels and the epistles focused on Yeshua's life and His resurrection. That is, of course, our great hope. He rose from the dead and has given us the means to do the same by the power of His Spirit. However, because of Constantine's vision, the cross was his inspiration and the sign from God to believe. Carroll says:

"Constantine put the Roman execution device, now rendered with a spear, at the center not only of the story of his conversion to Christianity; but of the Christian story itself.

"When the death of Jesus—rendered literally, in all its violence, as opposed to metaphorically or theologically—replaced the life of Jesus and the new life of Resurrection at the heart of the Christian imagination, the balance shifted decisively against the Jews. This was so because responsibility for that now pivotal death had long since been laid at their feet ...

One could almost say that for the Jews, the Age of Constantine came to an end only with David Ben Gurion"[187] (with Israel's rebirth in 1948).

This transformation of the Church was nothing less than catastrophic for the Jewish people. The Church fathers maligned the Jews with their words. The Roman emperor and self-proclaimed Vicar of Christ would take those attitudes and enact laws to reflect them and use the military to enforce them. Dark days were indeed ahead for the Jewish people but also for the state of the Church itself.

Constantine's great ambition was to unite and revitalize the Roman Empire, and he wanted to do under the Christian banner. In order to do this, he had to get the vast number of people of different faiths to convert. A great impediment to that came when explaining that Christianity came out of Judaism and had Jewish customs and traditions. The pagans pointed out that the Jews themselves rejected Yeshua, so why should they accept Him? The solution was to completely cut the connection between the two.

The ramifications of the Christianization of the Roman Empire and all of the pagan elements brought into it would be felt down through the ages for the Jewish people. Rome no longer persecuted the enemies of Rome but the enemies of Christ, and the first in line were the Jews. As the Church surfaced from the underground and became the establishment, Christian leaders became more and more vitriolic in their diatribes against the Jewish people, building upon what the Ante-Nicene theologians established.

In attempting to make the Empire unified, or "catholic," under the Christian banner, Constantine needed to unify Christian theology. Theologians spent the majority of their time discussing how God could become man and what was the substance of Messiah, etc. Constantine needed this issue settled, so he called together 250 bishops for the first of seven major ecumenical councils, the Council of Nicaea. The Nicene Creed was established, and in its first rendition, it didn't mention anything about the crucifixion or the suffering under Pilate. As mentioned, early Christianity had focused on the incarnation and resurrection of Yeshua. Now, however, since pagans were the enemy of the Empire, Pilate (a pagan) was fair game and was inserted into the creed. The problem for the Jews was that the responsibility for Yeshua's death had been, for two centuries, entirely their fault. It had now become a universal creed for the entire Roman world. Constantine's establishment of the cross as the universal symbol of the Christian faith and the Roman Empire further ingrained the death of the Lord and the Jews' responsibility for it in the minds of people. Messiah the victor becomes Messiah the victim, and someone needed to be blamed.

It was also established at this council that Easter would no longer be celebrated at Passover, thus beginning the separation of the two so that even today, many Christians don't know that Easter and the Lord's Table is the celebration of the Passover. As we explored in chapter 4, the timing of Easter was based on the cult of Tammuz and Semiramis.

Sunday worship was also established as law in the Roman Empire. Constantine was a worshipper of Mithras, the Persian sun god, and in 321, nine years after his "conversion," he decreed:

"On the venerable Day of the sun let the magistrates and people residing in cities rest, and let all workshops be closed. In the country, however, persons engaged in agriculture may freely and lawfully continue their pursuits: because it often happens that another Day is not so suitable for grain sowing or for vine planting: lest by neglecting the proper moment for such operations the bounty of heaven should be lost." [188]

Although Christianity had been moving away from its Hebraic roots for two centuries, laws would begin to be put in place that would force the issue and make it illegal to observe the very things God commanded his followers to do.

Constantine had a hostile attitude toward the Jews. In part of his letter to the bishops who were not present at the council, he wrote:

"It was, in the first place, declared improper to follow the custom of the Jews in the celebration of this holy festival, because, their hands having been stained with crime, the minds of these wretched men are necessarily blinded. By rejecting their custom, we establish and hand down to succeeding ages one which is more reasonable, and which has been observed ever since the day of our Lord's sufferings. Let us, then, have nothing in common with the Jews, who are our adversaries. For we have received from our Saviour another way. A better and more lawful line of conduct is inculcated by our holy religion. Let us with one accord walk therein, my much-honoured brethren, studiously avoiding all contact with that evil way."[189]

Eusebius is another major figure of Church history and anti-Jewish sentiment. As Bishop of Caesarea Maritima, he was considered a brilliant scholar and the first church historian. He also happened to be Constantine's obsequious biographer, whose writings attempted to practically deify the man. Amongst his many vile diatribes against the Jews, he wrote of the early Christians that:

"They did not, therefore, regard circumcision, nor observe the Sabbath, neither do we; neither do we abstain from certain foods, nor regard other injunctions, which Moses subsequently delivered to be observed in types and symbols, because such things as these do not belong to Christians." [190]

The trend would continue. St. Ambrose wrote:

" …the most worthless of all men. They are lecherous, greedy, rapacious. They are perfidious murderers of Christ. They worship the Devil. Their religion is a sickness. The Jews are the odious assassins of Christ and for killing God there is no expiation possible, no indulgence or pardon. Christians may never cease vengeance, and the Jew must live in servitude forever. God always hated the Jews. It is essential that all Christians hate them."[191]

Hilary said Jews were perverse and cursed by God forever. Gregory of Nyssa claimed they were "a brood of vipers and haters of goodness." Jerome referred to the synagogue as a brothel, the Devil's refuge and his fortress. He also said Jews don't understand their own scriptures, yet he was taught Hebrew by a Messianic Jew. It's obvious that he no longer considered his mentor to be Jewish, and that distinction would play a huge role in the attitudes of both Jews and Christians throughout Church history.

John Chrysostom

John Chrysostom, Bishop of Antioch, was called "Golden Mouth" for his charismatic preaching and is considered one of the early church's greatest orators. He is also well renowned for his eight hateful sermons about Jewish people, which were called "Adversus Judaeos," or "Against Jews." There has been some suggestion that the main target for Chrysostom's hate mongering was the Judaizers in his church, who were convincing others to participate in Jewish customs and go to the synagogues on the festival days. It seems that he was in danger of losing his parishioners, so he began to demonize the Jews in ways Christians never had before. Not only did he attack their practices but who they were as a people. Some of the things he said about the Jews were that they had fallen to the level of the lusty goat or pig, that they sacrificed their children to Satan, and like Jerome, that the synagogue was a brothel, a den of scoundrels, and dedicated to the worship of demons. Of the issue of deicide, which Origen first brought forth, he states that it was an unpardonable sin, there was no expiation possible for it, and that God had rejected them. He said he hated the Jews because they violate the Law. In one of his sermons, he even accused the Jews of being demons themselves.

Most disturbingly, in his first homily he states:

"And this is what happened to the Jews: while they were making themselves unfit for work, they grew fit for slaughter. This is why Christ said: 'But as for these my enemies, who did not want me to be king over them, bring them here and slay them.'"[192]

Chrysostom at first dehumanizes the Jewish people by equating them with livestock and then says they are fit for slaughter (i.e., it's ok to kill them). Worst of all, he claims that Yeshua says the same thing in one of his parables. For the first time, a leading member of the church had sanctioned violence and murder against the Jewish people, and all because he didn't like that his congregants were fellowshipping with Jews and worshipping with them. Shortly after his sermons, and without surprise, violent outbreaks occurred against the Jews in Antioch, which resulted in the destruction of the synagogue there.

Augustine

St. Augustine, a contemporary of Chrysostom, was equally as influential and condemning of the Jews. He said:

"A burning lamp is indeed capable at the same time of exposing to view other things which the darkness covered, and also of showing itself to thine eyes. So also the Lord Christ distinguished between His faithful ones and His Jewish enemies, as between light and darkness: as between those whom He illuminated with the ray of light, and those on whose closed eyes He shed his light."[193]

He also equates them to Cain, as having a mark on their heads, and says that Judas Iscariot is the true image of the Hebrew, who will never understand the scriptures. To his credit, Augustine did forbid killing the Jews with his proclamation "Do not slay them!" The popes in response did try to protect them for the next four hundred years, but there was a caveat. It was the desire to keep the Jews as an example of God's judgement on those who didn't accept the Messiah that this ambivalence and minimal protection was offered, but there was a constant tension in this reasoning. In the same breath, Jews were classified as sub-human but were then encouraged by Gentiles to be tolerated. It was a tension that would ultimately explode in the Crusades, for many who partook in them were not interested in the theological reasoning behind keeping the Jews safe but rather listened only to the hateful statements made about them. When you program the subconscious mind to hate, any reasoning to show restraint will eventually lose out to the much more powerful feelings that rule most people's decisions.

These are but a small sampling of the hundreds of quotations by those who formed Christian doctrine over the centuries. Despite Paul's warnings in Romans 11 for Gentiles not to be arrogant toward the Jews about their unbelief, theologians over the next two thousand years would produce statements and creeds that would marginalize and vilify the Jewish people, the very people that Messiah was born of, died for, and is coming back to save and redeem as His own.

The merging of an anti-Jewish church with the power of the government produced legislation that would further and further marginalize the Jewish people. Some examples are:

- 306: The church Synod of Elvira banned marriages, sexual intercourse, and community contacts between Christians and Jews.

- 315: Constantine published the Edict of Milan, which extended religious tolerance to Christians. Jews lost many rights with this edict. They were no longer permitted to live in Jerusalem or to proselytize.

- 325: The Council of Nicaea decided to separate the celebration of Easter from the Jewish Passover. They stated: "For it is unbecoming beyond measure that on this holiest of festivals we should follow the customs of the Jews. Henceforth let us have nothing in common with this odious people … We ought not, therefore, to have anything in common with the Jews … our worship follows a … more convenient course … we desire dearest brethren, to separate ourselves from the detestable company of the Jews … How, then, could we follow these Jews, who are almost certainly blinded."

- 337: Christian Emperor Constantius created a law that made the marriage of a Jewish man to a Christian punishable by death.

- 339: Converting to Judaism became a criminal offense.

- 343–381: The Laodicean Synod approved Canon XXXVIII: "It is not lawful [for Christians] to receive unleavened bread from the Jews, nor to be partakers of their impiety."

- 367–376: St. Hilary of Poitiers referred to Jews as a perverse people who God has cursed forever. St. Ephroem refers to synagogues as brothels.

- 379–395: Emperor Theodosius the Great permitted the destruction of synagogues if it served a religious purpose. Christianity became the state religion of the Roman Empire at this time.

- 380: The bishop of Milan was responsible for the burning of a synagogue; he referred to it as "an act pleasing to God."

- 415: The Bishop of Alexandria, St. Cyril, expelled the Jews from that Egyptian city.

- 415: St. Augustine wrote: "The true image of the Hebrew is Judas Iscariot, who sells the Lord for silver. The Jew can never understand the Scriptures and forever will bear the guilt for the death of Jesus."
- 418: St. Jerome, who created the Vulgate translation of the Bible, wrote of a synagogue: "If you call it a brothel, a den of vice, the Devil's refuge, Satan's fortress, a place to deprave the soul, an abyss of every conceivable disaster or whatever you will, you are still saying less than it deserves."
- 489–519: Christian mobs destroyed the synagogues in Antioch, Daphne (near Antioch), and Ravenna.
- 535: The "Synod of Claremont decreed that Jews could not hold public office or have authority over Christians."
- 538: The third and fourth Councils of Orleans prohibited Jews from appearing in public during the Easter season. Canon XXX decreed that: "From the Thursday before Easter for four days, Jews may not appear in the company of Christians." Marriages between Christians and Jews were prohibited. Christians were prohibited from converting to Judaism.
- 561: The bishop of Uzes expelled Jews from his diocese in France.
- 692: Canon II of the Quinisext Council stated: "Let no one in the priestly order nor any layman eat the unleavened bread of the Jews, nor have any familiar intercourse with them, nor summon them in illness, nor receive medicines from them, nor bathe with them; but if anyone shall take in hand to do so, if he is a cleric, let him be deposed, but if a layman, let him be cut off."
- 694: The seventeenth Church Council of Toledo, Spain defined Jews as the serfs of the prince. This was based, in part, on the beliefs by Chrysostom, Origen, Jerome, and other Church fathers that God punished the Jews with perpetual slavery because of their alleged responsibility for the execution of Jesus.
- 855: Jews were exiled from Italy.
- 1050: The Synod of Narbonne prohibited Christians from living in the homes of Jews.

- 1078: "Pope Gregory VII decreed that Jews could not hold office or be superiors to Christians."[194]

This is by no means an exhaustive list. When Cyril, the bishop of Alexandria, expelled all the Jews from Egypt in 415, it would be a hallmark of anti-Jewish tactics in the coming centuries. Anyone who didn't like the Jews just told them to pick up and leave. In 528, the Justinian Code was passed, prohibiting Jews from building synagogues, reading the Bible in Hebrew, or testifying against Christians in court. The systematic attempt to strip the Jews of their identity and force assimilation is the same tactic Antiochus Epiphanies used during the Maccabean revolt some 650 years earlier. In 612, Jews were banned from owning land or entering certain trades. This prohibition against an agrarian lifestyle necessitated the Jews to adopt other trades, especially where there was very little to take with them in case they had to leave quickly. Finance was a good option, especially since Christians looked at any kind of interest as usury. Therefore, they became adept at a profession that was scorned yet needed, and they were reviled because of it, especially because they were needed. In 613, serious persecution began in Spain with forced conversions or expulsion, and all children under six were taken and given a Christian education, the same thing that happened to the natives in Canada during the 1800s with the residential schools. In 722, Emperor Leo III outlawed Judaism and successfully had all Jews baptized. The Synod of Narbonne in 1050 prohibited Christians from living in homes of Jews. In 1078, another odious practice was instituted that required Jews to pay taxes to support the Church, the very institution that was persecuting them. The Church's attempts at humiliation knew no bounds and is one of the primary reasons for the hostility of Jewish people today at even the mention of the name of Yeshua.

The Crusades

The Holy Land and the Holy City had been overrun and captured by the infidel, and the Catholic Church was not about to let this lie. The Muslim conquest of Jerusalem had occurred late in the seventh century, and the rapid spread of this usurper across North Africa, the Middle East, and Southern Europe caused much political upheaval that eventually, in part, led to the splitting of the Church into the Catholics in the West and the Orthodox in the East. Millennial zeal, poor economic conditions, a restless population, and politico-religious wars between Emperors and Popes for over one hundred years all combined for anywhere from 100,000–600,000 to respond to Pope Urban II's cry, "Deus Volt (God wills it)!" to liberate the Holy Land from the Muslims at the end of 1096. A red cross (forming the word "croisade" or "crusade"—a military expedition under the banner of the cross)[195] was sewn on their garments, making them highly identifiable. Eight of these wars would occur, the last ending in 1270.

Throughout history, leaders have used a red herring or created an external cause as a diversion from economic or other problems that can't be easily solved to get the general populace to ask the very ones who created the problem to solve it. It's called the Hegelian Dialectic. Create in the mind of the people a common enemy, and one's troubles magically disappear. The idea of a Holy War to liberate the place of Yeshua's homeland seemed to be a good one, but as a learned rabbi once said, "An army moves on its belly." Supplying an army that large over such a long journey (the Christian countries didn't own the ports on the Mediterranean and therefore needed to take the much longer land journey) became an impossible task. The Crusaders consisted of many who were merely serfs (but some landowners as well) with no religious conviction, but rather mercenaries looking for a better opportunity. Many were attracted by Urban's promise that anyone who joined the Crusade would have their sins forgiven (a cry reiterated by Muslim leaders today who say those who die in jihad, or holy war, will automatically go to heaven) and wouldn't have to pay taxes.

Tens of thousands died along the way as fresh water and food ran out, and many were reduced to drinking sewage water or even their own urine. Disease was rampant. Many suffered from heat stroke. Conditions were miserable, and many Crusaders began looking for better opportunities. One Jewish survivor of the first onslaught is quoted as saying, "They said to one another 'Behold we travel to a distant land to do battle with the kings of the that land. We take our souls in our hands in order to kill and subjugate all those kingdoms that do not believe in the Crucified. How much more so (should we kill and subjugate) the Jews, who killed and crucified him.'"[196]

Although Jews weren't the only victims of the Crusades as the bloodlust and desperation caused people to run amok and hatred spread everywhere (the third and fourth Crusades caused untold carnage between the Greeks and Italians), the Jews suffered uniquely as Christ-killers. In 1099, the Crusaders rounded up a thousand Jews inside a synagogue, set it on fire, and herded those trying to escape back in, all the while singing "Christ, we adore Thee!"[197] amid the screams and victims jumping out of the windows. Entire communities were wiped out by hordes of crazed zealots, raping and pillaging anything in their path. Jews to this day are traumatized by the word "crusade," which makes it remarkable that Christian leaders would call their Evangelical meetings by this same name. If we're trying to present Yeshua to both Jews and Muslims, it might not be a bad idea to avoid using such an inflammatory term that didn't work out so well for them the last time. But this highlights the problem with Christianity today: there's a complete disconnect with the past and what our terminology and traditions mean, both to other people and to God.

Blood Libel

Propaganda is a very useful tool in demonizing one's enemy, and no group has suffered more than the Jews in this matter. The Nazis had a minister in charge of propaganda, and all Joseph Goebbels did was slander the enemies of the state to prepare the hearts of the people for their ultimate plan—complete annihilation.

In 1144 in Norwich, England, William, a young boy and tanner's apprentice, was found murdered in the woods. The Jews were blamed for this, and it just so happened that it occurred during Holy Week, so a retaliatory murder against a Jew was committed on Good Friday.[198] It's reported that a converted Jew laid the initial charge and set off a firestorm that continues to this day, almost nine hundred years later, as we see the Arab media printing cartoons claiming the same thing. The Blood Libel charge accused the Jews of taking young Christian boys, crucifying them, and using their blood to make their matzah to mock the crucifixion. In Luke 13:1, we see a similar act being committed against the Jews as Pilate mixed Galilean blood with their sacrifices. This charge spread like a cancer across Europe and was mentioned in both Chaucer's "The Prioress's Tale" and James Joyce's *Ulysses*. William was even sainted and enshrined in his hometown church.[199] Despite the fact that pope after pope denounced the charge as ridiculous, it nonetheless gained currency in the minds of people who had been indoctrinated over the past one thousand years that the Jews had killed Yeshua, so the stretch that they would want to re-enact the crime isn't such a far one.

The problem with the Catholic Church's renunciation of the libel is that it tried to make a distinction between "normal hatred" resulting from Christ's killing and fanciful hatred from fairy tales. Much like Pandora's box, once hatred is condoned, the propagators lose control of how far it goes. In this case, it cost the Jews hundreds of thousands of lives in the ensuing centuries.

The Blood Libel charge led to other lies against the Jews, for which they were hunted down, beaten to death, and even burned at the stake. Talmuds were burned in Paris in 1242 and also in other areas across Europe, usually in conjunction with physical persecution. Jews were accused of poisoning wells throughout Europe and kicked out of Paris in 1321. When the Black Plague struck Europe in 1348 and within two years had killed 25,000,000 people, or about a third of the continent, the well-poisoning claim took on a new frenzy. As mentioned before, the Jews, because of adherence to standards of cleanliness that far surpassed their Gentile neighbours, died in much fewer numbers. This was obvious proof that they were the ones causing it through well poisoning. Jews were tortured to confess to the crime and give up others who were co-conspirators and were then lynched, butchered, or burned at the stake. Some three hundred communities were utterly wiped out, and the devastation in Germany was so great that German Jewry wasn't revived for another three hundred years. It's estimated that 12,000 Jews were killed in Mainz alone during these pogroms.

Closely related to the Blood Libel was Host Desecration. In another attempt to ridicule Yeshua, Jews were accused of stealing the "host," or communion bread, and either stabbing it to make it bleed, burning it, or even sometimes burying it. In 1215 at the Fourth Lateran Council, transubstantiation became official Church dogma that claimed the bread and the wine became the actual body and blood of Yeshua. (This same council also first began forcing Jews to wear distinctive clothing, which later ended up being a yellow badge that the Nazis used.)[200] Therefore, the Jews were now stealing the literal body of the Lord and crucifying it all over again (this, of course, assumed the Jews believed in the metaphysical change of the elements too). The first accusation was made in 1243 in Berlitz, Germany, and the last recorded one was in Romania in 1836.[201] As a result, Jews were burned alive, synagogues were destroyed (with churches often being built on top of the ruins), and debts to Jews were cancelled. In many cases, debt cancellation was a prime motivator in Jewish persecution, as the Jews had become adept business people, and tradesmen were often in hock to them. Leveling a charge against them and then either killing them or expelling them from the land allowed these people to eliminate their debt the easy way. With the onset of the Reformation, the accusation began to die out, but it still rears its ugly head and is being used by the Arabs today in their programs to indoctrinate their people with hatred against the Jews—this despite the fact that Muslims don't believe in transubstantiation either. The great thing about lies and slander is you can use them and know they're not true. It doesn't matter. As long as they work.

The Spanish Inquisition

The Jewish people had had a thriving community in Spain for hundreds of years, and had even produced Moses Maimonides, known as the Rambam, considered to be probably the greatest Jewish mind in history. As a doctor and philosopher, he contributed more to rabbinic literature than anyone else. The first few centuries of the second millennium were a period of relative peace and harmony between Jews, Muslims, and Christians in the Iberian peninsula, as Maimonides wrote in Arabic and not Hebrew. However, this period fell apart as the Black Plague swept over Europe and with the establishment of the Dominican Order, whose friars were much more zealous in proselytizing than other sects. Spanish leaders weren't as welcoming to the Jews, and with the establishment of Kabbala after Moses de Leon wrote the Zohar, the Jews became more vocal in their opposition to the existing monarchy.

The conversion effort by the Dominicans was hugely successful, although their rabid anti-Semitism resulted in many "conversions" as the only alternative to some pretty harsh treatment. However, many Jews decided to stay in their new faith, but as they quickly found out, not all Christians were equal. Jews who were baptized were called *conversos*, stigmatizing them as still being different, and their Jewish brethren referred to them as *Marranos*, or pigs. Many *conversos* were very successful and had developed into a class of their own, even marrying into to well-to-do Christian families. However, with this success came suspicion, especially since many of the friars were of the merchant classes and were envious of the success of the Jews. Messages were increasingly anti-Semitic, and the pent-up frustration led to many attacks against them.

The Inquisition was initially set up to "inquire" as to the authenticity of people's faith. What transpired was a precursor to Nazi Germany as a police state filled with terror and suspicion. The Grand Inquisitor, Tomas de Torquemada, was the confessor of Princess (and later Queen) Isabella and set up a tribunal at Seville but eventually had two dozen offices across Spain. His job was to oversee the Inquisition and establish the legitimacy of people's profession of faith, especially that of the *conversos*. People were tortured, and heretics were burned at the stake by the thousands, since bloodshed was considered too barbaric! For the first time since the dawn of Christendom, anti-Semitism took on racial tones. Even though Jews professed Messiah in large numbers, they were still persecuted because they were Jewish by blood.

Torquemada eventually convinced King Ferdinand and Queen Isabella to expel all Jews from Spanish territory with the Alhambra Decree of 1492. (In the same year, a Jewish believer in Yeshua, Christopher Columbus, would find the Western Hemisphere, which would eventually provide a safe haven for Jewish people from all the persecution against them in Europe.) For the next several hundred years, this was a pattern right across Europe that would repeat itself over and over again. Jews would be told to leave a country and have their possessions confiscated. They became a nomadic people, suffering the whims of monarchies everywhere. Catherine the Great in 1791 imposed the Pale of Settlement, a boundary in Russia that Jews weren't allowed to cross that lasted until the Russian Revolution in

1917. (This is where our expression "beyond the Pale" originated from.) However, their expertise in finance and trade made them a necessity, so they would be invited back. Then, when things were good again, they would once again be forced out. The term "wandering Jew" certainly took on a legitimate meaning during this time.

The Reformation

The Catholic Church had stifled any kind of independent thought for so long that the pressure was bound to escape somewhere. It happened in 1517 when Martin Luther produced his Ninety-five Theses in opposition to Church practices of selling indulgences and nailed it to the door of Castle Church in his home town of Wittenberg, Germany. This eventually led to the breakaway from the Catholic Church itself. With the help of several other theologians around Europe, the Protestant Revolution was launched. It rejected the belief of Catholicism that the Church was what assured salvation and produced the doctrine of *Justificatio Solo Fide* (Justification by Faith Alone).

Luther, at the beginning of his revolt, was keenly sensitive to the plight of the Jews under the Catholic system and even said, "If I had been a Jew ... I should rather have turned into a pig than become a Christian."[202] Luther was indeed sympathetic to Jewish treatment by the Church ... for a time, that is. His initial overtures to the Jewish people were because he thought they were simply misled by anti-Jewish sentiment and rhetoric within the Church, and if they only heard the truth (including preaching from the Torah), they would respond to the gospel message. Despite his best efforts, however, he didn't get the response he expected and became very hostile to them. Many have suspected that Luther might have suffered from bipolar disorder, as he was known to have extreme mood swings.[203] He often felt like he was being assaulted from every side, and his bitterness against the Catholic Church no doubt contributed to his overall hostility to the Jews, as he viewed the failure to convert them as his own. He said of the Catholics:

"Because the Papists, like the Jews, insist that anyone wishing to be saved must observe their ceremonies, they will perish like the Jews."[204]

He went from writing "That Jesus Christ Was Born a Jew" in defense of Jewish people in 1523 to twenty years later penning "On the Jews and Their Lies." James Carroll calls it a "homiletic massacre."[205] Paragraph after paragraph of vile venom with no redemption offered anywhere. It's a wonder how this man could even call himself a Christian after demonstrating such a root of bitterness. I have often wondered what happens when someone who dedicates his life to serving the Lord gets to heaven and finds out he was so terribly wrong. Considering we will be judged for every idle word, it is frightening to think of when someone who hates the Jews has to stand in front of the Jewish Messiah to give an account.

Luther explains, "I have permitted this booklet to go forth that I might be found among those who have resisted such poisonous undertaking of the Jews, and have warned the Christians to be on their guard against them. I would not have thought that a Christian would permit himself to be fooled by the Jews to share their exile and misery."[206] This book was an entire treatise that simply repeated the vituperation of thousands of sermons and harangues against the Jewish people over the previous 1,400 years. However, Luther also devised a detailed blueprint on how to ensure God's perceived wrath against them could be carried out. It was a systematic plan that could now be designed and implemented. In it, he asks a rhetorical question and then answers it himself:

"Now what are we going to do with these rejected, condemned, Jewish people? We should not suffer it after they are among us and we know about such lying, blaspheming and cursing among them, lest we become partakers of their lies, cursing, and blaspheming. We cannot extinguish the unquenchable fire of God's wrath (as the prophets say), nor convert the Jews. We must practice great mercy with prayer and godliness that we might rescue a few from the flame and violent heat. We are not permitted to take revenge. Revenge is around their neck a thousand times greater than we could wish them. I will give you my true counsel:

"First, that we avoid their synagogues and schools and warn people against them. And such should be done to the glory of God and Christendom, that God may see that we are Christians and have not knowingly tolerated such lying, cursing and blaspheming of His Son and His Christians. For what we so far have tolerated in ignorance (I myself did not know it), God will forgive us. Now that we know it, however, and in spite should before our very noses tolerate such a building for the Jew in which they blaspheme, curse, spit upon, and disgrace Christ and us, that would be simply too much, as if we did it ourselves and much worse, as you well know. Moses writes in Deuteronomy that where a city practiced idolatry, it should be entirely destroyed with fire and leave nothing. If he were living today he would be the first to put fire to the Jew schools and houses. [Followed by proofs from scripture.]

"Secondly, that you also refuse to let them own houses among us. For they practice the same thing in their houses as they do in their schools. Instead, you might place them under a roof, or stable, like the Gypsies, to let them know that they are not lords in our country as they boast, but in exile as captives; like with-out ceasing they howl bloody murder and complain about us before God.

"Thirdly, that you take away from them all of their prayer books and Talmuds wherein such lying, cursing, and blaspheming is taught.

"Fourthly, that you prohibit their Rabbis to teach. For they have forfeited the right to such an office, because they keep the poor Jews captive with the passage of Moses 7:11–12, who there commands them to obey their teachers under threat of losing body and soul. Moses clearly adds, 'What they teach you according to the law of the Lord.' This the profligates pass over, and use the obedience of the poor people for their own willfulness against the law of the Lord, and pour out for them such poison and blasphemy.

"Fifthly, that protection for Jews on highways be revoked. For they have no right to be in the land, because they are not lords, nor officials. They should stay at home. I am told that at this time a wealthy Jew is riding with twelve horses in our country. He wants to become a Kochab. [Star Bar-Kochba, 'Star Son,' false Messiah, was leader of the last rebellion of the Jews against the Romans 132/5 after Christ.] He practices his usury on princes and lords, land and people. High officials close an eye to it. If you princes and masters do not forbid land and highways to such usurers, I would like to assemble a cavalry against you, because you will learn from this book what the Jews are and how they are to be treated and their activities not to be protected. For you should not and cannot protect them unless you want to be partners of their abominations. What good would be the result, you may well consider and perish.

"Sixthly, that, their usury be prohibited, which was prohibited by Moses, where they are not lords in their own country over strange lands, and take away all the currency and silver and gold and put it away for safe-keeping. For this reason, everything they have they have stolen from us (as said above) and robbed through their usury, since they have no other income. Such money should be used as follows: whenever a Jew is truly converted, he be given one, two, or three hundred flo [measure of money] according to his person, that he may begin to support his poor wife and child and/or support the aged and infirm. For such property which was obtained dishonestly is cursed where it is not turned to good use with God's blessing.

"Finally: That young, strong Jews be given flail, ax, spade, spindle, and let them earn their bread in the sweat of their noses as imposed upon Adam's children, Genesis 3:19, 'In the sweat of thy face shalt thou eat bread, till thou return unto the ground; for out of it wast thou taken: for dust thou art, and unto dust shalt thou return.' For it will not do that they should let us cursed Goyim work in the sweat of our brow, while they, the holy people, devour our bread in laziness behind the stove and then boast that they are masters over the Christians, but their laziness should be driven from their back."[207]

When Kristallnacht (The Night of Broken Glass) was enacted in 1938, again in Germany as another pogrom, the blueprint could be clearly seen from a document from the sixteenth century. Luther's invective also coincided with his translation of the Bible into German and marked the beginnings of the rise of nationalism within Germany, which would result in the Holocaust four hundred years later.

Although the Reformation saw Jews obtain some individual rights and would eventually lead to their emancipation through the Age of Enlightenment, it was also a bitterly dark time for the Jews in Europe. As they were driven from Western Europe to the East, they began to face pogroms, state-sponsored riots against them, primarily for religious reasons. The peasantry would often get whipped up by charges of deicide or something else, and villages would be attacked. One of the most heinous instances was the Chmielnicki Uprising of 1648–49. Bands of Cossacks and Tartars went to war against the nobility who had tried to steal Bohdan Chmielnicki's land, but as usual, the Jews got caught in the crossfire. Ultimately, the Jews of Poland and beyond were savaged and almost wiped out.[208] While it's impossible to know the exact number that perished, it is known that three hundred communities were destroyed, with loss of life in the hundreds of thousands.

The Holocaust

The Holocaust, without question, is the nadir of Jewish history. With over five million perishing in the death camps, never before had an entire society been set up to exterminate a particular people. Death squads roamed throughout Europe looking for Jews to kill because, according to Hitler's *Mein Kampf*, the Jews were a problem and needed to be solved. Although it was quite obvious that Hitler, an occultist and Free Mason, had no regard for the God of the Bible, the question is: Would he have been able to do all he did without the help of the Church, whether it be actively or passively? The entire world could be held accountable for the abandonment of the Jewish people, as was witnessed by the saga of the St. Louis (the ship full of over nine hundred Jewish refugees that no country would allow in and which eventually had to return to Europe, with every passenger perishing in the camps). However, few had the power to intervene or could be held responsible for the prevailing sentiment about Hitler's number one victims as the Church did. Poland's decimation of over three million Jews could be laid at the feet of the Catholic Church, whose ongoing anti-Semitic attitudes were bred into the peasants' psyche until the Nazis invaded. The populace couldn't wait to hand them over. Much to the shock of their Polish accomplices, the Nazis had no more regard for them, and after the Jews were eliminated, they were next to the camps. In 1936, Cardinal Augustyn Hlond said in a sermon, "There will be the Jewish problem as long as the Jews remain. It is a fact that the Jews are fighting against the Catholic Church, persisting in free thinking, and are the vanguard of godlessness, Bolshevism and subversion."[209] This letter was read from the pulpits of Poland as the Catholic Church officially endorsed the boycott of Jewish businesses in Germany. Contrast this with the Danish

THE RED MARK ON GOD'S FOREHEAD

king, who wore a yellow star himself and eventually led all of Denmark to do the same so that not one Danish Jew perished in the Nazi onslaught.

Not all Catholics or Protestants were complicit, and the stories about the *Goyim Tzadikim* (Righteous Gentiles) are numerous. Many Catholics, including priests, and Protestant Christians went to their deaths in the camps alongside the Jews while trying to help stop the slaughter. It's also known that Pope Pius XII did make some attempts to protect the Jews at the end of the war and that he had equal disdain for the barbarism of both the Nazis and the Communists, but he remained officially silent when the Church could have prevented much more than it did. Pius held the same ambivalence toward the Jews as his predecessors because of the view that they are destined to suffer because of their crime against Yeshua. He actually put away a letter the previous pope had written against racism and anti-Semitism and abstained from signing the Allied declaration decrying the liquidation of European Jewry.[210] It's also known the Lutherans were quite complicit with the roundup of the Jews by handing over the baptismal records to identify which Christians had Jewish blood. By this time anti-Semitism was fully a racial issue due to the influence of occultists like Helena Blavatsky, 33rd degree Mason and founder of the Theosophic Society, who promoted the idea of the superiority of one race over another. The religious convictions of a person mattered little now. One's blood was the determinant of worthiness. In his book *Hitler's Pope*, John Cornell sums it up by saying:

"While there is an arguable distinction between racist anti-Semitism and religious anti-Judaism, this material, published in Rome during Pacelli's (the future Pope, Pius XII) school days, exemplifies a groundswell of vicious antipathy. That views such as these were promoted by the leading Jesuit journal, enjoying papal auspices, indicates their potential outreach and semblance of authority. Such prejudices were hardly inimical to the racist theories that would culminate in the Nazis' furious assault upon European Jewry in the Second World War. It is plausible indeed that these Catholic prejudices actually bolstered aspects of Nazi anti-Semitism."[211]

And it wasn't just Germany that got caught up in the anti-Jewish sentiment of the nineteenth and twentieth centuries. Captain Alfred Dreyfuss, a Jewish soldier in France, was falsely accused of treason by selling secrets to

Germany in 1894. Although he was exonerated twelve years later, L'Affaire, as it is known, deeply divided the country, and all the old hatred of predominantly Catholic France came to the surface. This no doubt played a part in the Vichy government's willingness to so readily cooperate with their German masters during WWII, including rounding up and sending over 77,000 French Jews to their deaths.

The human mind is the most powerful machine ever created. It has the ability to appreciate and worship God, unlike any other creature on earth. It can make incredible things, plan, design, and build societies, and has the capacity for love and beauty. It can write astounding music, poetry and literature, imagine breathtaking paintings, and create recipes that will produce untold pleasure. However, with the wrong information, it can also be an incredibly destructive power. Programmed with lies from the evil one, it will hate, kill, destroy, and ultimately reject the Creator. Most of humanity's history is dotted with murder, atrocities, and indescribable acts of cruelty and selfishness. God had to create a nation to give His Word to and bring through them the Saviour of the world. When Yeshua went to heaven, He sent the Holy Spirit to establish the Body of Messiah, the Commonwealth of Israel. One would think that the Gentiles within the Church would be grateful to the Jewish people for being the vehicle of their salvation from the flames of hell and do everything they could to overcome the satanic unbelief they are cursed with that prevents them from the receiving the same gift. Sadly, that has not been Christendom's legacy.

For almost the entire history of the Christian Church, starting even during the apostolic era, anti-Jewish attitudes were cultivated, promoted, and spread throughout every land. No institution has more Jewish blood on its hands than the Church itself through its demonization of the Jews. The Body that Yeshua died and rose again to create turned against the very people He came from. The Church fathers, wanting to separate Christianity from Judaism, aided their cause by making Jews and Jewish things hateful. Anything associated with the Jews was to be avoided, disdained, spoken against, and loathed. Calling Jews "beasts fit for the slaughter" and "cursed without redemption" allowed them to be viewed as subhuman. It led to Luther creating a detailed plan as to how to deal with them and culminated in the fires of the crematoriums in Auschwitz during the 1940s. It will also aid in the coming Holocaust of the Antichrist during the Great Tribulation. Zechariah 13:8 tells us two-thirds of the Jewish people will be slaughtered, amounting to double the victims of the Nazi genocide, as there won't be a North America they can hide in this time.

The human mind will accept whatever it is told, whether true or not. With close to two thousand years of obloquy and scorn directed at the Jews through lies, deceit, false and often ridiculous accusations, and disparaging attitudes, it's no wonder even well-meaning Christians don't accept what they consider to be "Jewish" things as important or required of them, even if in scripture.

Most believers today would strenuously deny they were anti-Semitic, and many would even profess a great love for the Jewish people and Israel. Yet because of the influence of the virulently anti-Jewish attitudes of the men who defined our theology, anything associated with being Jewish is looked at as needing to be separated from and avoided. One mega-church pastor recently declared:

"Peter, James, Paul elected to unhitch the Christian faith from their Jewish scriptures, and my friends, we must as well. And I'll tell you why. It's actually the same reason they did: because we must not make it difficult for those Gentiles who are turning to God. They didn't. We shouldn't either. The faith of the next generation may depend on our willingness and our ability to get this right. The faith of your neighbor may depend on it. And who knows? Someday, your faith may depend on it as well."[212]

So much for our faith being founded upon the apostles and the prophets. This is Marcion speaking from the grave, and the virus of his heresy plagues the vast majority of Christian theology today.

Furthermore, though Christians love Israel and the Jews, some will still use the name "Palestine" to refer to the Holy Land, and many Bibles even have the name on their maps. They will advocate a two-state solution to the Middle East conflict with the Palestinian people, who didn't even start using that name until after the Six-Day War in 1967. Why would believers who claim to hold true to the scriptures denigrate the land of the Messiah and God's chosen dwelling place by continuing to call it the same name given to it by a conquering pagan emperor who wanted to erase even the memory of Israel from history? Why refer to the place of God's promise by the name of a vile people who were hated enemies of the Israelites and have been gone from history for thousands of years? Why advocate for splitting up the land and sharing it with a people whose leaders refuse to make peace with their Jewish neighbours, whose stated aim is to "drive them into the sea"? God said the land will never be divided again and that Jacob's descendants would inherit it forever. The tendrils of anti-Semitism are everywhere in our faith.

Back to our original question in this chapter. Why has the Church strayed so far from the truth? Because it believed the lies, originating from Satan, that the Jews are cursed, are killers of the Messiah, and therefore the Hebrew scriptures have no part in what we believe today. Our justification for changing the Sabbath to Sunday (or any day we please), or ignoring the Feasts of the Lord and exchanging them with vile, pagan holidays, or eating animals that God, with much wisdom, told us not to eat—or whatever of the other multitude of ways we walk in disobedience—is because we think those things are somehow Jewish, and since we've been told God is done with the Jews, He's done with their things too. Compare this with what God says to Zechariah:

"So the angel who was speaking with me said to me, 'Proclaim, saying, "This is what the Lord of armies says: 'I am exceedingly jealous for Jerusalem and Zion. But I am very angry with the nations who are carefree; for while I was only a little angry, they furthered the disaster.' Therefore the Lord says this: 'I will return to Jerusalem with compassion; My house will be built in it,' declares the Lord of armies, 'and a measuring line will be stretched over Jerusalem.' Again, proclaim, saying, "This is what the Lord of armies says: 'My cities will again overflow with prosperity, and the Lord will again comfort Zion and again choose Jerusalem.""' (Zec 1:14–17).

The treason against God's Word runs very deep.

Antinomianism comes out of anti-Semitism, and just because Christians today might not have negative attitudes toward the Jewish people themselves, the men who established our theology certainly did; therefore, those who practise such things share in their errors.

Chapter 10—The Messianic Way

"Well, here's another nice mess you've gotten me into."

Oliver Hardy

"Now when they heard this, they were pierced to the heart, and said to Peter and the rest of the apostles, 'Brothers, what are we to do?' Peter said to them, 'Repent . . .'"

Act 2:37-38

Several years ago, I was asked by some friends to officiate a bar mitzvah for their son. They were not believers in Yeshua, and they knew I was. When they asked, I told them that if I did it, I would be sharing with their families what I believed. When they said no problem, I asked them more than once if they were sure, and they assured me that what I was proposing was ok. At one point a few months later, I again asked if they were really certain they wanted to do this. They replied that I was making a bigger deal out of it than it really was. I smiled, for little did they know.

For the next eight months or so, I taught their son the Hebrew alphabet and trained him to chant his parsha (Torah portion). On the big day, we had the ceremony in front of about one hundred people. The young man finished his part and then I did my speech. For the next fifteen minutes or so, I spoke about how it was impossible to keep Torah, but God promised one who would on our behalf. While I didn't directly say the name of Yeshua, everyone knew exactly what I was talking about. Several people walked out during my speech, and afterward at dinner, you could have sworn I had leprosy the way people avoided me. It was a hostile environment to be sure. However, right after I finished speaking and was tidying up, very unsettled by the anger of the people, one woman ran up to me and said, "God bless you!" She was probably the only believer in the crowd that day. Despite the intense rejection I experienced from everyone else, including the parents of the boy I bar mitzvahed, my relationship with whom I knew was now over, she reaffirmed that I had glorified God and had spoken truth to people who might never hear it again. It was just the encouragement I needed then.

I imagine it must have been very similar for a man almost two thousand years ago in a virtually identical situation.

"Now a Jew named Apollos, an Alexandrian by birth, an eloquent man, came to Ephesus; and he was proficient in the Scriptures. This man had been instructed in the way of the Lord; and being fervent in spirit, he was accurately speaking and teaching things about Yeshua, being acquainted only with the baptism of John; and he began speaking boldly in the synagogue. But when Priscilla and Aquila heard him, they took him aside and explained the way of God more accurately to him" (Act 18:24–26).

Preaching the gospel to a bunch of people who have been told their whole lives that Yeshua isn't for them is no mean task. It can make the most stout-hearted of people uneasy at the least. I knew the reaction I was going to get from my bar mitzvah crowd, and no matter how much you try to prepare for it and tell yourself to God be the glory, only a sociopath wouldn't be affected by that kind of anger and rejection. Add that to the grieving in your heart about the blindness, hard-heartedness, and lostness of the audience and it's a heavy burden to bear. It helps us to understand how God feels about people who reject Him and choose an eternity away from Him in the torment of flames, despite Him doing everything He can to convince them of His love.

I'm certain that although Apollos spoke with boldness and eloquence, facing people he knew were going to reject his message would be difficult. I remember being on a street outreach campaign back in New York City many years ago, handing out tracts to Jewish (and other) people. I had many wonderful conversations and led some people to the Lord, but there were times it was still pretty intimidating, and I believe it might very well have been for Apollos too. But just as God did with me at the bar mitzvah, He sent Apollos two people who believed to encourage him. Aquila and Priscilla, who had spent time with Paul making tents and no doubt received some wonderful instruction from him, were God's reinforcements to a man stepping out in faith to be a witness for Him.

What I love about the telling of this event is that when they heard him preaching, they realized he was missing something. He only knew of the baptism of John, which was for repentance. He wasn't aware of the baptism of the Holy Spirit, the infilling of the Spirit of God after we repent and come to believe in Yeshua. And how did they respond to this realization? They took him aside and explained to him the way of God more accurately. They didn't condemn or criticize him. They didn't go on Facebook or Twitter and denigrate him to their followers. They took him aside privately and filled in where he was lacking. After all, this man was doing the work of the Lord. He was boldly preaching where others were afraid to open their mouths. He was their ally, and they all worked for the same team. They didn't publicly rebuke or correct him like so many in the Body do today. They helped him.

It's the very reason God commissioned me to write this book and why I've used that verse as the subtitle. It's not for the purpose of condemnation but rather exhortation and correction. I love the Body of Messiah. Believers are my spiritual family, and I want only the best for them. I want to see the worldwide Body grow and prosper so we can have the abundant life Yeshua promised us in John 10:10 and win many souls for the kingdom. However, Christianity is in serious trouble today. There's very little blessing or power coming from it, certainly in North America. It's not influencing society to come back to God. Instead, it's adopting the ways of the world and conforming itself to the Babylonian/antichrist system that God says He will destroy in the last days. Because of this, God is being rejected by society. We've made the Church and its message so similar to the world, the world doesn't see any difference in what the Church offers, so it doesn't see any need for it. Why give up some of the pleasures in life when there's no real benefit? The message of salvation and eternal life are a lot harder to believe if there's no tangible evidence here and now. It's the radically changed life that convinces people that there's something to the gospel message. When someone who struggled with addiction or anger or depression is now delivered and has joy, or when someone can be content even in difficult circumstances, knowing God is going to take him or her through the situation and there's a purpose to our suffering, that's what people want and need in this life. Not some candy floss message about how God loves me but there's no proof behind it.

Ever since I came to faith over twenty-three years ago, I've seen what the Bible says the Church should be like and then looked at the Church and said, "They ain't the same." How is it that the book of Acts speaks about how the disciples had all things in common, and power and fear came over the people who saw them, yet today the Body is mocked, ridiculed, and isn't considered a threat? The kingdom of darkness should be terrified of the Church. It isn't. What has neutralized the power that Yeshua Himself endowed it with? Disobedience. In trying to be like the world, we have rejected God's commandments and compromised on just about everything. James tells us, "*You adulteresses, do you not know that friendship with the world is hostility toward God? Therefore, whoever wants to be a friend of the world makes himself an enemy of God*" (James 4:4).

The Messianic Lifestyle

As with all things of God, when the enemy of our souls sees a work or movement of God, he immediately sets forth to corrupt it and render it ineffective. The priesthood was established, and immediately Nadab and Abihu came and offered strange fire, which God forbade. The Church was launched, and Ananias and Saphira lied about what they were doing to receive honour from men. God dealt with both of these situations fairly quickly, but the problem never stops there. The corruption and watering down of the spiritual effectiveness of anything God does is a continual process, like waves in the ocean crashing against the rocks. Remember, all Satan and his hordes have on their hands is time to frustrate us until they are judged. He's got nothing better to do. God never sleeps, but neither does Lucifer, and the moment we let our guard down, he's there to get in and mess things up.

This entire book has addressed a serious problem: that we have rejected God's commands and told Him we're going to do it our way. It's the Frank Sinatra gospel. Not only has the Church done that, but Christians get mad when you try to explain to them what God's Word says, as I've demonstrated several times. The fact that an entire book needed to be written to help convince you that God's Word hasn't changed, nor has Yeshua's expectation that if you love Him, you'll keep His commandments, shows just how far we've strayed and been deceived. We haven't been careful as Paul was when he told the Corinthians " ... *so that no advantage would be taken of us by Satan, for we are not ignorant of his schemes*" (2 Cor 2:11). We've been duped, and it shows. However, the solution isn't difficult. As a matter of fact, it's written all over the Bible. It's *teshuva*. Repentance. We need to change our minds about how we approach God. He's already made it quite clear how He wants that to happen. We just need to believe His Word when He says so in it.

Messianic Judaism is a little-understood concept within Christianity today. While there are many different flavours of it, in essence it's a lifestyle. Yeshua was the Jewish Messiah. The apostles were all devout Jewish men. The Bible was written by Jews about a Jew. He is known as the God of Israel, of Abraham, Isaac, and Jacob. We're not talking about theological positions here. Again, that's Greco-Roman thinking. It's about a way of life. Again, why do the feasts and food cause so much consternation? Because those are part of our life-cycle. God is interested in the daily things and has given us a program to follow to make sure we're safely tucked away under His hand of protection by doing so. If Christianity were only about salvation, it wouldn't work. It's about how a saved person lives. In Hebrew it's called הֲלָכָה (halacha – to walk). We need to be so busy doing the things God called us to do that we don't have time to think about what lies and garbage the devil is trying to tempt us with. People are going to be drawn to Yeshua when we live like He did and we experience the power, freedom, and favour that comes with being obedient to God's loving instructions for our daily lives.

Romans 8:37 says we're to be *more than* overcomers. Today, the Church is full of underwhelmers. Instead of pillars in our congregations and society, we have caterpillars (thank you, David Jeremiah, for that one).

Instead of healing the sick, raising the dead, casting out demons, speaking in new tongues, and not being harmed by poison, Christianity today is being savaged by false teaching, failed marriages, debt and poverty, failed health, an inability to overcome life's basic challenges, and being ineffectual in influencing society. Why? Disobedience. We're told the blood has the power to defeat death, but if the sin hasn't been repented of, the blood can't wash us clean. We don't have the armour on to deflect the enemy's flaming darts. Christians are being taken out like wild turkeys in a field.

People will argue strenuously about what I've said in this book, but show me I'm wrong. You will know them by their fruit, and much of the fruit of Christianity is overripe, soft, and mushy. I once had the head of a denomination tell me he disagreed with Messianic congregations and wished that they were all "true New Testament congregations." I asked him what that meant, and his reply was that they would all have Sunday services. I replied, "That's your definition of a true New Testament congregation?" I was incredulous. This man had a PhD in theology too. Shows how much a theological education can be worth today. I retorted and asked that if his way was the correct way and mine wasn't, where were all the Jewish people coming into the Church then? He just kind of looked at me blankly. Sorry, but leaning on your credentials when you obviously don't know what your Bible clearly says because you've bought into the anti-Semitic theology of the Church fathers you studied to get your degree leaves you falling over. By the way, this same man, when we went to Yad Vashem, the Holocaust Museum in Israel, told our unbelieving Jewish tour guide about how wonderful Augustine's *City of God* was to read, while a quote from him demonizing the Jews was literally hanging right behind them. You can't make this stuff up. Another forehead slap.

Terminology

Many of the problems we have detailed come from a lack of understanding about what the Church actually is. First of all, the word "church" isn't even in the Bible. The word translated to church is usually ἐκκλησία, (*ekklésia*—Strong's # 1577),[213] which is more accurately translated an "assembly" or "congregation." The other times worship gatherings were described, the word "synagogue" was used. Never church.

The word church actually has its origins in, you guessed it, Greek mythology.

"In his classical study, 'The Myth of Kirke,' Robert Brown gives extensive meanings in the ancient Greek world and concludes that Circe's simple meaning is 'Circle' or 'Circular.' But it not only referred to a building or monument that was 'circular,' but one of its main meanings was its reference to the ancient Goddess 'Kirke' or 'Circe.' Circe was the great heathen daughter of the Sun God, famous for taming wild animals in her 'circus.' She also met Ulysses returning from the Trojan War and had an adulterous relationship with him that produced, as one of the children, Latinus, the supposed founder of the Latin race. And how is Circe pictured in the classical accounts? She is shown holding a golden cup in her hand mixed with wine and drugs through which she controls the kings of the world (like Ulysses)."[214]

Can we find a reference to this in the Bible? I'm glad you asked.

"Then one of the seven angels who had the seven bowls came and spoke with me, saying, 'Come here, I will show you the judgment of the great prostitute who sits on many waters, with whom the kings of the earth committed acts of sexual immorality, and those who live on the earth became drunk with the wine of her sexual immorality.' And he carried me away in the Spirit into a wilderness; and I saw a woman sitting on a scarlet beast, full of blasphemous names, having seven heads and ten horns. The woman was clothed in purple and scarlet, and adorned with gold, precious stones, and pearls, holding in her hand <u>*a gold cup full of abominations and of the unclean things of her*</u> <u>*sexual immorality*</u>*, and on her forehead a name was written, a mystery: 'BABYLON THE GREAT, THE MOTHER OF PROSTITUTES AND OF THE ABOMINATIONS OF THE EARTH.' And I saw the woman drunk with the blood of the saints, and with the blood of the witnesses of Jesus. When I saw her, I wondered greatly"* (Rev 17:1–6, emphasis mine).

So we've named our gatherings and even the Body of Messiah itself after a pagan goddess who God tells us is the spirit called the Whore of

Babylon that murders the saints. Each day of the week and month of the year in our calendar is named after a pagan god or goddess. How did the Hebrews refer to the days of the week? Day one, day two, day three … The paganization of society is literally everywhere we look, which is to be expected, but God's set-apart (holy) assembly, His own Body, should not take part in it, yet almost every aspect of our language and practices have been defiled by the Antichrist system. Most Jews today walking into a church service wouldn't recognize that Christianity came out of Judaism, despite the fact our entire worship service is founded on the first-century synagogue system.

Our terminology is extremely important. For those of us in Jewish ministry, it becomes all the more so, but it should be for everyone. Translating Hebrew concepts, written in Greek to Latin or other languages, leads us far away from the original meaning and intent. Many nominal church-goers think Christ was Yeshua's last name. *Christos* was the Greek translation for *Mashiach* (Messiah), or Anointed One. There were many messiahs in the Old Covenant. When someone took an office, whether prophet, priest, or king, they were anointed, but Daniel 9 speaks of *the* Anointed One. Even the name "Jesus" doesn't convey what His name meant. Yeshua means salvation. I'm not opposed to using the name Jesus per se, as untold millions have been saved by it over the centuries. God doesn't insist we say His name a certain way to be saved, so however it's pronounced in any language is fine. However, cultural sensitivities must also be taken into account when we witness. Talking to a Jewish person about Jesus Christ, worshipping on Sunday, or enjoying ham sandwiches while going to church on Christmas Day and you are no longer speaking about the Jewish Messiah.

The Commonwealth of Israel

What the Church actually is, as Paul tells us in Ephesians 2:11, is the Commonwealth of Israel. Countries that are part of a commonwealth, such as Britain's, share in special privileges and preferred relationships, such as trade and finance, military protection, education, and systems of government. While being part of the Commonwealth from another country such as Australia, Canada, India, or Jamaica didn't make their citizens British, they got to experience the advantages of the British people.

Israel's Commonwealth works the same way. Although becoming a believer doesn't make one Jewish (as some would like to believe, spiritually or otherwise), Gentiles get all the of the perks that Israel did in its relationship with God. All the covenants God made with Israel, especially the New Covenant, are now extended to anyone who believes that Yeshua shed His blood to cleanse us of sin's wages, which is death.

The big issue concerns how that Commonwealth works. What are the expectations? The simple and obvious answer is "What God told Israel to do." If Gentiles are being grafted into Israel, as Paul tells us in in Romans 11, does it not make sense that they would be expected to live the same way God told His firstborn to live, through the Torah? While we dealt with this extensively in chapter 5, I reiterate that, logically, it only makes sense that when you become part of a unit, whether a family, community, organization, etc., you adopt that unit's customs and practices. If Israel is the root, then the branches need to be fed by it. If we're worshipping the God of Israel and become part of the Commonwealth of Israel, we ought to live and worship as Israel was instructed to do through the commandments of Torah. There is no other way given to us in scripture. I've heard so many people say, "Now we're called to walk by the Spirit." Amen. And just how do you think the Spirit is going to tell you to walk? By the very commands He gave Moses. God cannot and will not contradict Himself. If you get a rhema (spoken word) that contradicts the logos (written word), it is not of God. It's another spirit. The God who gave Israel, His firstborn, the Shabbat will not tell the younger child that Sunday, or any day, is fine with Him. He will tell that child, who is now part of Israel's family, to worship on Shabbat. If He told Israel His appointed times were mandatory, the newest members to the family don't get to choose their own days and customs to practise on those days, especially when they originated from pagan origins.

"The Romanized Western Church has historically taken a perversion, modified it to some extent— sometimes not at all—then added it to an already non-scriptural man-made observance and stamped 'Holy' on it. Now they have their 'tradition.'"[215]

Ruth said it best:

"Do not plead with me to leave you or to turn back from following you; for where you go, I will go, and where you sleep, I will sleep. Your people shall be my people, and your God, my God. Where you die, I will die, and there I will be buried. May the Lord do so to me, and worse, if anything but death separates me from you" (Ruth 1:16–17).

Your people shall be my people, and your God, my God. Ruth clung to her mother-in-law because she knew that God was with her, even though it might have appeared He had abandoned her. How is it people figure they can march into an institution that began after 1,500 years of preparation with a particular nation and change all the furniture, the locks, and the terms of the lease? The expected attitude a Gentile should have is that God adopted them into His family so they should be respectful of the rules of the house. These are the days Israel is to show up? I'm part of Israel, so I show up. These are the animals that we don't eat? I don't eat them either because Israel's God said not to. Anything else is arrogance and an offense to God. In the Millennium, Zechariah tells us:

"The Lord of armies says this: 'It will yet turn out that peoples will come, that is, the inhabitants of many cities. The inhabitants of one city will go to another, saying, "Let's go at once to plead for the favor of the Lord, and to seek the Lord of armies; I also will go." So many peoples and mighty nations will come to seek the Lord of armies in Jerusalem, and to plead for the favor of the Lord.' The Lord of armies says this: 'In those days ten people from all the nations will grasp the garment of a Jew, saying, "Let us go with you, for we have heard that God is with you"'" (Zec 8:20–23).

In the Millennium, the Gentiles, like Ruth, will ask the Jews to take them to God because they understand that God is with them. Even in Ephesians 2:12, Paul says it was the Gentiles who were far off from God, not the Jews. Even though most don't believe in Yeshua as Messiah today, He's still in the midst of them, hidden right in the Torah and their biblical customs and practices, waiting to be found.

In Revelation 12, John sees a vision of Satan being cast to the Earth and he says:

"So the dragon was enraged with the woman, and went off to make war with the rest of her children, who keep the commandments of God and hold to the testimony of Yeshua" (Rev 12:17).

And again, he tells us:

"Here is the perseverance of the saints who keep the commandments of God and their faith in Yeshua" (Rev 14:12).

The description of a remnant believer during the Tribulation period is one who keeps the commandments first and then believes in Yeshua. We need both. The commands without Yeshua are a works-based righteousness, but Yeshua without the commands leads to lawlessness, which is anarchy. Everyone does what is right in his own eyes.

The prophet Jeremiah had a tough ministry. He called the people of Israel to repent for years, yet most refused, even after judgement came. The heart of God is revealed when the Lord tells Jeremiah to write:

"This is what the Lord says: 'Stand by the ways and see and ask for the ancient paths, where the good way is, and walk in it; then you will find a resting place for your souls'" (Jer 6:16).

Just reading this lowers my heart rate and blood pressure. It was a call to come back to Torah. God calls the ways of the Law the "ancient paths." They are good, and when we do walk in His commandments, we find shalom for our souls. Where is the shalom in the Assembly today? Is there peace in the family, in the congregations? By and large, I'd have to say no, and I've been in enough churches to know. And the reason? Disobedience. Belief is not enough. Faith without works is dead. Works are defined by God in His Torah. It's simple. We're the ones who complicate it. And God has a red mark on His forehead.

Dr. Robert Heidler says in his book *The Messianic Church Arising*:

"*Once upon a time* ... there was a church that *worked*. Its members loved each other, took care of widows and orphans, fed the hungry, and transformed cities. It taught the Bible, built believers to maturity, and satisfied the longing in their hearts to touch God. This church didn't just *talk* about the power of God: it healed the sick, raised the dead, and cast out demons.

It won the lost with incredible effectiveness, discipled its converts, and equipped them to minister. Its effectiveness was not limited to one culture or ethnic group. It grew with explosive power wherever it was planted.

"It's the church we have all been looking for, but never found … a church you and I have never seen, but I fervently believe we soon will. This church has often been called the *early* church, the *New Testament* Church, or the *first-century* church. For reasons we will soon see, I like to call it the *Messianic Church*. It's a church that would work in any generation. It's the Church as GOD designed it."[216]

Replace the word "church" with "community," "congregation," or "the Body" and is this not, like he said, exactly what we're looking for? I too long to see the Body of Messiah walk in its authority and *dunamis* (power). That's the reason for this book. Not to condemn but to call God's Assembly to *teshuvah*, to return to Him and live a sanctified life, free from the defilement of the world.

God's people today aren't completely in error. Many still preach salvation. However, there is a more accurate way, one filled with blessing, favour, power, joy, unity, assurance, and the peace that surpasses all understanding. It's through obeying His commandments, His loving instructions for us to be safe and prosper in this world. This is not a secret formula that only a few favoured initiates find. It's available to anyone who desires to know. If you seek, you shall find. Let's all walk the ancient paths and find that shalom.

Acknowledgements

No book has ever been written in a vacuum and this one is no different. Although the author is the one who gets the credit and accolades, there are always people behind the scenes who have supported, sacrificed and been there to encourage us to get the job done.

I first want to thank my wife Milena and son Yossi who championed my long hours in my office. Knowing that this book was a calling, you both encouraged me every step of the way and kept telling me this book was necessary. Milena has always been a rock for me in ministry and does so much to take the burdens off so that I can do what God has called me to do, many times at great inconvenience to herself. Yossi is a constant source of encouragement and uplifting words. For someone so young to have just the right words and actions so often is a marvel to me and he often convicts me that I need to be more like that. You make your dad proud and hopeful about humanity when the desire to blow the whole thing up hits me hard.

To all of my supporters at the Lamb Video Network (www.lambnetwork.tv), it was for you this book was written. The emails, texts and phone calls I got speaking about how excited they were about the book and pushing me along when I struggled made the journey easier. Mark Smith, founder of the Lamb Network has given me a platform to air my ravings about what I think the Bible says and anytime I needed something done, he has been right on it.

To my friend Tracy from Kyoto Coffee in Peterborough, Ontario, your wares often kept my eyes open and heart beating long after they wanted to quit. The expression I can do all things through Yeshua and coffee certainly was true for me in this journey. Your coffee is truly the best in the world and I've tried enough all over the place to say that with confidence. Many nights I stumbled out of my office barely missing walls and furniture after writing longer than I should have but the next morning was all right after that first glorious sip.

To my friend and homeopath Lloyd, were it not for your help over the years to keep my health in order, I literally don't think I would be alive to have written this book. You have helped me overcome so many physical challenges, come of them in the truly bizarre category that I am forever grateful. We will always have our rabies-tainted coffee story too.

Thank you Linda and Jackie, my web, advertising and social media team. Your creative ideas helped make the promotion of this book a reality and none of this could have been done without you and your belief in the project encouraged me. I also want to thank Friesen Press for the professional way they walked me through the whole process. Writing the book is easy. Getting it to market is the hard part and the team at Friesen worked their magic so you the reader can actually enjoy what I've done.

Finally, all glory goes to God through Yeshua the Messiah. This book was my stewardship and I recall after dragging my heals for several years the day when I was in prayer and He asked me ever-so quietly "Are you going to write My book?" I knew I had to get on it at that point. This book is to bring honour to His name and His word and I trust that I was successful in doing that. John the Baptist said "He must increase but I must decrease." I pray that is the case with The Red Mark On God's Forehead.

Endnotes

Chapter 1

1. Terry J. Woychowski, *The Energy To Lead: The Thermodynamics of Leadership,* (Commerce Township, MI: Level V Advising, 2007), 130.

2. "The Facts and Stats on '33,000 Denominations,'" *Evangelical Catholic Apologetics*, accessed 4/13/2022, http://www.philvaz.com/apologetics/a106. htm.

3. "Antinomianism," *Theopedia*, accessed 4/13/2022, https://www.theopedia. com/antinomianism.

4. *Merriam-Webster.com Dictionary*, s.v. "antinomian," accessed April 13, 2022, https://www.merriam-webster.com/dictionary/antinomian.

5. Michael Lake, "Examining the Son of Perdition—Part 1," *Kingdom Intelligence Briefing*, last modified 2/23/2015, accessed 4/13/2022, http://kingdomintelligencebriefing.com/examining-the-son-of-perdition-part-1/.

6. Dr. Michael K. Lake, *The Shinar Directive: Preparing the Way for the Son of Perdition*, (Crane, MO: Defender Publishing, 2014), 104.

7. *ProCon.org*, accessed August 16, 2018, http://israelipalestinian.procon.org/view.answers.php?questionID=000359.

8. "Whether sin is fittingly defined as a word, deed, or desire contrary to the eternal law?" *Summa Theologica*, accessed April 25, 2022, https://www.ccel. org/ccel/aquinas/summa.FS_Q71_A6.html.

9. Kenny Jahng, "Eyebrow-Raising Facts About Church Tithing That Clearly Defines the Generosity Gap," *Kenny Jahng. com*, accessed April 13, 2022, http://www.kennyjahng.com/facts-church-tithing-clearly-defines-generosity-gap/.

10. Scott McKnight, "Jesus Vs. Paul," *Christianity Today*, last modified December 3, 2010, accessed April 13, 2022, https://www.christianitytoday. com/ct/2010/december/9.25.html.

11   Accessed August 19, 2018, https://www.jesuswordsonly.com/books/80-paul-admits-often-uninspired.html.

12   Dr. Michael K. Lake, *The Kingdom Priesthood*, (Seymour, MO: Biblical Life Publishing, 2020), 167.

13   Roy Zuck, *Job*, (Chicago, IL: The Moody Bible Institute, 1978), 9.

14   Ellen O'Gorman, "Cato the Elder and the destruction of Carthage," *The Free Library*, last modified March 22, 2004, accessed April 14, 2022, https://www.thefreelibrary.com/Cato+the+Elder+and+the+destruction+of+Carthage.-a0127009576.

15   Joel Stucki, "Not Under Law But Under Grace," *Unlocking the Bible*, last modified January 24, 2017, accessed April 18, 2022, https://unlockingthebible.org/2017/01/not-undr-law-but-under-grace/.

16   A. J. Jacobs, "The Year of Living Biblically," (New York, NY: Simon & Schuster, 2007), 328.

17   "Ecthra," *Bible Hub*, accessed April 18, 2022, https://biblehub.com/greek/2189.htm.

18   "Temple Warning," *Bible History*, accessed September 17, 2018, https://www.bible-history.com/archaeology/israel/temple-warning.html.

19   Jack Wellman, "What Is the Biblical Definition Of Holy?" *What Christians Want to Know*, accessed September 17, 2018, https://www.whatchristianswanttoknow.com/what-is-the-biblical-definition-of-holy/.

20   Matt Slick, "What Is Legalism?" *Christian Apologetics and Research Ministry*, last modified May 19, 2010, accessed April 18, 2022, https://carm.org/about-the-church/what-is-legalism/.

21   Cecil Maranville, "What Is the Teaching of Galatians on Law and Grace?" *Life, Hope & Truth*, accessed April 18, 2022, https://lifehopeandtruth.com/bible/law-and-grace/galatians-law-and-grace/.

22   Ibid.

Chapter 2

23   Fred Burner, "Get out of the Box, *The Discussion Table Blog*, accessed April 18, 2022, https://thediscussiontable.wordpress.com/about/.

24   "Notes on Customs, Traditions, Folkways, Mores ..." *Christ's College*, last modified July 26, 2007, accessed April 18, 2022, https://christcollegemsw.blogspot.com/2007/07/notes-on-folkways-mores.html.

25   Scott Manning, "Process of Copying the Old Testament by Jewish Scribes," *Scott Manning*, last modified March 17, 2007,

accessed April 18, 2022, https://scottmanning.com/content/
process-of-copying-the-old-testament-by-jewish-scribes/.

26 "Why Are Cultural Traditions Important?" *Reference.com*, last modified
April 12, 2020, accessed April 18, 2022, https://www.reference.com/
world-view/cultural-traditions-important-371702b90743ebec.

27 Phillip Schaff, *History of the Christian Church Vol. 1*, second edition,
(Peabody, MA: Hendrickson Publishers, Inc., 2002), 460.

28 "The Freedom of Slavery," *Christian Ambassadors*, last modified May
2014, accessed April 18, 2022, https://christambassadors.files.wordpress.
com/2014/05/the-freedom-of-slavery-romans-612-23.pdf.

Chapter 3

29 Yusha Evans, "Pagan Origins of Birthdays," *Just Dawah*, accessed
April 18, 2022, https://www.justdawah.org/resources/festivals/
pagan-origins-of-birthdays.

30 "Birthdays: Pagan/Occult Origins & The Highest of All Holy Days
(Holidays) in the Satanic Bible," *Still Waters Revival Books*, last modified
August 2, 2018, accessed April 18, 2022, https://www.sermonaudio.com/
new_details3.asp?ID=18801.

31 Ibid.

32 "The Book of Enoch," *Hidden Bible*, accessed April 18, 2022, http://www.
hiddenbible.com/enoch/online.html.

33 Bill Salus, "Are Demons the Disembodied Spirits of the Nephilim?"
Prophecy Depot Ministries, last modified February 7, 2021, accessed
April 18, 2022, http://www.prophecydepotministries.net/2021/
are-demons-the-disembodied-spirits-of-the-nephilim/.

34 Dr. Michael K. Lake, *The Shinar Directive: Preparing the Way for the Son of
Perdition*, 73.

35 Thomas Horn, *Zenith 2016*, (Crane, MO: Defender Publishing, 2013), 189.

36 "Nimrod," *The Rain*, accessed April 18, 2022, https://therain.org/appen-
dixes/app28.html.

37 "Who Was Nimrod?" *Associates for Biblical Research*, accessed
April 18, 2022, https://biblearchaeology.org/research/
founders-corner/4126-who-was-nimrod.

38 Dr. Michael K. Lake, *The Shinar Directive: Preparing the Way for the Son of
Perdition*, 91.

39   "Nimrod & Semiramis," accessed January 23, 2021, http://whale.to/c/nimrod.html.

40   Wikipedia, "Occult," *Wikipedia*, last modified March 13, 2022, accessed April 18, 2022, https://en.wikipedia.org/wiki/Occult.

41   Mark O'Connell and Raje Airey, *The Complete Encyclopedia of Signs & Symbols*, (Leicester, UK: Southwater, 2012), 6.

42   Wikipedia, "Remphan," *Wikipedia*, last modified April 1, 2022, accessed April 18, 2022, https://en.wikipedia.org/wiki/Remphan.

43   "How Saturn's Golden-Age Celebration Became Christmas," accessed April 18, 2022, *Astrology Hub*, https://astrologyhub.com/io-saturnalia-a-celebration-of-a-golden-age/.

44   "What Are the Origins of Common Christmas Symbols?" *United Church of God*, last modified November 9, 2011, accessed April 18, 2022, https://www.ucg.org/the-good-news/what-are-the-origins-of-common-christmas-symbols.

45   Jo Adetunji, "The Holly and the Ivy: How Pagan Practices Found Their Way into Christmas, *The Conversation*, accessed April 18, 2022, https://theconversation.com/the-holly-and-the-ivy-how-pagan-practices-found-their-way-into-christmas-52343.

46   "Danteworlds," *University of Texas at Austin*, accessed April 18, 2022, http://danteworlds.laits.utexas.edu/circle9.html.

47   Matthew Sewell, "Thor, St. Boniface, and the Origin of the Christmas Tree," *Church Pop*, last modified December 24, 2014, accessed April 18, 2022, https://www.churchpop.com/2014/12/24/thor-st-boniface-and-the-origin-of-the-christmas-tree/.

48   Heather Taylor, "Meet Haddon Sundblom, Creator of Coca-Cola's Santa Claus," *Advertising Week*, accessed April 18, 2022, https://www.advertisingweek360.com/meet-haddon-sundblom-creator-coca-colas-santa-claus/.

49   Tanya Basu, "Who Is Krampus? Explaining the Horrific Christmas Beast," *National Geographic*, last modified December 5, 2018, accessed April 18, 2022, https://www.nationalgeographic.com/history/article/131217-krampus-christmas-santa-devil.

50   "The Pope and the Bent cross—Core Satanism Revealed," *Am Redeemed*, last modified May 12, 2016, accessed April 25, 2022, https://amredeemed.com/pope-bent-cross-core-satanism-revealed/.

51   "Gaal," *Biblehub*, accessed April 18, 2022, https://biblehub.com/hebrew/1350.htm.

52   "Qadash," *Biblehub*, accessed April 18, 2022, https://biblehub.com/
      hebrew/6942.htm.

53   "Changing Sabbath to Sunday," *Pilgrim's Rest Presents*, modified July 7, 2005,
      accessed April 18, 2022, https://www.sdadefend.com/MINDEX%20Tracts/
      BS-26-Sabbath-to-Sunday.pdf.

Chapter 4

54   "What Are The Origins of Easter?" *Got Questions*, accessed April 18,
      2022, https://www.gotquestions.org/easter-origins.html.

55   "The Truth about Easter Traditions," *Alpha Omega Publications*, last
      modified April 5, 2012, accessed April 18, 2022, https://www.aop.com/blog/
      the-truth-about-easter-traditions.

56   Michael Scheifler, "The 40 Days of Weeping for Tammuz (Lent)," *Hope of
      Israel*, accessed April 18, 2022, https://www.hope-of-israel.org/lent.htm.

57   Austin Cline, "The Pagan Origins of Valentine's Day," *Learn Religions*, last
      modified February 20, 2018, accessed April 18, 2022, https://www.learnreli-
      gions.com/christian-holiday-pagan-origins-of-valentines-day-250892.

58   "The Violent, Sexy, Pagan Origins of Valentine's Day," *Universal
      Life Church Monastery*, last modified February 8, 2021,
      accessed April 18, 2022, https://www.themonastery.org/blog/
      the-violent-sexy-pagan-origins-of-valentines-day.

59   Austin Cline, "The Pagan Origins of Valentine's Day."

60   "10 Theories on the Origins of the Valentine's Heart," *List Verse*, last
      modified February 8, 2013, accessed April 18, 2022, https://listverse.
      com/2013/02/08/10-theories-on-the-origins-of-the-valentines-heart/.

61   Sarah LeDuc, "The History of Cupid," *Wedding Bee*, last modified
      February 9, 2021, accessed April 18, 2022, https://www.weddingbee.com/
      engagement/the-history-of-cupid/.

62   "Who is that 'Angelical' Cupid? Tammuz, Nimrod?" *The Manifestation of
      Reality*, last modified February 14, 2009, accessed April 18, 2022, https://
      therealtemple.blogspot.com/2009/02/who-is-that-angelical-cupid-tammuz.
      html.

63   "Samhain," *History*, last modified October 19, 2021, accessed April 18,
      2022, https://www.history.com/topics/holidays/samhain.

64   Joe Schimmel, "Halloween: A Satanic Holiday," *Good Fight Ministries*,
      accessed April 18, 2022, https://www.goodfight.org/articles/cults-occult/
      halloween-satanic-holiday/.

65 Ibid.

66 Les Hewitt, "Stingy Jack and the History of the Jack-o'-Lantern," *Historic Mysteries*, last modified October 27, 2015, accessed April 18, 2022, https://www.historicmysteries.com/the-legend-of-stingy-jack/.

Chapter 5

67 Charlotte Hempel, "Community Structures in the Dead Sea Scrolls: Admission, Organization, Disciplinary Procedures," *Academia*, last modified 1999, accessed April 18, 2022, https://www.academia.edu/3662483/Community_Structures_In_the_Dead_Sea_Scrolls_Admission_Organization_Disciplinary_Procedures.

68 "Ger," *Biblehub*, accessed April 18, 2022, https://biblehub.com/hebrew/1616.htm.

69 Phillip Schaff, *History of the Christian Church Vol. 1*, second edition, (Peabody, MA: Hendrickson Publishers, Inc., 2002), 337.

70 Ibid.

71 Ibid.

72 Joel Stucki, "Not under Law but under Grace," *Unlocking the Bible*, last modified January 24, 2017, accessed April 18, 2022, https://unlockingthebible.org/2017/01/not-under-law-but-under-grace/.

Chapter 6

73 "Shabath," *Biblehub*, accessed April 19, 2022, https://biblehub.com/hebrew/7673.htm.

74 "Napahs," *Biblehub*, accessed April 19, 2022, https://biblehub.com/hebrew/5314.htm.

75 Victor P. Hamilton, *The Handbook on the Pentateuch*, (Grand Rapids, MI: Baker Academic, 2006), 27.

76 Michael McLain, *Numerology*, accessed June 17, 2021, http://www.astrology-numerology.com/numerology.html.

77 Samuele Bacchiocchi, *From Sabbath to Sunday*, (Rome: Pontifical Gregorian University Press, eighteenth printing, 2005), 21.

78 Richard Amiel McGough, "The Biblical Meaning of the Number Seven," *Bible Wheel*, accessed June 17, 2021, http://www.biblewheel.com/topics/Seven_Meaning.asp.

79 Dr. Gary Baxter, The Seventh Day, A Defence of the Bible, last accessed May 31, 2022, https://www.adefenceofthebible.com/2022/04/13/the-seven-day-week/

80 *Sabbath vs. Sunday*, accessed June 17, 2021, http://sabbath-vs-sunday.net/hs/hschp3.htm

81 "The Sabbath and the 8th day," *Catholicism and Adventism*, last modified December 31, 2003, accessed April 19, 2022, http://blog.theotokos.co.za/?p=266.

82 Ibid.

83 Dan Vander Lugt, "Do We Disobey God When We Don't Worship on Saturday, the Sabbath?" *Questions.org*, accessed April 20, 2022, https://questions.org/attq/do-we-disobey-god-when-we-dont-worship-on-saturday-the-sabbath/.

84 Samuele Bacchiocchi, *From Sabbath to Sunday*, 22.

85 Ibid, 20.

86 Henry Sheldon, *The History of the Christian Church, Vol. 1*, (Peabody, MA: Hendrickson Publishers, Inc., 1988), 274.

87 Phillip Schaff, *History of the Christian Church Vol. 1*, second edition, (Peabody, MA: Hendrickson Publishers, Inc., 2004), 202.

88 Ibid. 478.

89 "Methodist Quotes About the Sabbath," *Sabbath Truth*, accessed April 19, 2022, https://www.sabbathtruth.com/sabbath-history/denominational-statements-on-the-sabbath/id/methodist.

90 Samuel Owusu, "Vatican Declares: The Catholic Church Is above The Bible," *Am Redeemed*, last modified July 15, 2018, accessed April 19, 2022, https://amredeemed.com/vatican-declares-the-catholic-church-is-above-the-bible/.

91 "Olam," *Biblehub*, accessed April 19, 2022, https://biblehub.com/hebrew/5769.htm.

92 "Holy Convocation—What does the Bible say about Convocation," accessed July 3, 2021, http://messianicjews.com.au/articles/details/8/Holy-Convocation-What-does-the-Bible-say-about-Convocation.

93 Samuele Bacchiocchi, *From Sabbath to Sunday*, 90.

94 Ibid., 93.

95 Ibid.

96 Ibid., 108.

97 "What Is the 'Lord's Day' of Revelation 1:10?" *Sabbath*, accessed April 19, 2022 https://www.sabbath.org/index.cfm/fuseaction/Basics.FAQ/ID/168/ What-is-Lords-Day--Revelation-1-10.htm.

98 "The Book of Revelation," *Cranfordville.com*, last modified May, 9, 2009, accessed April 19, 2022, http://cranfordville.com/IBC%20Cologne/ BibleSession10.pdf.

99 Samuele Bacchiocchi, *From Sabbath to Sunday*, 127.

100 "What is the 'Lord's Day' of Revelation 1:10?" *Sabbath,* accessed April 19, 2022, https://www.sabbath.org/index.cfm/fuseaction/Basics.FAQ/ID/168/ What-is-Lords-Day--Revelation-1-10.htm.

101 Wikipedia, "Red Herring," *Wikipedia*, last modified March 25, 2022, accessed April 19, 2022, https://en.wikipedia.org/wiki/Red_herring.

102 John T. Lowe, "Didache," *World History Encyclopedia*, last modified July 22, 2015, accessed April 19, 2022, https://www.worldhistory.org/Didache/.

103 *The Didache*, accessed April 19, 2022, http://www.thedidache.com/.

104 "The Didache and the Sabbath," *Church of God News*, last modified July 7, 2017, accessed April 19, 2022, http://www.cogwriter.com/news/ church-history/the-didache-and-the-sabbath/.

105 Ibid.

106 "DIalogismos," *Biblehub*, accessed April 19, 2022, https://biblehub.com/ greek/1261.htm.

107 Bob Pickle, "Lord's Day???" *Pickle Publishing*, accessed April 19, 2022, http://www.pickle-publishing.com/papers/sunday-fraud.htm.

Chapter 7

108 Ola Rybacka, "Quotes About Time," *Time Camp*, last modified January 3, 2022, accessed April 19, 2022, https://www.timecamp.com/blog/2016/06/ quotes-about-time/.

109 Stephen Hawking, *The Illustrated A Brief History of Time*, (New York, NY: Bantam Books, 1996), 34.

110 John Fuller, "Does Time Change Speed?" *How Stuff Works*, accessed April 19, 2022, https://science.howstuffworks.com/science-vs-myth/everyday-myths/time-dilation1.htm.

111 Daniel Fuchs, *Israel's Holy Days in Type and Prophecy*, (Neptune, NJ: Loizeaux Brothers, 1985), 10.

112 "Questions and Concepts for Parsha Vayikrah," *Torah Resource Center*, accessed April 19, 2022, http://www.yashanet.com/shabbat/parsha/vayikrah.htm.

113 Brad Scott, "Hebrew Mind vs. Greek Mind," *Wild Branch Ministry*, accessed April 20, 2022, https://www.wildbranch.org/teachings/hebrew-greek-mind/lesson7.html.

114 Robert Heidler, *The Messianic Church Arising*, (Corinth, TX: Glory of Zion International Ministries, 2006), 97.

115 "Bedikat Chametz: Search for Chametz," *Chabad*, accessed April 20, 2022, https://www.chabad.org/holidays/passover/pesach_cdo/aid/117217/jewish/Bedikat-Chametz-Search-for-Chametz.htm.

116 "Chamets," *Biblehub*, accessed April 20, 2022, https://biblehub.com/hebrew/2557.htm.

117 "Seor," *Biblehub*, accessed April 20, 2022, https://biblehub.com/hebrew/7603.htm.

118 "Nuph," *Biblehub*, accessed April 20, 2022, https://biblehub.com/hebrew/5130.htm.

119 Roger Waite, "The Resurrection and the Wave Sheaf Offering," accessed April 20, 2022 http://www.rogerswebsite.com/articles/TheResurrectionandtheWavesheafOffering.pdf.

120 Alfred Edersheim, *The Temple, Its Ministry and Services*, (Peabody, MA: Hendrickson Publishers Inc., 1994), 210.

121 Wikipedia, "Pentecost," *Wikipedia*, last modified April 20, 2022, accessed April 20, 2022, https://en.wikipedia.org/wiki/Pentecost.

122 "Renewed Covenant," *Third Mill*, accessed April 20, 2022, https://thirdmill.org/answers/answer.asp/file/40555.

123 Natan Lawrence, "New Covenant or Renewed Covenant? What Are Its Terms and Conditions?" last updated Novermber 17, 2017, accessed August 10, 2022, https://hoshanarabbah.org/blog/2017/11/17/new-covenant-or-renewed-covenant/

124 Jamie Geller, "What's the Deal with Dairy On Shavuot?" last updated May 11, 2021, accessed April 20, 2022, https://jamiegeller.com/holidays/whats-the-deal-with-dairy-on-shavuot-an-easy-guide-to-the-holiday/.

125 Elon Gilad, "Rosh Hashanah Wasn't Always the 'New Year.' Here's This Jewish Holiday's History," *Haaretz*, last modified, September 5, 2021, accessed April 20, 2022, https://www.haaretz.com/jewish/the-history-of-rosh-hashanah-which-wasn-t-always-the-new-year-1.5301295.

126 "How the Feast of Trumpets Became Rosh Hashana," *One for Israel*, last modified September 4, 2018, accessed April 20, 2022, https://www.oneforisrael.org/holidays/rosh-chodesh-celebrating-the-new-moon-2/.

127 Allan R. Aguirre, *The Feasts Unlocked*, (Park City, UT: Planet Blue Media, 2018), 16.

128 "Teruah," *Biblehub*, accessed April 20, 2022, https://biblehub.com/hebrew/8643.htm.

129 "Tishrei—The Head of the Year," *The Rooted Kafe*, last modified September 22, 2020, accessed April 20, 2022, https://www.therootedkafe.com/blog/Tishrei.

130 "Harpazo," *Biblehub*, accessed April 20, 2022, https://biblehub.com/greek/726.htm.

131 "Shub," *Biblehub*, accessed April 20, 2022, https://biblehub.com/hebrew/7725.htm.

132 Nissan Dovid Dubov, "Teshuvah," *Chabad*, accessed April 20, 2022, https://www.chabad.org/library/article_cdo/aid/361890/jewish/Teshuvah.htm.

133 Alfred Edersheim, *The Temple, Its Ministry and Services*, 242.

134 Daniel Fuchs, *Israel's Holy Days in Type and Prophecy*, 60.

135 Julia Blum, "Two Goats of Yom Kippur," *Israel Institute of Biblical Studies*, last modified October 13, 2016, accessed April 20, 2022, https://blog.israelbiblicalstudies.com/jewish-studies/yom-kippur-two-goats/.

136 "Sacrificial goat, Scapegoat … What about the Lamb? Not on Yom Kippur," *Sinai 6000*, last modified October 12, 2016, accessed April 20, 2022, http://sinai6000.net/sacrificial-goat-scapegoat-what-about-the-lamb-not-on-yom-kippur/.

137 Ibid.

138 "Taher," *Biblehub*, accessed April 20, 2022, https://biblehub.com/hebrew/2891.htm.

139 Skip Moen, "Spring Cleaning," *Skip Moen*, last modified April 28, 2013, accessed April 20, 2022, https://skipmoen.com/2013/04/spring-cleaning/.

140 Skip Moen, "Yom Kippur," *Skip Moen*, last modified October 11, 2016, accessed April 20, 2022, https://skipmoen.com/2016/10/yom-kippur-2/.

141 Daniel Fuchs, *Israel's Holy Days in Type and Prophecy*, 76.

142 Dafna Langgut, "The Four Species of Sukkot Explained," *Tel Aviv University*, last modified October 2, 2017, accessed April 20, 2022, https://english.tau.ac.il/news/four-species-of-sukkot.

143 Daniel Fuchs, *Israel's Holy Days in Type and Prophecy*, 78.

144 Rabbi Mendel Weinbach, "Chanukah: The Dispute Between Beit Hillel & Beit Shammai," *Orthodox Union*, last modified June 29, 2006, accessed April 20, 2022, https://www.ou.org/holidays/some_talmudic_insights/.

Chapter 8

145 "Kashrut: Jewish Dietary Laws," *Judaism 101*, accessed April 20, 2022, https://jewfaq.org/kashrut.htm.

146 Hope Eagan, *HOLY COW! DOES GOD CARE ABOUT WHAT WE EAT?* (Littleton, CO: First Fruits of Zion, Inc., 2005), 32.

147 Ibid.

148 Ibid, 33.

149 "DIONYSUS CONNECTION," *Jewish Expert*, accessed April 20, 2022, https://live.jewishexpert.com/dionysus-connection.

150 Emilee Unterkoefler, "Do You Really Need to Cook Lobsters Alive?" *Lifesavvy*, last modified June 26, 2020, accessed April 20, 2022, https://www.lifesavvy.com/30842/do-you-really-need-to-cook-lobsters-alive/.

151 George Lujack, "BEETLES: UNCLEAN," *Scripture Truth Ministries*, last modified March 23, 2018, accessed April 20, 2022, http://scripturetruthministries.com/2018/03/23/beetles-unclean/.

152 "Poisonous Mushrooms," *Mushroom World*, accessed September 13, 2021, https://www.mushroom.world/mushrooms/poisonous.

153 Brandi Walker, "The 10 Most Poisonous Fruits in the World," *World Atlas*, last modified March 11, 2020, accessed April 20, 2020, https://www.worldatlas.com/articles/the-10-most-poisonous-fruits-in-the-world.html.

154 Roy Zuck, *Job*, (Chicago, IL: The Moody Bible Institute, 1978), 61.

155 Hope Eagan, *HOLY COW! DOES GOD CARE ABOUT WHAT WE EAT?* 107.

156 Sam Nadler, *Messianic Foundations*, (Charlotte, NC: Word of Messiah Ministries, 2010), 173.

Chapter 9

157 Shad Helmstetter, "What tToSay When You Talk tToYourself," *Semantic Scholar*, accessed April 20, 2022, https://pdfs.semanticscholar.org/f16d/3d87fb862e651989960a66f4aaedafc3492e.pd

158 Vince Poscente, "the ant and the ELEPHANT," (Dallas, TX: Cornerstone Leadership Institute, 2004), 111.

159 "Phobia," *Miriam Webster Dictionary*, accessed April 20, 2022, https://www.merriam-webster.com/dictionary/phobia.

160 Wikipedia, "Wilhelm Marr," *Wikipedia*, last modified March 21, 2022, accessed April 20, 2022, http://en.wikipedia.org/wiki/Wilhelm_Marr.

161 Thomas Cahill, *The Gifts of the Jews*, (New York, NY: Nan A Talese/Anchor Books, 1998), 3.

162 "Proton," *Biblehub*, accessed April 20, 2022, https://biblehub.com/greek/4412.htm.

163 Wikipedia, "Antisemitism in Christianity," *Wikipedia*, last modified April 20, 2022, accessed April 20, 2022, http://en.wikipedia.org/wiki/Christianity_and_antisemitism.

164 "Nazarenes," *Triumph Pro*, accessed Sept 15, 2021, http://www.triumphpro.com/nazarenes.htm.

165 *RBC Ministries*, accessed Sept 15, 2021, http://www.rbc.org/bible_study/answers_to_tough_questions/answers/47969.aspx.

166 Max I. Dimont, *Jews, God and History*, (New York, NY: New American Library, 2003), 151.

167 Alexander Roberts and James Donaldson, *Ante-Nicene Fathers Vol. 1*, (Peabody, MA: Hendrickson Publishers, Inc., 2004), 63.

168 Alexander Roberts and James Donaldson, *Ante-Nicene Fathers Vol. 3*, (Peabody, MA: Hendrickson Publishers, Inc., 2004), 155.

169 Phillip Schaff, *History of the Christian Church Vol. 2*, second edition, (Peabody, MA: Hendrickson Publishers, Inc., 2004), 484.

170 Julian Spriggs, "Marcion—'The First-born of Satan,'"*Julian Spriggs,* accessed Sept 16, 2021, https://www.julianspriggs.co.uk/Pages/Marcion.

171 "Testament," *Miriam Webster Dictionary*, accessed April 20, 2022, www.merriam-webster.com/dictionary/testament.

172 Phillip Schaff, *History of the Christian Church Vol. 2*, 484.

173 James Carroll, *Constantine's Sword*, (New York, NY: Houghton Mifflin Co., 2001), 147.

174 "Justin Martyr," *Jewish Virtual Library*, accessed April 21, 2022, https://www.jewishvirtuallibrary.org/justin-martyr-x00b0.

175 "Dialogue with Trypho" (Chapters 10–30), *New Advent*, accessed April 21, 2022, https://www.newadvent.org/fathers/01282.htm.

176 Iibid.

177 Iibid.

178 Iibid.

179 Iibid.

180 "Against Heresies" (Book III, Chapter 21), *New Advent*, accessed April 21, 2022, https://www.newadvent.org/fathers/0103321.htm.

181 Bill Tammeaus, "Anti-Judaism in Christian History," *Bill's Faith Matter blog*, accessed April 21, 2022, https://billtammeus.typepad.com/my_weblog/anti-judaism-in-christian-history.html.

182 David Anthony, "Romans 11:18–23," *Pastor's Study*, accessed April 21, 2022, https://pastors-study.com/romans/chapter-11/1118-23/.

183 "Epistle of Barnabas," *Global Catholic Network*, accessed April 21, 2022, https://www.ewtn.com/catholicism/library/epistle-of-barnabas-11350.

184 "Cyprian of Carthage, 'On the Lord's Prayer' (252)—ch 1–11," *Council of Centers on Jewish-Christian Relations*, last modified December 19, 2008, accessed April 21, 2022, https://ccjr.us/dialogika-resources/primary-texts-from-the-history-of-the-relationship/cyprian.

185 James Carroll, *Constantine's Sword*, 167.

186 Ibid., 171.

187 Ibid., 175.

188 Walter Veith, "Constantine and the Sabbath Change," *Amazing Discoveries*, last modified April 24, 2010, accessed April 21, 2022, https://amazingdis-coveries.org/S-deception-Sabbath_change_Constantine.

189 Phillip Schaff, *Christian Classics Ethereal Library*, accessed April 21, 2022, https://ccel.org/ccel/schaff/npnf203.iv.viii.i.x.html.

190 James Richardson, "Quotes from Early Church Fathers: the Sabbath, Lord's Day, and Worship," *Apostles Creed*, last modified August 10, 2018, accessed April 21, 2022, http://apostles-creed.org/confessional-reformed-christian-theology/ecclesiology/quotes-from-early-church-fathers-on-the-sabbath-and-the-lords-day/.

191 David Turner, "The Jewish Problem: Adversus Judeaos (Against the Jews)," *Jerusalem Post*, last modified September 26, 2014, accessed April 21, 2022, https://www.jpost.com/Blogs/

The-Jewish-Problem---From-anti-Judaism-to-anti-Semitism/
The-Jewish-Problem-Adversus-Judeaos-Against-the-Jews-376333.

192   Paul Halsall, "Saint John Chrysostom (c.347–407): Eight Homilies Against
the Jews," *Fordham University*, last modified October 2, 2013, accessed April
21, 2022, http://www.fordham.edu/halsall/source/chrysostom-jews6.html.

193   Alexander Roberts and James Donaldson, *Ante-Nicene Fathers Vol. 7*, 205.

194   B.A. Robinson, "Two Millennia of Jewish Persecution Anti-Judaism: 70
to 1200 CE," *Religious Tolerance*, last modified February 7, 2010, accessed
April 21, 2022, http://www.religioustolerance.org/jud_pers1.htm.

195   "Crusade," *Online Etymology Dictionary*, accessed April 21, 2022, https://
www.etymonline.com/word/crusade.

196   James Carroll, *Constantine's Sword*, 237.

197   Wikipedia, "History of the Jews and the Crusades," *Wikipedia*, last modified
February 1, 2022, accessed April 21, 2022, http://en.wikipedia.org/wiki/
History_of_the_Jews_and_the_Crusades.

198   James Carroll, *Constantine's Sword*, 272.

199   Max I. Dimont, *Jews, God and History*, 241.

200   Jennifer Rosenberg, "History of the Yellow Star Inscribed With 'Jude,'"
ThoughtCo., last modified August 15, 2019, accessed April 21, 2022, http://
history1900s.about.com/od/holocaust/a/yellowstar.htm.

201   Wikipedia, "Host Desecration," *Wikipedia*, last modified April 21, 2022,
accessed April 21, 2022, http://en.wikipedia.org/wiki/Host_desecration.

202   James Carroll, *Constantine's Sword*, 367.

203   Steven Wedgeworth, "Luther's Personality: Fearsome or Fun?" *The
Calvinist International*, last modified August 29, 2013, accessed April 21,
2022, https://calvinistinternational.com/2013/08/29/luthers-personality/.

204   James Carroll, *Constantine's Sword*, 367.

205   Ibid.

206   "The Jews and Their Lies by Dr. Martin Luther," *Christian Nationalist
Crusade*, last modified September 4, 2019, accessed April 21, 2022, https://
www.truthfromgod.com/pdf/The%20Jews%20and%20Their%20Lies.pdf.

207   Ibid.

208   Wikipedia, "Khmelnytsky Uprising," *Wikipedia*, last modified April
6, 2022, accessed April 21, 2022, http://en.wikipedia.org/wiki/
Khmelnytsky_Uprising.

209 James Carroll, *Constantine's Sword*, 272.

210 *Jeruslaem Post*, accessed Sept 29, 2021, http://www.jpost.com/servlet/Satellit e?cid=1176152809534&pagename=JPost%2FJPArticle%2FShowFull.

211 John Cornell, *Hitler's Pope–The Secret History of Pius XII*, (London, UK: Penguin Group, 1999), 28.

212 Garret O'Hara, "Revisiting Andy Stanley's 'Unhitch' Remark," *Things Above Us*, accessed April 21, 2022, https://thingsabove.us/ andy-stanley-unhitch-old-testament/.

Chapter 10

213 "Ekklesia," *Biblehub*, accessed April 21, 2022, https://biblehub.com/ greek/1577.htm.

214 "Church as Circe, The Whore on the Beast's Back," *Geniemusic.com*, accessed April 21, 2022, https://geniemusic.com/?w=694.

215 Allan R. Aguirre, *The Feasts Unlocked*, (Park City, UT: Planet Blue Media, 2018), 56.

216 Robert Heidler, *The Messianic Church Arising*, (Corinth, TX: Glory of Zion International Ministries, 2006), 15.

Printed in the USA
CPSIA information can be obtained
at www.ICGtesting.com
LVHW052035151023
761010LV00001B/72